Statistical Studies
of Historical
Social Structure

POPULATION AND SOCIAL STRUCTURE

Advances in Historical Demography

Under the Editorship of

E. A. HAMMEL

Department of Anthropology
University of California, Berkeley

Kenneth W. Wachter with *Eugene A. Hammel* and *Peter Laslett*, Statistical Studies of Historical Social Structure

In preparation

Nancy Howell, Demography of the Dobe !Kung

Statistical Studies of Historical Social Structure

Kenneth W. Wachter

Department of Statistics
Harvard University
Cambridge, Massachusetts

With

Eugene A. Hammel

Department of Anthropology
University of California, Berkeley
Berkeley, California

Peter Laslett

Trinity College
Cambridge, England

With the participation of
Robert Laslett *and* Hervé LeBras

Academic Press
New York   San Francisco   London
A Subsidiary of Harcourt Brace Jovanovich, Publishers

ACADEMIC PRESS, INC.
111 Fifth Avenue, New York, New York 10003

United Kingdom Edition published by
ACADEMIC PRESS, INC. (LONDON) LTD.
24/28 Oval Road, London NW1 7DX

Library of Congress Cataloging in Publication Data

Wachter, Kenneth W
  Statistical studies of historical social structure.

  (Population and social structure: Advances in historical demography)
  Bibliography: p.
  1. Family––England––History. 2. Households––England––
History. 3. England––Population––History. 4. Demography
––Data processing. I. Hammel, Eugene A., joint author.
II. Laslett, Peter, joint author. III. Title.
HQ613.W3   301.42'1'0942   78–51232
ISBN 0–12–729150–4

PRINTED IN THE UNITED STATES OF AMERICA

Contents

List of Exhibits

Foreword

Statistics makes exacting demands on the imagination. How can I shape my speculations, the user of statistical approaches is required to ask, so that evidence is capable of bearing on them? From each interpretation, what is it which follows which can be tested and brought within established theoretical knowledge? You have to figure that out for yourself—a revealing American phrase, this—which can be a peremptory, sobering task.

For a full third of the contents of this book, in those chapters which deal with microsimulation, the reader is wholly caught up in an invented, an imaginary statisticians' world, entirely created by them in collusion with computers and those who tell computers what to do. It might seem at first sight that nothing could be further removed from the intellectual arena occupied by the student of society, whether anthropologist, psychologist, sociologist, or, more particularly, historian. This book, historians might be disposed to think, is not a book for them. On the contrary. It is the working historian whose possible indifference to a work with our title we are most anxious to overcome.

There is surely a sense in which the activity of all historians is to some extent an activity of simulation. They are perpetually simulating to themselves past situations, past processes; the plans, intentions, and proceedings which might or must have taken place in the minds of men and women now long dead. The interesting thing is that, as they reflect on what happened and try to make up their minds why it happened and what it meant then, what it means now, historians and other students of society are more often engaged in simulating to themselves what could have been the case, but was not, than in simulating what they finally decide must have been the case.

Historians simulate occurrences in fact in order to dispose of them. They do so to discover what would have happened if the simulated succession of events had also taken place. If it turns out that these other eventualities never transpired, they conclude that the events they have conjured up as possibilities, and the choices and attitudes which went with them, could not have ever been realities. This is the mood in which we have mounted our simulation experiments about household composition. Historians, I think, usually carry through such reasoning intuitively and descriptively. They are here being offered an overt, principled, arithmetically exact exposition of their ordinary intellectual procedures. We have done our simulation in public and we now offer the outcomes for everyone to inspect. Household composition as a subject of course is exemplary: Though important in itself, at least to us, we have all simulable processes in our purview.

I am aware, of course, that to dispose of what could not have happened is not to decide what must have happened. All the intricate issues as to counterfactuals are raised by an argument of this kind. My own position, set out in 1968,[1] is that no historical judgment can be passed unless counterfactuals are taken into account, that is, unless we try to judge what would have happened if what did happen had not happened. Systematic treatment of hypotheticals is the vocation of statistics, par excellence. It is one thing, however, for us to be presented with a technically formulated and statistically argued comparison between what might have happened and what did happen and another thing to understand the details sharply enough to make this comparison our own.

To this I can only respond in a personal way by insisting on the advantage of my own opacity. In the lengthy interchange between Professor Wachter and myself, the principle has always been that no point should be allowed to pass until I understood it. We hoped in this way to insure that every literary reader of our text would understand it too.

A similar principle of interchange used to inform the addresses which took place in what are sometimes called the heroic days of cultural broadcasting, in Britain in the 1940s and 1950s, the heyday of the Third

---

[1]Laslett (1968) "History and the Social Sciences," in Sills, ed., *Encyclopedia of the Social Sciences*.

Programme. It gave rise, for example, to the explicatory prose of such books as Fred Hoyle, now Sir Fred Hoyle, on the *Nature of the Universe*, in 1949.

It would be wrong to pretend that we have succeeded in following this principle throughout the whole of this volume. There are parts of the argument about variances in age pyramids in Chapter 11 and even about baronetcies in Chapter 7 which I do not always understand. All of those who, like myself, stand in the anteroom so to speak of mathematical and statistical knowledge will recognize the sense of comprehension which means that you understand it on Mondays, Wednesdays, and Fridays, but do not on Tuesdays, Thursdays, and Saturdays. However, the few implacably technical steps in the arguments have been confined to sections of their own, leaving the main portions of the text as accessible as possible.

Having done our best for that part of our wished-for readership which is entirely historical and literary in its background and outlook, it is to be hoped that the mathematically and technically informed will not feel that they have been the losers. For these statistical studies of historical social structure are addressed in all sincerity to the whole society of those for whom the problems of social understanding are important, in the past or in the present.

Peter Laslett

Hall of Graduate Studies
Yale University

Preface

Tyche, Goddess of Chance, is the patron of this book. First, because the book grew out of a purely happenstance encounter, and, second, because its principal theme is the need and opportunity, in studying historical social structure, for giving chance its due.

The researches reported here are the fruits of collaboration between an historical sociologist, a social anthropologist, and a mathematical statistician. Careful planning would scarcely have brought the three of us, Peter Laslett, Gene Hammel, and myself, together. But accident arranged for us to be in the same room in Bishop's Hostel at Trinity College, Cambridge, on a sunny Tuesday afternoon in June of 1971. We were all expressing curiosity—casual enough on my part—about the households in which people used to live. Like many people, I was a vague believer in a once upon a time when households had been large, hierarchical, full of kin with diverse roles and relationships, and with a niche for everyone. I should have cited *Buddenbrooks* or *A Child's Christmas in Wales* as survivals of families as they used to be, before industrialization brought nuclear family households to the fore. That there were reasons for doubting this picture came as news to me.

Household and Family in Past Time, which Peter Laslett coedited, was in preparation when we chanced to meet in Bishop's Hostel. It described listings of members of households in preindustrial settlements in which coresident kin were rare. That was surprising to anyone with the picture I then held, and since 1971 it has become a matter for general surprise and controversy. But what, if anything, did these data prove? Could not the relative absence of kin be plausibly explained as an artifact of demographic rates? *Household and Family in Past Time* left the question in the air. Gene Hammel, with experience in computer simulation, was arguing that a computer should be used to model the impact of demography on household composition. Each of us for different reasons found that proposal intriguing, and our work together began.

The problem which tempted us into collaboration was the problem of demographic constraints on English preindustrial household kin composition. The originality in our approach was to be the substitution of computer simulation technology for guesswork. We intended a short sequel to *Household and Family in Past Time*. But our research gradually taught us that the problem was wider and the computer technology secondary. Building models was easy, but making models interlock with historical data tightly enough for inferences to remain tenable in the face of random effects proved delicate. Our different backgrounds made us leery of different evasions, and the great merit of the computer turned out to lie in forcing us to make our assumptions explicit. We came to regard the household composition problem as an initiation into working out new ways to take seriously and view systematically the uncertainties of historical data. What was called for was a contribution to the statistical conceptualization of historical issues.

Our computer simulation experiments, then, established a legacy of interpretive concerns, concerns which tie the household problem to other problems. Maneuvers devised for household data have been elaborated and refined for other sorts of data, partly collaboratively and partly individually, but with continual interchange among us. This background explains the structure of the book. The first six chapters form a connected report of our findings on household composition and demographic influences. The other five chapters take the methodological preoccupations developed during the household study and carry them over into studies of five other problems in historical social structure. The unity is a unity of approach.

Of the six chapters on household composition, the first four are devoted single-mindedly to the computer simulation experiments. Chapter 5 presents new data on English household composition and analyzes it in the light of the simulation outcomes. Chapter 6 broadens the discussion to the European Continent and ends with general reflections on stem-family hypotheses. The last five chapters branch out into other subjects.

Chapter 7 considers data on the extinction of English patrilines and their relevance to the measurement of rates of social mobility. Chapter 8 studies wealth and taxation practices reflected in a medieval Balkan document. Chapter 9 proposes an answer to the question of how many different ancestors a person may expect to have had alive at some time in the past. The last two chapters concentrate on the aspect of the demography of a population which impinges most directly on its social structure, namely, its age distribution. Chapter 10, a translation of a French article by Hervé LeBras, deals with numbers of living parents, grandparents, and great-grandparents in a stable population. Chapter 11 offers methods for taking account of random variability in the age distribution of small populations.

Application of statistics to history is nothing new. But what is commonly meant by the application of statistics to history is not what this book offers. A glance will show that there are few tables, compared to the number of pages of text. There is some appeal, but relatively little, to standard statistical procedures, correlation coefficients, linear regressions, t or F or χ^2 tests. We are not taking and using methods of statistics. We are engaged, rather, in articulating and applying concepts from statistics in historical investigations.

For many purposes, in other works, the collection, processing, and presentation of appropriate numbers suffice to shed light on historical problems. The numbers, once gathered, speak for themselves, or are supposed to speak for themselves. For our purposes, on the contrary, the numbers tell us little, taken on their own. What they have to say only emerges after a large investment of time and ingenuity in models which can serve, so to speak, as sounding boards for the data. Supplying a framework of expectations, models amplify and focus systematic messages in the data and dampen out random noise. The effort of data analysis exceeds the effort of data collection and processing. The investment is only justifiable when the data are rare and precious, as are the few numerical clues to preindustrial social structure which survive.

Readers of this book, then, should not expect compendia of numbers or routine statistical computations. Readers should expect arguments about uncertainty written in English prose.

Some subjects undeniably lend themselves to careful treatment of uncertainty more readily than others, and so our methodological concerns and our choice of subjects are interrelated. The role of models during data analysis which has just been mentioned puts a premium on areas where model-building has some sound foundation. The preeminent area of this kind is demography. Demographers understand basic facts about the statistical regularities of human births, marriages, and deaths;

this understanding gives us leverage over other social processes on which demography impinges. For this reason, interactions of social structure with demography are the natural proving ground for statistical approaches to history, and all the problems studied in this book involve demography.

All the problems studied in this book likewise involve preindustrial Europe. The choice of preindustrial Europe reflects the backgrounds of the authors, but it also has statistical ramifications. Most data about preindustrial European social structure pertain to small populations like parishes or settlements. Random variability is especially prominent for such populations. Furthermore, the individuals in such settlements cannot be taken to constitute statistically independent units for analysis. They are, after all, each other's parents, children, spouses, and so on, and these relationships introduce statistical dependencies between their ages and other characteristics. Textbook statistical methods generally assume the availability of a sample of independent individual cases, and they are therefore inappropriate to these situations. Thus our subject necessitates the development of new statistical methods. This methodological challenge, in its turn, gives our problems a wider interest. Much of this book reports basic statistical research. However, passages of technical statistical argument are introduced only with explicit warning, in order that the text as a whole remain accessible to readers interested in the substantive problems.

We do assume some basic statistical nomenclature in the text—means, standard deviations, variances, random variables, constants, expectation values, distribution functions—but we mostly draw on statistics not for technical material but for certain habits of mind. These are not things we could cover in a technical appendix, nor are they the exclusive province of those who have taken statistics courses. Experience worrying about randomness is what is at stake. Those statistical approaches that we do employ are reshaped to suit our needs. In terms of the dichotomy between "exploratory" and "confirmatory" methods introduced by John Tukey (cf. Tukey, 1977), the distinctive character of our approach may be described as the use of confirmatory strategies as exploratory tools. Thus for many confrontations between data and theory we imitate the setup of Neyman–Pearson hypothesis testing and its asymmetrical treatment of its two types of errors, without any commitment to significance levels or the assumptions required for their validity. Thus also we rely repeatedly on formal probabilistic models, not in order to work within one of them at estimation or testing, but in order to elaborate a variety of sharply formulated points of comparison for our data. These approaches are especially evident in Chapters 4, 7, and 11.

For the other major methodological thrust of this book, developed in the first four chapters, we coin the name "experimental history." The name aims to provoke some free association. How can we perform experiments on history? What is the laboratory? How are controlled conditions to be guaranteed? How are results to be made replicable? What can we undertake that deserves the name experimental history, short of sending an omnipotent scientist back into the past in a time machine? Without omnipotence, how could we hold all relevant historical conditions constant so that we can observe the differences in historical effects produced by varying one isolable factor?

Many scholars have sought for controlled conditions, controlled after the fact instead of before, by hunting for cases from history which happen to share as many conditions as possible. That is one kind of experimental history, but not the kind we mean. Our first four chapters report experimental history conducted by the aid of a computer, a computer programmed with a model to simulate demographic and social processes. By this method controlled conditions are achievable, for over the processes in the computer we have complete control.

Even a little corner of the historical world is more complex than anything we can model inside a computer. But we are not trying to model the world with our experiments. We are trying to model ideas about the world. We are trying to test claims that certain patterns of conditions, other things being equal, should account for certain consequences. In our case, the patterns are patterns of demography and social choice, and we can take theories about these patterns and reduce them to computer programs in full detail. We can also incorporate effects of random variability. Thus, when we run our computer program, not only can we test whether the assumptions do produce the consequences they are supposed to produce, but we can also measure the randomness to be expected in historical data.

Computer simulation is easy to misunderstand, for it is easy to jump to the false conclusion that an experiment must propose to re-create some particular historical reality inside a computer, rather than to recreate and test the ideas that scholars have. To articulate an experimental approach to an historical problem, as we attempt in Chapter 1, is to struggle against false starts at every turn. Chapters 2 and 3 document the assumptions for our particular experiment on demographic constraints on household structure and Chapter 4 reports the results. We are especially proud of two aspects of this work. First, while preliminary studies and illustrations of method abound in the field of computers and their applications, this is one experiment that has been carried through in full detail to address actual historical questions. Second, these researches are strictly subject to replication and the methods are accessible to others, since the computer programs are fully documented in a separate volume (Hammel *et al.*, 1976) and remain available. Complete documentation has seemed to us an essential requirement of scientific work. We offer our version of experimental history as one path toward a more genuinely scientific social science.

In the text we emphasize that simulation experiments and the other approaches we develop are not substitutes for data, but rather aids in the interpretation of data. Hand in hand with predictions of random variability and relationships between variables under controlled conditions goes the need for data assembled in a manner which facilitates sound statistical comparisons. All our chapters bear on the analysis of data and several chapters present new sets of data. While these data are important in their own right, attention to statistical issues in their collection and analysis gives them their special significance. The prime example is in Chapter 5, which presents new data on the kin composition of 64 English places between 1574 and 1821. The point of the three tables in Chapter 5 is not to say, "Here are some places where the following proportions of households are recorded as containing the following types of coresident kin. . . . There are more kin here than there. . . ." The point is that these places have been selected out of the whole body of available listings of preindustrial English settlements in a special way. Their selection has been designed to guard against prejudicing the proportions in favor of particular household forms and to approximate as far as possible a genuine statistical sample. We believe this to be the first time an attempt has been made in this field to assemble something approximating a sample as opposed to an assortment of special cases. This application of statistical ideas to historical data collection puts the ongoing controversy about living arrangements in the preindustrial past on a new basis.

Opinion has shifted in one direction and another in the period since our meeting at Trinity College initiated our simulation experiments and collection of the new English sample. Attribution of the low levels of complex households in English listings to the effects of demography and the life cycle is not so popular at the moment as it was a short time ago. But the status of the debate, in terms of the evidence that can be adduced for and against the explanation, has not shifted very much up until now. In the absence of a rigorous analysis, such as we attempt here, views about household composition would remain vulnerable to fashion and ideology and the surprise-value of each newly discovered document. The arguments in this book are complex, but only with complex arguments can we hope to anchor the debate.

Not only household composition and demography, but the other subjects that we study—social mobility, wealth, ancestors, ages—have emotional associations. They are subjects where vivid impressionistic evidence, however unrepresentative, has initial persuasive power. But the problems with which we grapple in this book—selection bias, random variability, the proper allowances for factors like demography—are not eluded by resorting to nonquantifiable sources. They become, in fact, more severe, and they threaten to reduce argument to old wives' tale or old husbands' tale. We press this point in Chapter 1. Lip service about limitations of evidence or the difficulties of generalization is meaningless, if the conclusions are left to stand. It is right to feel impatience with social history that consists of a collection of instances and a rehearsal of anecdotes, without methods for distinguishing the typical from the incidental and contrived. To carry history beyond instance and anecdote demands respect for statistical issues. Our research is intended as a stroke in behalf of statistically serious history.

It must be clear that this book's recurrent theme is the importance of random variability. Among the worries of historical data analysis, randomness might seem to be just one more complicating factor making life harder for the scholar. But the contrary is true. Giving chance its due entails rewards. Data are always full of patterns clamoring for our attention. When most patterns can be written off to chance, our attention is freed to dwell on the few patterns that do stand out above random noise. We end up with less to explain, and so we may hope for more trenchant explanations. For example, the literature on European households is already complicated, full of contrasts between places, periods, and circumstances—so much so that a pessimist might wonder whether anything of general validity or interest can be gleaned out of the welter of details. When we see that many contrasts disappear if chance is given its full due, while some contrasts remain, the subject gains appeal. The homogeneity of the English household samples asserted in Chapter 5 is an example of a regularity that takes on new importance in the light of results on random variability. Statistics is a tool for simplicity. It is one of the few.

All these concepts we have been dwelling on are abstractions, as is inevitable when our project is to make knowledge more secure. But it is good to remember that our data are the traces of people, people like "Her Majestie's mowltaker" who makes his appearance in Chapter 5. Her Majestie's mowltaker, Richard Hampton, worked for Queen Elizabeth catching moles and left his name as the two-hundred-second entry on the earliest known listing of an English settlement with ages and households of inhabitants. Most of the people of the past who are known to us at all directly are only known, like Richard Hampton, through occasional and accidental mention in listings, registers, and similar documents. The impulse to write the history of the many, after centuries of historians writing the history of the few, requires work with sparser and more accidental sources. Sparse and accidental sources imply a common ground between history and statistics, leading inevitably to the concerns which tie this book together.

Research into the features which the lives of people like Richard Hampton shared connects with questions of broad appeal and baffling difficulty. Most of the people represented in our data lived during the couple of centuries when the population explosion was beginning its course in England and then in Europe. Disentangling demography from social structure and evidence about social structure over this period forms a part of any inquiry into the origins of the population explosion and the limits on our understanding of it. Data about many aspects of this subject, particularly economic aspects, are very scant; the availability, such as it is, of data about household composition singles out this corner as one where progress may be made. The old picture of preindustrial households and their supposed later transformation, the picture I brought to our chance meeting at Trinity College in 1971, has shaped beliefs for a long time. How to redraw that picture may prove to be one of the few things we can know, within the so much wider circuit of the things we should like to know.

The fundamental and commonplace way in which my own experience differs from that of Her Majestie's mowltaker and the other people represented in our data is something we do not yet know how to study. It is a difference in vocabulary, where the word "millions" has taken the place of "hundreds." This change of scale has psychic costs. As scholars, we worry over distinguishing the typical from the random in the circumstances and behavior of people in the past at least partly because as people we have to worry over these distinctions in our everyday alignment to the world. Statistics, as a humanistic and conceptual discipline, can be an effort to make the vocabulary of "millions" more nearly comfortable. For this reason I think of statistically serious history as the natural form of history for us today to try to write.

Kenneth W. Wachter
Berkeley, California
May 1978

Acknowledgments

The order of the names following each chapter in the Table of Contents attempts to indicate the relative contributions of each of us to the research as well as the presentation, though our collaboration has been so close that these contributions are hard to separate. As for the text itself, I have been responsible for the first four and last three chapters, Peter Laslett for Chapter 6, and Eugene Hammel for Chapter 8, while Chapters 5 and 7 were produced in a memorable sortie into joint composition by Peter Laslett and myself. Robert Laslett selected, extracted, and processed the data and prepared the tables for Chapters 5 and 6. Chapter 10 is the work of Hervé LeBras, which I have translated from the French. I am indebted to him for reading and suggesting improvements in my translation and for discussing and approving substantive revisions for the English version.

The National Science Foundation of the United States has generously supported the SOCSIM Project in Computer Microsimulation of which the experiments reported in the first four chapters are a part. Grant numbers have been SOC73-09214, SOC76-10923, SOC77-16129, and SOC78-18010. At different stages the Institute of International Studies at Berkeley and the Social Science Research Council of London have also aided the research. Conceptual progress was furthered by seminar-workshops at Cambridge University in 1974 and at the Center for Advanced Study in Palo Alto, California, in 1975, the former sponsored by the Social Science Research Council of London and the latter by the Mathematical Social Science Board of Washington, D.C. A fellowship from the Miller Institute at the University of California, Berkeley aided completion of the book.

Several individuals have made special contributions. Chad McDaniel has helped clarify our thinking on many occasions. David Hutchinson programmed the SOCSIM routines on which the first four chapters depend and kept us out of vagueness. Robert Lundy and Ruth Deuel shouldered responsibility for auxiliary computer programs for the experiments. David Kendall has been a faithful supporter, giving us precise suggestions for improvements. David Sacks's criticisms led to important changes in Chapter 5. John Hajnal, James Trussell, E. A. Wrigley, and Roger Schofield guided us to needed revisions, while Georgia Kingson and Mauriça Anderson gave invaluable assistance in preparation of the final typescript. Most of all, Janet Crockett Laslett and Joan Swingle Hammel have patiently nurtured our collaborative endeavors.

Trinity College, Cambridge, Harvard University, the University of California, Berkeley, and St. Catherine's College, Oxford, have left their imprint on this work and helped it grow.

Kenneth W. Wachter

1

Demographic Rates and Complexity of Households: Rationale for Experiments

The demography of a population imposes constraints upon its household composition. In the simplest case, certain combinations of expectations of life with ages at marriage can obviously prevent grandparents, parents, and children in most cases from living together under the same roof for large parts of their lifespans, no matter what their intentions. In more complicated cases, two assertions may appear equally plausible in the abstract: either that, to interpret any data on prevalence of household types, detailed information about demography and its influence is indispensable; or, alternatively, that demography impinges on household composition only in extreme circumstances, and that within broad limits an explanation of the occurrence of some household types rather than others will not stand or fall on demographic considerations. Choice between these assertions is a theoretical problem which precedes the interpretation of data, and it embraces the narrower question whether a rarity of instances of various types of complex household found in data for parts of preindustrial Europe is still compatible, due to the demography, with theories that those societies in one sense or another favored complex households.

To investigate these questions we have used computer microsimulation. A series of hypothetical events is constructed by the computer, in a random fashion but in accordance with specified probabilities. Often called Monte Carlo, this technique allows us to trace the consequences for aggregate behavior of assumptions about individual behavior. It comes into its own with complicated processes like population and household composition where we seek knowledge of statistical variability as well as central tendency. The same instructions and probabilities can be given to the computer not merely once but many times, holding everything the same except random numbers, the "throws of the dice." Like a batch of movie retakes, a collection of views arises of what might have been, of how different a community might look on account of random variations without any change in its structural characteristics.

This ability to repeat or replicate a process under the same conditions suggests the name "experiments" for microsimulation studies of our kind. An analogy with experiments in physical and biological science will be our recurrent theme, as we argue that computer microsimulation offers to historical social science many of the aids to conceptual clarity of laboratory research. History delivers us no retakes. But the computer can show us what the retakes ought to look like if we believe some one of our own descriptions of the processes in motion. Arraying for us the observable incidental and essential features implicit in the description, the computer can give us theoretical insight with which to make the most of historical data.

Our experiment explores the extent to which particular sets of demographic conditions constrain observable proportions of household types under three variants of one particular hypothesis about household residence choices of individuals. The particular demographic conditions are conditions which aim to be relevant to English settlements of the 1600s and 1700s. The particular household hypotheses abstract the implications for behavior of an often revived and controversial general picture of traditional European households, the stem-family hypothesis associated with P. G. Frédéric Le Play. This stem-family hypothesis, or, for our purposes, its reduction to hypotheses about individual decisions to join and leave households, is interesting not so much for its own sake as for its position as a reasonably strictly specifiable example of practices which might promote large, complex, multigenerational households.

Specifying and recasting, in the form of computer instructions, demographic conditions and hypotheses as to residence choices makes an intricate story which we postpone to Chapters 2 and 3 of this volume. Chapter 2 relates the demographic assumptions for our experiment. Chapter 3 relates the hypotheses about household choice. For vital events and for household membership equally, the computer demands complete and exact instructions for every eventuality. Historical data are not rich enough to dictate all the instructions we give the computer, but, as in any argument, we are better off spelling out the arbitrary assumptions we have to make than concealing them in muddle. Except for the prohibition against the inconclusive and the vague, our problems are the problems of any modelling of human social structure, and Chapter 3, especially, formulates possible stances for a debate over historical household listings as much as for trial by computer runs. Such a debate, admittedly, might take an unfamiliar shape, for a formal approach like ours is relatively new to household studies, Fischer (1958), Goodenough (1956), and Geoghegan (1975) being perhaps the nearest parallels. Just as new is the appeal to microsimulation at all, although the literature on related applications is growing (cf. Dyke and MacCluer, 1974; Zubrow, 1977). To show how the building blocks are meant to fit together in the inferential edifice we are constructing, we spend this chapter setting out the questions we want our experiment to answer. We carry through the analysis of computer outputs in Chapter 4. Chapters 5 and 6 discuss the best existing quantitative evidence on English preindustrial households and its relation to Continental evidence in the light of these results.

At the present time the question that we are tackling by microsimulation, the question of demographic constraints on household structure, especially in the context of preindustrial England and with reference to hypotheses of practices promoting complex households, is a pivotal problem of social structure and social history. Its pivotal role is partly accidental. Widely held expectations concerning English households before the first national censuses have happened to collide with the first quantitative data that have become available. Briefly put, a variety and prevalence of complex households, which would have fitted the popular image of a traditional family, were conspicuously absent from the English listings reported at the 1969 Cambridge conference which led to the volume *Household and Family in Past Time*, Laslett and Wall (1972). Complex households were so little in evidence that any suggestion which might reconcile the older picture with the new data and reduce the surprise of the data has come to command attention beyond what it might otherwise deserve.

If one must relinquish a belief that many English preindustrial villagers did actually live in complex households, one might still be able to maintain a belief that they tried to do so and were prevented by demography. What we see in listings of settlements is a highly selective picture of the households people were inclined to form. Demography makes the selection. It grants people so and so many years with such and such living relatives. People can decide to exclude or include in their households only the relatives they have, giving only limited rein to inclination and prevailing practice. Demographic processes act like a filter between individual decisions and the evidence for their execution. They filter some tendencies out and let others pass through to be recorded. Thus the possibility arises of redrawing the older picture in terms of social practices of choice of residence instead of in terms of actually occurring types, and to defend it in the face of the data in this weaker form by an appeal to the effects of the demographic filter.

This special role of demographic constraints as the cornerstone for a possible second line of defense for a traditional picture is typical of its more general importance. Analysis of historical listings alone can never yield inferences about social practices in household formation directly. Theory is required as well as data in order to calibrate or standardize the data for the demographic background, in other words, to make allowances for the demographic filter between the choices of individuals and the occurrences of household types. On the simplest level such theory is needed to say how much is much. Suppose 30% of households in the listing of a place turn out to include three lineally related generations. Is 30% close to the maximum that could be expected, or is it so small in comparison with the maximum that it might occur reasonably often, as a random event, among communities with no special practices favoring multigenerational households? Until such questions can be answered, as far as social practices are concerned, a figure like 30% remains evidence for nothing. Similarly, if one listing shows 30% stem-family households and another shows 20%, is this 10% difference a large one or a small one? Does it suggest a real cultural contrast? May it be a by-product of demographic dissimilarities? Or is it likely to have occurred, without any systematic difference, by chance alone?

The results of computer simulations of demography and household structure can be read in four main ways. First, they support or discourage a general claim that demography does strongly influence types of households that occur. Second, when simulations with different sets of rates can be compared, the results indicate which variables in the model are most potent determinants of household proportions. Third, they furnish benchmarks against which to compare proportions of household types found in empirical data, aiding deductions about the residence choices of persons over their life cycles from data on residence at a fixed point in time. Fourth, they reveal the amount of random variability for which, at a minimum, allowance must be made. We discuss each of these facets at greater length before describing the batches of computer runs in the experiment.

In the first place, as we have said, computer runs pairing any one set of demographic conditions with any one household formation hypothesis tend to confirm or contradict a general principle that demography does exercise a major influence over types of households. Can household patterns observed in lists be taken at face value, as reflecting directly a pattern of choices that individuals make about residence, whatever the demography? Put the other way, do the leitmotifs of an hypothesis about decisions manage to make their implications evident in the pattern of households, whatever the demography? Let us expand the metaphor of a filter, saying what it is that can be filtered out or let to pass. An hypothesis ordains choices like "eldest daughters with two living parents and no brothers remain in their parents' household upon marriage," or perhaps the opposite. We start with dozens of such rules, but as the computer constructs a series of births, marriages, and deaths only some of the rules get the chance to operate very often. There may be many brotherless eldest daughters or few. The demographic circumstances filter out households producible by some rules and let others through. We talk of passing an hypothesis through the demographic filter to yield a pattern of occurring household types. In this manner of speaking, we are asking how permeable a demographic filter is.

For this question, the sharper and more stylized the hypothesis about residential decisions, the more cogent is the experiment. Two of the three versions of a stem-family hypothesis to be defined in Chapter 3, the so-called "primonuptial" and "ultimonuptial," are highly stylized hypotheses expressly tailored to this question. Now a fuzzy (if realistic) hypothesis passed through the "demographic filter" is liable to produce a fuzzy pattern of household types and to give only ambiguous support or discouragement to the general principle that demography matters. But a sharp (if unrealistic) household hypothesis passed through the demographic filter may give either a sharp pattern or a fuzzy pattern of household types and so either deny or confirm the general principle for the cases concerned. The stylization and lack of realism in the hypothesis are advantages and not drawbacks, because the question at issue is not one of historical description but of the plausible relationships between variables.

We come to our second point, namely, that we can chart relationships between variables in some detail when enough batches of simulation runs with different rates and different hypotheses concerning household formation are available. Our experiment contains 15 such batches, each consisting of 64 replications, 64 runs entirely alike except for different random numbers. Holding some variables fixed and changing others from batch to batch, we can ask which variables exercise the greatest leverage over household types. For instance, does growth rate affect household types more than death rate? Does death rate affect them more than the choice whether to let brotherless eldest daughters stay with parents? Do choices about eldest daughters affect them more than choices about youngest sons? We want such information for two reasons. We want to know how sensitive our results are to the exact assumptions that we frame, and how far we may dare to generalize from them. We also want to be able to distinguish potentially important variables from irrelevant variables when we venture explanations of historical material.

Extreme enough values of any variable, needless to say, have large effects. We are really asking how large are the effects due to differences of a size that would be found within an historical context of interest. For instance, did growth rates in Stuart England differ enough to alter household types more than differing death rates could? To confront such questions we must select demographic assumptions for our experiment which span a suitable range of possibilities for the historical case; this requirement is one of the issues of Chapter 2. Going further, we may then ask whether differences in hypotheses about household formation large enough to provoke argument in the present state of discussion have effects on household types larger or smaller than the demographic effects.

Our third point states that simulation results furnish benchmarks against which to compare data. Taking practices which would promote complex households, demography aside, the computer shows how much complexity of households is promoted, demography included. Ideally, we should like a procedure for going the other way, starting with the outputs, the pattern of households, demography included, and telling us what inputs, that is, what practices, demography aside, could correspond to them (under some fixed demographic conditions). We should call such a procedure "inverting the demographic filter." This ideal is out of reach, at least directly, and we must learn how to go backward, from outputs to inputs, by going forward, from inputs to outputs, with test cases strategically devised.

Our test cases are our three variants of household hypotheses in Chapter 3 called primonuptial, primoreal, and ultimonuptial. They are like three patches on a standard color chart which a photographer uses to gauge the effects of a color filter in front of a camera lens. Of course, our demographic filter and a camera filter are quite analogous. We might think of a mix of stem-family household tendencies, nuclear household tendencies, and other tendencies much as we think of a mix of the primary colors red, blue, and green. Our three household hypotheses are, pursuing the metaphor, three shades of stem, like three shades of red. Our different demographic conditions in different simulation batches are like interchangeable color filters on a camera, differently distorting and transmitting the hues. A breakdown of households by their type of kin composition in a classification scheme is like the exposed camera film, and running our simulations is like photographing the test patches on the color chart.

With a given filter, a photo of a deep red patch will register some mixture of red, blue, and green on the film, which we could pinpoint on a conventional Newton–Young Color Diagram, an equilateral triangle whose vertices are pure red, pure blue, and pure green and whose interior points are mixtures more red, blue, or green the nearer to the vertices they lie. In Chapter 4 we shall actually pinpoint each simulation output on a kind of triangle plot, where the vertices represent 100% stem, 100% nuclear, and 100% other households, and the interior points represent mixtures of the three types. Now, just because one color patch with one filter registers a certain color on film, that would not make it the only pair of color patch and filter that would register that color. Likewise, just because the listing of a settlement gives proportions of households much the same as the average proportions from a simulation, say a simulation with primoreal household rules, brides' ages in the low twenties, etc., it need not follow by any means that the settlement members can only have made decisions that accord with primoreal rules or that their daughters married in their twenties. The inverse of the demographic filter need not be unique. But that does not mean that our test cases are uninformative. Suppose household proportions from a listing fall close to outcomes from a late-marriage primonuptial simulation and also close to outcomes from an early-marriage primoreal simulation, but not to other outcomes. That does invite us to adjust our rating of the strength of stem-family household practices by our suppositions about age at marriage for the settlement. This is the sense in which simulations furnish benchmarks for inferences about historical data.

We may liken, then, the activity of interpreting historical listings to the job of retinting pictures. Test photographs of color patches with different camera filters, like simulations with different demographic rates, teach us how nearly exactly we need to know which filter was in front of the lens for a picture we seek to retint and teach us how pale our inks should be. Of course, such tests are not always worth the cost. Passport snapshots are not on a par with Viking transmissions of the Martian landscape. Like the issues of inference with which we deal, color charts and test photos are not the first worries of a photographer. They are later worries that become preeminent when the photographs are rare and precious and the great point of studying them is to get the color right.

Another way of describing the demographic filter calls it a black box which transforms residence behavior of individuals over time, as they live out their life cycles, into a community pattern of residency at a fixed instant of time. It transforms a vertical into a horizontal time slice. The problem of inverting or undoing this transformation has been emphasized in household research especially by Lutz Berkner, whose paper "Inheritance, Land Tenure, and Peasant Family Structure" (1976) we discuss in Chapter 6 of this volume. Berkner, like Fortes (1949) or Hammel (1961), uses cross-tabulations of household types by age of household head to infer the presence of certain overlapping developmental cycles from single listings. Computer simulation permits more detailed allowance for the differing rates at which individuals move from childhood into marriage perhaps and childbearing and widowhood and death, under the limitations, it must not be forgotten, of explicit assumptions about the demographic conditions, which are never precisely verifiable for any particular community under study. It is clear that even under the strictest practices favoring complex households, at some points in the life cycles of household members some households will be simple. It is also clear that under some circumstances a stage of complex composition could be experienced by every household while at any one time only a small proportion of all households were complex. What is far from clear, and what the computer helps reveal, is what circumstances are likely to lead to what ratios between complex households and simple ones. This question is part of a larger subject, how the human life cycle expresses itself in available, quantifiable data, a subject discussed from many points of view in Hareven (1978).

It would have been possible in our experiments to record the lengths of time that individuals spend in households of each type, the sequence of types, and the frequencies of transitions from type to type. Analyzing these data, however, would have been a large research project in its own right, and we elected not to undertake it. Thus, we have only limited information on the ratios which connect domestic group cycles with community profiles at an instant of time, limited compared to what is potentially obtainable by simulation. This aspect, still more than others, awaits further treatment.

In the fourth place, computer simulations garner clues to the extent of randomness sure to enter into proportions of household types. How big a gap between two villages in, say, the proportions of nuclear households should be written off to chance effects? How big a gap begins to be statistically significant? In small populations like preindustrial villages, random variability is bound to be sizable. This assertion should not sound obscure, but two phrases in it need glossing, "random variability" and "small populations."

The random variability at stake is not fluctuation over time, although this is certainly present, but rather random spread about mean values.

Villages with identical structural characteristics, vital rates, and social practices, if they existed, would still differ in their appearance due to the haphazard element in the timing of each single birth, death, or other event. Measurements on them would show statistical dispersion around a central value. In practice, as we said early in this chapter, we cannot find such "movie retakes" among historical villages. The replications of a simulation under identical controlled conditions substitute for them. They supply an artificial random sample from which we can estimate not merely means but variances and shapes of whole probability distributions of statistics like proportions of household types. Our sample size is the number of replications of the simulation. We can increase it freely to obtain estimates as accurate as we desire. The relevance of the estimates of course hinges on the suitability of the random components in our computer programs, discussed at length at the end of Chapter 2.

On the matter of small populations, we intuitively expect proportions based on small populations to be more subject to random variability than those based on large ones. It is important to remember, however, that the different persons or households in a village are not statistically independent units, so that the population size or number of households is not a sample size in any strict sense. The village contains fathers and daughters whose ages are correlated. It contains siblings in separate households, one of which can include a mother only by the others foregoing her. The system is full of these weak statistical dependencies. Thus random sampling theory forms at best a questionable guide to the variances of village statistics and their relationship to village size. How much of this theory carries over to our more complicated setting is one of the questions about random variability we shall ask of our simulation results.

We have now completed our four-point summary of ways in which simulation experiments can be read. It should be clear that our simulations address issues about populations raised and attacked with other methods by several authors in recent times. On pages 131 to 135 of *Population and History*, E. A. Wrigley (1969) gives a rough calculation of the proportion of three-generational households that might arise from rules for choice of residence under which all married children leave their parents' household but where upon widowhood a parent rejoins some one married child. This calculation assumes all couples married at the mean age at marriage, all children born at the mean age of childbearing, and no remarriage, and is admittedly very crude. But it early focused attention on the subject of benchmark proportions just discussed as our third point; desires to refine this calculation provided impetus for the present experiments.

Wrigley's calculation has been modified and extended by Bradley and

Mendels (1977) who go on to the important question of random variability, just discussed as our fourth point. Their paper offers a formula for the sampling variance of the proportion of extended households under the same rules for choice of residence as Wrigley. Their formula evaluates variance due to randomness in survival from birth to the mean age of married couples and from that mean age to the mean age of parents of married couples, under binomial probability models and the assumption of statistical independence between all households in a settlement. Comparing their expressions for variance against differences in observed proportions for settlements including some of those in our Exhibits 5.1, 5.2, and 5.3, Mendels and Bradley reach a discouraging conclusion which may be rephrased as saying that the power of statistical tests of hypotheses about household organization is bound to be too low to distinguish between interesting alternatives. They endorse the appeal to other sources and methods for household studies.

The mean ages for Wrigley's example taken over by Mendels and Bradley are close to mean ages in several of our simulations, including the batches labeled $P4$, $R5$, and $U2$ (see Chapter 2 of this volume). The model for choice of residence is very different from our models, but their rules are such that three-generational households under their model ought to show up under our model as households whose label of classification we call "extended lineal" or else as an occasional solitary household (cf. Chapter 3 of this volume). Our simulations produce estimates below 15% for mean proportions of these households where Mendels and Bradley estimate 31%. Also, Mendels and Bradley find household proportions to be much more sensitive to marriage rates than we find them in our results presented in Chapter 4. In the absence of other explanations, we contend that the startling disagreement between these analytic results and our simulation results is to be blamed on oversimplification in the analytic model.

Three other points come to the fore in connection with Mendels and Bradley's paper. First, the column labeled "incidence of extensions" in their empirical table, when compared against the cited sources, seems to lump multiple households and laterally extended households together with the lineally extended households to which their formula applies. Thus to compare the tabled figures directly with the benchmarks from their formula would be misleading. This problem highlights the importance of using the same standard classification scheme for households while modeling as while analyzing data and motivates the care we devote to this matter in Chapters 3–5 of this volume.

Second, although like Mendels and Bradley we find in Chapter 4 that variances are large, our conclusions are less discouraging. The hope of making sound inferences even in the face of large variance is enhanced when a collection like the one in our Tables 5.1 and 5.2 can be assembled so that all need not turn on a single listing of a settlement. Examining together proportions of several types of households rather than a single proportion, such as we do in Chapters 4 and 5, also helps.

Third, a word on "other sources and methods" other than the analysis of numerical proportions of household types for household studies is in order. Of course other sources and methods should never be ignored. But neither should anyone belittle the danger of using "other sources"— literary, legal, epistolary, and anecdotal, for instance—in the way they are often used. All such sources are themselves subject to random variability and selection bias. But the danger is that because, unlike the situation with numerical evidence, the randomness and bias cannot be measured and so controlled, they will be ignored. Conclusions will not be adjusted to take the limits of knowledge in the face of randomness into fair account. Until methods are found to allow concretely for the extent of random variability and bias in nonnumerical sources—methods that go beyond lip service in an introductory or concluding paragraph—it is hard to see how serious studies of household organization can avoid resting largely on the sometimes frustrating numerical data that we have.

Issues like those discussed under our first point were broached as early as 1965 by Marion Levy, Jr. (1965), prompting analytic calculations of effects of demographic rates on household size by Coale (1965) and generating a vigorous literature (cf. Levy and Fallers, 1971). Levy (1965) argues that

> In societies of the first type (i.e., societies devoid of modern medical technology) the relative uniformity and magnitude of death rates, etc., is such that despite radical variations in ideal family structures from one society to another, the actual variation in vertical and horizontal proliferation of membership and all that those proliferations affect substantially is much more restricted than preoccupation with the ideal structures has led most of us to believe [page 49].

Without embarking on a discussion of the many broader questions treated in Levy's work, it is interesting to ask how our simulation results bear on this particular hypothesis. The answer depends on the meaning of "much more restricted." Certainly the span of household percentages from the simulations found in Exhibits 4.1 and 4.2 is more restricted than one might imagine it being a priori. That is in line with the hypothesis put forward. On the other hand, Chapter 4 does show that within this range the constraints that demography puts on household composition are surprisingly loose. Practices regarding residence choice differing only moderately from each other can produce patterns of household composition differing unmistakably. That holds for a period before the onset of modern medical technology, at least for northwestern European demographic rates. On this level, then, our results argue against a strong form of Levy's hypothesis. It is hoped that Chapter 4 provides a good deal of material for this continuing debate.

We proceed now from the background for our study in previous literature to the features of our particular experiment. Early versions of these four chapters were presented in 1974 at the Cambridge Seminar on Microsimulation mounted by the Social Science Research Council of London. They reported a single batch of 100 replications in an experiment with a single set of birth, death, and marriage rates and other demographic assumptions and a single version of household formation practices, very close to the "primonuptial" rule system described in Chapter 3 of this volume. That highly stylized hypothesis aimed to maximize proportions of stem-family households in order to mark an upper limit against which proportions in English historical listings could be judged. The upper limit fell so far above the historical levels as to cast severe doubt on any proposal to ascribe the low levels in the listings to demographic intervention instead of residential decisions. But the conclusions remained provisional. Tests were needed, first, to show how much the proportions of stem-family households and other complex households would drop under a less rigid pattern of stem-family choices than the primonuptial system. Second, the sensitivity of the conclusions to the exact choice of demographic conditions demanded investigation.

The first question was taken up in the authors' paper "Primonuptiality and Ultimonuptiality: Their Effects on Stem Family Household Frequencies" presented at the M.S.S.B. Philadelphia Conference on Historical Demography in November 1974 and published in Lee (1977). That paper refers back to the early version of the present chapters, which were not published and which are superseded by the present version. The second question, of sensitivity to demographic rates, has awaited the present experiment. It consists of 15 new batches of simulations, with 64 replications in each batch. Some nine different sets of demographic rates are tried in various combinations with three different versions of a stem-family hypothesis. Our 15 batches not only extend the range of questions we can answer but allow fuller answers to the questions at stake in the original one-batch experiment. The detailed specification of the batches is given, for the demographic assumptions, in Chapter 2 and, for the household organizational assumptions, in Chapter 3.

2

Demography in the Computer

Experiments require apparatus. The experimental apparatus for our study of relationships between demography and household structure consists in computer routines which generate records of "births," "marriages," "deaths," "shifts of residence," and similar events in random sequences governed by certain laws and matching certain long-term rates. That the numbers of these artificial events, their timing, and links between them be a reasonable mimicry of the human world is one aim. The other aim is that enough of the peripheral complication of the real world be excluded so as to display particular interactions under controlled conditions, stylized like the laboratory conditions of physical science. This chapter is a study of those aims in tension, being an account of the demographic assumptions for our experiment.

Computer simulation routines resemble a machine with many dials and knobs. After demographic mechanisms have been reduced to a representation in computer code, the experimenter must select rates for vital events and specify the particular demographic regime for the experiment. The "machine" we are using, the SOCSIM demographic–social microsimulation program running on a Control Data Corporation 7600 computer, is described in detail in the *SOCSIM Manual* (Hammel, Hutchinson, Wachter, Lundy, & Deuel, 1976), so that we can restrict our summary of it to salient features. But the settings of dials and knobs—the choices of rates and input parameters for the computer runs—demand more extensive review; the specific relevance of the experiment turns on them. Our series of rates attempt to span a range of plausible demographic situations for England in the two centuries surrounding 1700, because our first goal is to provide theoretical background for the interpretation of the English household listings which are the subject of Chapter 5 of this volume. No small series can be exhaustive, but we do claim to have covered cases that should be informative for all but extreme examples of the English parishes for which listings from this period survive. We shall try to document the demographic rates in our experiment at sufficient length so that readers acquainted with the historical literature can judge this claim for themselves.

Under the heading of realism fall three questions which occupy us in this chapter. First, as we have said, there is the relevance of the overall vital rates and of programming options to historical cases. Second, there is the consistency of secondary statistics with our general knowledge about populations. Rates under the direct control of the experimenter like age-specific death and marriage rates have consequences for dozens of secondary statistics like age distributions of widows or duration of marriage which are not explicitly controlled. Sane values for these statistics bolster confidence in the computer model. These two questions call, then, primarily for documentation, first, of the choices of vital rates, and, second, of the resulting values of secondary statistics. The third question which occupies us is a knottier one, whether the randomness incorporated in our computer process and in mathematical stochastic population theory more generally, captures that randomness with which historians must cope in making inferences about social structure in the past. This question does not appear to have been raised or treated satisfactorily in previous literature. It clearly demands subtler answers than we have to offer, but we shall claim at the conclusion of the chapter that some present knowledge can be brought to bear.

Our hope of imitating inside the computer the timing of human life cycles rests on our confident basic knowledge at the individual level of how births, marriages, childbirths, and deaths tend to follow each other. Some of this is too simple for words. Some of it is hard-won observation of statistical independences and regularities from a tradition of mathematically-informed demography dating at least to Edmund Halley and John Graunt. However poorly understood the more complex interactions like marriage markets may be, and however unforeseeable the upshot in the aggregate of individual behavior, there is solid foundation for composing computer instructions about the main events happening to individuals. This advantage for demographic simulation is one that simulation in other areas of social science must often forego. The "micro" in microsimulation emphasizes that in our routines the computer programming implements assumptions about events and interactions for individuals. Summary statistics printed by the computer are accumulated from hundreds and thousands of individual random contributions.

The special demographic assumptions of the experiment are fed into the computer in the form of tables of birth, death, and marriage rates and a listing of a starting "population." The general demographic assumptions are built into the computer code itself for determining births, birth intervals, marriages, selection of spouses, fertility multipliers, remarriages, deaths, and their probability distributions and interrelationships for the "population" in the long run. By a "population" in the computer we mean an artificial population whose existence is only as entries in a listing stored in the computer, entries which refer to notional individuals, not to any real historical people. At any time during the simulation this list can be printed out and resembles the listing of a settlement that might be found for an actual parish except that it substitutes identification numbers for names and shows much more information about the life histories of the inhabitants and their relationships to each other, with greater detail and exactness, than any historical listing. The computer keeps track of time in notional "months." The population list is updated each month to assimilate events generated for the individuals by the computer with its random number generator, and the simulation itself is best imagined in terms of this ever-changing list. Of course we shall refer to the individuals entered in the list as if they were human beings acting out their fates themselves.

The *SOCSIM Manual* describes the computer programs in their state of development at the time the present experiment was run. The 50 some pages of sample inputs and outputs in the manual make more vivid than we can here the nuts and bolts of experimentation. Also, aspects of the model secondary to understanding the results, passed over here, are treated there. For each person each month, the probabilities of each event appropriate for the person depend on his or her characteristics and—a basic assumption—they are otherwise independent from month to month. Death rates depend on sex and age within 5-year age groups, except that the first month of life, the next 11 months, and the next 4 years form separate age groups. Childbirth probabilities depend on a woman's age within the age groups 15–16, 17–19, 20–24, 25–29, 30–34, 35–39, and 40–44, on her marital status (single, married, or widowed) and on her parity, the number of children she has already borne. They also depend on a fertility multiplier, assigned at random to the woman at birth and carried with her through life, making some women consistently subfertile and others superfertile relative to the average fertility in the population. This provision for heterogeneous fertility seeks to enhance the realism of ratios of variances to means of completed family size, a statistic potentially important to household structure. A random birth-spacing routine adjusts a woman's probability of giving birth soon after bearing a child depending on whether the earlier infant survives or dies.

Marriage rates for females depend on age, marital status, and position in a household, and when a woman is assigned an event of marriage, her groom is chosen from all eligible males by criteria which relate the age of the groom to the age of the bride. The model is a closed model; if a groom is found at all, he is found from within the existing population, and the marriage precipitates changes of residence and household status for related members of the population. Assumptions about household membership are pursued in Chapter 3 of this volume. There is no divorce, and the polygyny option in SOCSIM was not exercised, but illegitimate births can occur, and widows and widowers are able to remarry. Retirement is not an event in its own right. The somewhat intricate routines for selection of grooms allow postponement of marriage in some cases and so involve a very weak feedback between numbers of eligible males and population growth, but no direct feedback from numbers of people or numbers of households to population growth or household numbers is in force.

The most serious simplification in SOCSIM's demography is the absence of provision for migration. The artificial population in the computer is a closed population. An individual joins it only by being born and leaves it only by dying. We know that in English preindustrial settlements mobility was considerable. Some evidence from England and the Continent further suggests that families often migrated as units and that younger age groups tended to migrate more than others (cf. Laslett, 1977, Chapter 1). However, the information is much too scanty to supply plausible age-specific, household-specific rates for a simulation. It seems unwise to guess at rates and expose every conclusion of the experiment to the objection that it might be a side effect of inappropriate migration rates. And, in our state of ignorance, to try enough alternative sets of migration rates to span the range of possibilities would be to conduct a full-scale new experiment, albeit one that should eventually be mounted. In this experiment, absence of migration is one of the controlled conditions. This fact must be kept in mind throughout the evaluation of its conclusions. Fortunately, it is at least feasible to argue a priori about the direction, if not the magnitude, of the adjustments to be made to our conclusions to allow for different kinds of migration, and we shall do so in Chapter 3 after we explain the systems of rules for household formation and dissolution.

We come now to the more specific demographic assumptions of our experiment, involving rates and probabilities. As we have said, they are selected to span a range broadly appropriate to English villages of the 1600s and 1700s. It is important, however, not to misunderstand the role of these assumptions by thinking that they are meant to capture an actual historical situation as exactly as possible. They are not. Our experiment is studying relationships between variables, relationships between demographic rates and household proportions. We wish our demographic rates to be plausible rates for the historical context in which we are interested, so that any demographic influences on household proportions which we observe in the experiment will be the kind of influences we might reasonably expect the actual demographic conditions, whatever they were in English preindustrial settlements, to have exercised over household proportions. But we are never going to know enough about any preindustrial village to specify all the rates we must specify for a computer simulation with reference to data for that settlement. It is more essential to observe the whole range of random variation which can occur for a single fixed set of rates than to worry over a precise choice of rates. Within a band of more or less equally plausible rates, the choice is not critical to our kind of conclusions.

We map out the range of random variation which occurs for a single set of rates by repeating our simulation experiment using different random numbers each time. For each of 15 sets of rates, the present experiment has been repeated (or replicated) 64 times, tracing the evolution of a population for 150 years each time. We control the rates to be the same each of these 64 times, and we start each of our 15 times 64 = 960 simulations with the same artificially constructed starting population, to be described shortly. The random numbers are statistically independent (speaking more technically, they result from separate calls to a congruential generator), so the 64 readings on each variable of interest supply 64 statistically independent observations. From these observations we gain information we could not gain by comparing historical villages, for we cannot in practice be confident that different historical villages are sensibly considered as independent identically-distributed cases nor that the same fixed demographic rates applied. The random effects are crucial for any questions pertaining to small village populations, in which random fluctuations are often very large.

The 15 combinations of demographic rates in the experiment are apportioned among tests with the three systems of rules for household formation to be described in Chapter 3, eight batches (labeled R1 to R8) for the so-called "primoreal" (R) rules, five (P1 to P5) for the "primonuptial" (P) rules, and two (U1 and U2) for the "ultimonuptial" (U) rules. R6, for instance, is a batch of 64 independent simulations with primoreal household rules (Chapter 3), populations declining slowly on average, low mortality, low fertility, and late marriage. The prohibitions on marriages between persons of certain statuses in their households under each rule system imply that runs with the same birth, death, and marriage probabilities specified as input cards by the experimenter have somewhat different growth rates and other demographic characteristics. R2, with an average crude yearly growth rate of +.00144, P2 with growth +.00155, and U1 with growth +.00220 share the same input parameters, as do R7 (−.00516), P4 (−.00573) and U2 (−.00456) as well as each pair

$$
\begin{array}{ll}
\text{R6} \ (-.00263), & \text{P3} \ (-.00219) \\
\text{R1} \ (+.00332), & \text{P1} \ (+.00350) \\
\text{R8} \ (-.00628), & \text{P5} \ (-.00632).
\end{array}
$$

There is a loose but not a sharp separation between the demographic and the household structural assumptions in the experiment.

Exhibits 2.1 and 2.2 give a demographic profile of the 15 batches in

EXHIBIT 2.1   Average Demographic Rates Realized in Simulation Batches

	Growth[a]	POP[b]	HH-size[c]	NRR[d]	Birth[e]	Death[f]	e_0f[g]	$e_{15}f$[h]	e_0m[i]
P1	+.00350	702	5.32	1.107	.0320	.0281	40.6	44.7	37.9
P2	+.00155	531	4.89	1.034	.0284	.0267	40.3	44.6	38.2
P3	−.00219	304	4.82	.899	.0225	.0244	40.1	44.5	38.0
P4	−.00573	181	4.41	.812	.0267	.0312	26.7	39.2	25.8
P5	−.00632	165	4.50	.811	.0251	.0299	26.8	38.9	26.3
R1	+.00332	692	4.94	1.102	.0316	.0279	40.5	44.8	38.0
R2	+.00144	518	4.37	1.023	.0281	.0266	40.2	44.6	38.2
R3	+.00085	476	4.51	1.009	.0274	.0264	40.3	44.5	38.1
R4	−.00090	359	4.57	.970	.0355	.0363	27.3	39.3	25.9
R5	−.00129	351	4.36	.956	.0355	.0365	27.3	39.5	25.5
R6	−.00263	288	4.28	.888	.0223	.0244	40.2	44.6	37.8
R7	−.00516	198	4.05	.830	.0273	.0314	27.2	39.2	25.7
R8	−.00628	168	4.21	.822	.0250	.0298	27.3	39.2	25.9
U1	+.00220	584	3.62	1.053	.0295	.0271	40.2	44.6	38.1
U2	−.00456	214	3.46	.855	.0285	.0322	27.3	39.1	25.4

[a] Average crude yearly growth rate across 64 simulations in a batch.
[b] Average total population after 150 years of simulation.
[c] Average total population divided by average number of households.
[d] Average net reproductive rate.
[e] Average crude yearly birth rate.
[f] Average crude yearly death rate.
[g] Average female expectation of life at birth.
[h] Average female expectation of life at age 15.
[i] Average male expectation of life at birth.

EXHIBIT 2.2.   Marriage and Parity Statistics Realized in the Simulation Batches

	Bride age (a)	Age gap (b)	S-S gap (c)	Mother age (d)	First birth (e)	Mean parity (f)	Var/ mean (g)	Child- less (h)
P1	25.3	5.8	2.3	31.5	26.4	3.98	2.76	.193
P2	25.3	1.0	.1	31.3	26.3	3.74	2.71	.202
P3	28.9	5.2	1.3	33.1	28.9	3.49	2.78	.225
P4	25.5	1.0	−.2	31.7	26.4	4.36	2.81	.180
P5	19.3	8.5	4.1	27.8	22.2	3.98	2.74	.196
R1	25.3	6.6	2.6	31.4	26.5	3.97	2.77	.192
R2	25.4	1.2	−.3	31.4	26.6	3.72	2.75	.209
R3	28.7	.6	−.7	33.1	28.7	3.78	2.85	.211
R4	19.1	8.8	4.4	27.8	21.6	4.59	2.77	.166
R5	25.2	.8	−.3	31.6	25.9	4.91	2.95	.161
R6	28.9	6.0	1.4	33.2	29.1	3.48	2.79	.226
R7	25.3	1.1	−.7	31.6	26.3	3.37	2.82	.177
R8	19.3	9.2	4.2	27.9	22.3	3.99	2.75	.194
U1	25.3	.6	−.6	31.4	26.3	3.82	2.66	.191
U2	25.3	.4	−1.3	31.6	26.3	4.45	2.83	.172

Explanation of these variables:

(a) Average of the bride's mean ages at first marriage.

(b) Average of the average age differences in years between spouses including all marriages.

(c) Average of the average age differences in years between spouses with both partners never before married.

(d) Average of the mean ages of mothers at childbirth.

(e) Average of the mean ages of mothers at first birth.

(f) Average parity of all women dying older than 45.

(g) Ratio of mean parity to the variance in parity of all women (married or not) dying older than 45.

(h) Proportion of all women dying older than 45 who are childless.

terms of averages taken over the 64 simulations in each batch. When we average over this many independent cases most—though not all—of the randomness cancels itself out, so the numbers in Exhibits 2.1 and 2.2 reflect quite directly the input parameters, the death, birth, and marriage rates chosen for the batches, which we now discuss in turn.

Two mortality levels can be discerned showing their effects in the tables, with expectations of life at birth (e_0) around 40 and around 27. The sex and age-specific death rate schedules are both taken from Ledermann (1969), *Nouvelles Tables—Types de Mortalité*. The low mortality levels are from the page labelled $Q = 350$ in Ledermann's Table 103, adjusted so that female and male monthly death rates are .092222 and .105226 in the first month of life and .008757 and .010057 in each of the next 11 months. For females e_0 equals 40.15; for males, 38.21. These levels are chosen to accord with the mortality rates for the age group 0–15 for Colyton, England, in the 1600s reported in Wrigley (1966). The more severe mortality levels are from the page labelled $Q = 30$ in Ledermann's Table 100 with adjusted first month rates of .128420 and .141357 and next 11 month rates of .014390 and .018282. For females e_0 equals 27.15; for males, 25.80. In retrospect, some batches with still more severe mortality would have been desirable for comparison with unlucky communities of the early 1600s, but the spread is already substantial. Peaks and troughs of mortality occur throughout each simulation run, the product of random variability, although no spurts of crisis mortality are prearranged for the runs.

The shape of the marital fertility curve for most of the batches is based on the parish reconstitution of Aldenham for 1600–1649 by the Cambridge Group for H.P.S.S. (unpublished). For $R8$, $R4$, and $P5$ rates peaking at slightly earlier ages were used. The levels of the fertility curve were picked to attain various growth rates. Growth rates are, however, hard to predict from the input parameters, because of special SOCSIM features like heterogeneous fertility and birth-interval adjustment. Choosing the fertility levels proved to be a game of trial and error, in which the four large negative growth rates were errors, still useful for the experiment but unintended. Illegitimate rates and parity-specific gradients were guesses. The birth interval parameter BINT described in the *SOCSIM Manual* was set to 18. The columns showing mother's average age at birth and mother's average age at first birth, average first birth interval, net reproductive rate, and total fertility rate give a picture of the fertility structures that result.

The choice of marriage rates is more involved than mortality or fertility. Marriage probabilities are statistics which cannot be obtained directly from family reconstitution because there is no way of calculating person–months at risk. What can be recovered from parish registers, however, are statistics about the distributions of ages at marriage. Computer simulation can then be used, working backwards, to determine marriage probabilities that will yield a distribution of ages at marriage like the observed distribution in the presence of appropriate death rates. Marriage rates determined in this way are not uniquely determined in general, but any set of marriage rates that yields an appropriate distribution of ages at marriage is appropriate for our experiment, for which the distribution of ages at marriage and not the rates are of primary significance. For this experiment this technique was applied to find rates of marriage using the ages at marriage for Colyton 1600–1649 and again for Aldenham 1600–1649 from the files of the Cambridge Group for H.P.S.S. The former give bride's mean age at first marriage near 28 in $R6$, $R3$, and $P3$. The latter give that mean age near 25, in all the other batches except

*R*8, *R*4, and *P*5. Batches *R*8, *R*4, and *P*5 employ rates resulting in bride's mean age at first marriage near 19, constructed for a separate experiment to test effects of crisis mortality on age gaps between spouses. These last marriage rates lead to marriage ages lower than any English family reconstitution studies before the immediate precensus years, but they supply interesting contrasts since household structure proves to be sensitive to marriage age.

So far we have been talking exclusively about averages. Of course the 64 independent simulations within a batch look very different from each other, due to random variability, so the spread of observed characteristics in the simulations is much greater than the spread of average values among batches. The stem and leaf diagrams in Exhibit 2.3 indicate the extent of this spread. A stem and leaf diagram is a popular variant of a histogram described in detail in Tukey (1977). The number of digits stretching to the right of the vertical line shows the number of cases, out of the 64 in a batch, with values of the displayed statistic whose highest significant figures equal the number to the left of the vertical line. The digits themselves give the next significant figure for each case, thus preserving extra information that would be lost if, for instance, we drew *X* to the right of the line for each case. For instance, in batch *P*5, we find two cases with bride's mean age at first marriage between 18.3 and 18.4, cases with values 18.32 and 18.39. Where a + appears we have separated out the cases with last digits above 5 in a separate bar.

Each of six statistics is represented in Exhibit 2.3 by a stem and leaf diagram for a different batch. These batches have been chosen by actual flips of a coin by the author in order to remove any selection bias. Within the limitations of space, it seems preferable to give full sample distributions for some batches rather than less informative summary statistics for all.

Exhibits 2.1 through 2.3 should enable the reader to judge how well the sets of demographic rates in the experiment embrace conditions relevant for comparisons with rural England around 1700. We shall refer again to these tables in Chapter 4 of this volume, when we investigate which demographic parameters exercise the strongest influence on household structure by contrasting proportions of household types in different batches. As a theoretical question about relationships between variables, this question is meaningful no matter what the particular rates, but as background for interpretation of English listings its interest is enhanced if, with reference to the historical context, rates differ enough to count as significant alternatives while remaining credible possibilities.

A number of the columns in Exhibits 2.1 and 2.2 shed light on the consistency between our demographic model on the one side and realistic expectations on the other. For instance, the separations between mean

EXHIBIT 2.3.   Stem and Leaf Diagrams from Randomly Selected Batches

Bride's mean age at
first marriage   P5

18.2	3
18.3	29
18.4	15
18.5	8513
18.6	09109520
18.7	21524110976
18.8	14460801
18.9	239812860011
19.0	1320647
19.1	496286
19.2	6
19.3	0
19.4	8

Mother's mean age at
childbirth   R3

32.7	4
32.8	96
32.9	660980571442
33.0	08079892093592943
33.1	6733505169237
33.2	2256159
33.3	9790
33.4	2
33.5	428236
33.6	3

Net reproductive rate   R1

.9+	572
1.0	344042424
1.0+	8867787687766968769579
1.1	30023330231
1.1+	5729689766558757
1.2	300

Female life expectancy
at birth   P5

22.	98
23.	98
24.	1735
25.	47769178
26.	87044560186139297
27.	100667739950944910
28.	141351689
29.	5571

Female crude birth rate   P1

.024+	7
.025	40
.025+	878
.026	420010431
.026+	56996668
.027	10434331
.027+	958667668696
.028	0323111120
.028+	998557
.029	140
.029+	6

Male crude death rate   R7

32+	699
33	
33+	667
34	040324
34+	887688
35	333022
35+	67588578885
36	32003222
36+	68687
37	2063300130
37+	55
38	
38+	87
39	4

age of mothers at first birth and at all births are consequences of many factors built into the model but not under the experimenter's direct control, including marriage probabilities, spouse selection criteria, age-specific birth rates, and birth-interval adjustments. That these separations are relatively stable at around 5 years is heartening. So is the stability of the proportion of women surviving their fertile period childless in the last column of Exhibit 2.2. The age gaps between spouses are partly determined by the age selection criteria for grooms, which were varied from batch to batch, but also by the interaction of population size and sex ratios with these criteria. The absence of wild values and the regular relationship between age gaps between all spouses and between spouses both never previously married are encouraging. The mean parities of women dying over the age of 45 correspond well with the mean ages of mothers at childbirth. Flaws in the model might have produced flukes in such statistics. One known anomaly in the model pointed out by Dr. Barbara Anderson, in a personal communication, turns out fortunately to have negligible effect. The computer code for birth spacing and for women scheduled for marriage who fail to find a groom in the first year of search removes some women from risk of death for some months. The observed and expected life tables (not reproduced here for reasons of space) are in such close agreement, however, that for our rates this anomaly is of no consequence.

On the subject of family size, the mean parities in Exhibit 2.2 give some indication of completed family size, although they count unmarried as well as married women. Unfortunately, parity distributions by marital statuses were omitted from computer printouts of the simulations. If we divide each mean parity figure by one minus the proportion childless, we obtain an index of conditional completed family size conditional on the birth of at least one child. Calling the last three columns of Exhibit 2.2 f, g, and h, the ratio of the conditional variance to the conditional mean completed family size conditional on at least one child equals $g - fh/(1 - h)$. It ranges from 1.76 in batch $P2$ to 2.10 in batch $R7$.

In our description of input parameters for the experiment, we reserve little space for the composition of the starting population which all 64 runs in all 15 batches have in common. The choice of population, except for its size, is of only minor concern, since the evolution of these populations whose vital rates are not changing over time becomes rapidly independent (within little longer than a generation) of the composition of the initial population. This independence of initial state could be inferred for processes like ours which lack strong nonlinearities by analogy with Stable Population Theory (cf. Coale, 1972, Chapter 3). It is also easy to observe directly in the simulations themselves. The actual starting population used was the terminal population of a trial simulation of 100 years with "primoreal" household rules, rates mostly like those for batch R6, and near zero growth, starting with a population characterless but for sex and age, with a stationary age distribution. The practice in the earlier household experiment reported in Hammel and Wachter (1977) of taking an historical population like that in the 1599 listing of Ealing in place of the characterless population was abandoned in this experiment. That picturesque touch did not seem worth added effort combatting the false notion that a simulation starting with the Ealing population must be seeking to recreate in the computer the historical evolution of Ealing. For our runs the starting population consisted of 206 men and 203 women in 84 households, and its important feature is that it is identical across all runs.

No simulation can do without some starting population, whether a primordial couple or a full-fledged community, but history offers no clear counterpart to such a starting population. It makes no sense to dream of identifying some group of founding fathers and mothers at some well-defined era in the past for the typical English parish of the 1600s. This remark brings us to the difficult question of the nature of randomness at stake in historical inferences about the social structure of communities.

Consider the dilemma in which historians find themselves. They need to regard a settlement as an instance handed them at random out of some larger collection of possible settlements with the same structural characteristics. For, they want their assertions to be stimulated by systematic features of social phenomena, not, for instance, by the vagaries of sperm cells hunting eggs. Thus they want to allow at least for the variance introduced into community statistics from year to year by the inherent variability of demographic processes, the sources of randomness incorporated into the computer simulation. To allow for variances, or for other expressions of statistical dispersion, means to discount any contrasts in data which are too small to be statistically significant in the face of that much variance or dispersion. Historians certainly want to allow for variances from demographic processes. Indeed, it would appear that they ought to regard variances calculated for these sources as bare minima. For, at first blush, it makes sense to regard the demographic rates—held fixed in the experiment—as themselves at least slightly random, responding to the vicissitudes of community ecology, politics, and economics. But, if historians include in their reckoning even the minimum demographic fluctuations from the more and more distant past, the total contribution to variances of many statistics can be shown, in principle, to grow ridiculously large. Evidently, there exist long-term historical processes which suppress variance and balance out the accumulating short-term variances. These take the form, presumably, of slow feedback and control mechanisms, sociological or Malthusian, including systematic migration.

These are not obvious points, and it may help if we repeat them, point by point, in terms of computer simulations instead of historical settlements. No one run of our computer program reveals what model we have selected, for the random numbers in the simulation have a large say in the outputs. At best we can regard any one run as one handed us at random out of a collection of possible runs. But with simulations, unlike historical settlements, we can turn the possible runs into actual runs and assemble a collection we can observe. We can measure the dispersion among the different runs in a batch in the values of any given statistic. The dispersion would be still greater if we increased the realism of our model by introducing more random features.

Now, notice that the amount of dispersion, measured for instance by the variances, depends on the length of time the simulations run. If this time equals zero, these variances are all zero, for the initial populations for the different runs are the same and there is no dispersion. As we lengthen the timespan over which the populations in the different runs are allowed to evolve out of the common initial population, most variances increase. The runs come to differ more and more. If we simulated forever, most variances would creep or zoom to infinity. How rapidly depends on the size of the initial population, for much of the variance of many statistics can be traced back to the variance of the size of population and the sizes of age and sex groups. This dependence holds as much for variances in proportions of household types, chief outputs from our experiment, as for anything else. Obviously, variances headed for infinity signal that some forces present in history are missing from our model, forces which suppress variances over the long run.

Independent processes add variance, by and large. For a process to suppress variance, it must be dependent on the processes generating variance. For example, if numbers of immigrants are random and independent of events in a parish, then taking account of them will raise the variance in population size. To depress the variance of population size we would need to assume streams of immigrants likely to increase when the parish starts to shrink and to taper when its size surges. We would need to assume statistical dependence.

It is a fact of life that joint probabilities for dependent processes require vastly more data to estimate than those for independent processes. In the absence of compelling and precise external information, the outlook for estimating the contributions of long-term control mechanisms with anything like the statistical rigor—itself limited enough—that we are beginning to apply to births, marriages, deaths, and household types appears dim.

The obvious resort is to ignore beyond some fixed point of time the contributions to variance from the distant past, recognizing that at some distance in time long-term variance-suppressant processes must begin to dominate over short-term variance-augmenting processes. This strategy corresponds to choosing some fixed timespan to let the simulations run. But that places a premium on understanding the impact of different timespans on variances. The validity of the strategy depends on finding the major variances to be relatively insensitive to the exact choice of timespan within plausible bounds.

The simulation study of age pyramid variances reported in Chapter 11 of this volume does tackle this problem of sensitivity of variances to timespan from a limited point of view. It suggests that a period does exist after the influence of the initial population wears off during which the variances of the age pyramid remain relatively stable. This finding lends support to our choice in the experiment of a timespan of 150 years. It is likewise encouraging to note that inspection of household statistics after 100 years of simulation in our batches reveals few glaring differences from the 150-year statistics we report, although a full-scale analysis of timespan dependence is a large undertaking which must await another occasion.

Variances are functions not only of timespan, as we have said, but of population size. The problem of randomness we have been discussing interlocks with the problem of a closed population. Viewed another way, migration affects variances directly. In the computer, the marriage pool consists of all and only those suitable mates already in the population. Of course English parishes were not closed in this strict sense. But evidence from family reconstitution of adjacent parishes by the Cambridge Group does indicate that numbers of marriages fall off rapidly with distance beyond a point. We would argue that the present evidence for villages of the size typical for those described in Chapter 5 of this volume is compatible with the assumption of an approximate effective breeding population in the range of 200 to 700 persons. In this range, starting from an initial population of 409, most of our terminal simulation populations fall. It would be pleasant to be able to make a stronger claim, but the state of our knowledge does not oblige us.

Our populations in the computer are not only closed, in the sense of being self-contained breeding groups, but they are also homogeneous, in the sense that the same demographic rates and household formation rules apply to all their members equally. We introduce no stratification in our populations, whether by class or occupation or tenant status or religion or any other variable. We may imagine that demographic rates and social practices did vary across certain strata in preindustrial communities, though the gentry, for instance, must usually have been too few among too many to alter the overall picture. So long as strata may be assumed only rarely to intermarry, our results continue to apply, separately to separate strata with their own rates and household formation rules. Even if strata often intermarried, first approximations for a stratified village are surely obtainable by taking weighted averages of results for separate strata, weighted by the hypothetical sizes of the strata, and adding some extra margin of uncertainty.

Readers should be cautioned, in all fairness, that no splitting and weighting of strata has been attempted for our own comparisons between simulation outcomes and historical listings in Chapters 5 and 6 of this volume. The figures that are given should, however, allow readers who are interested in such possibilities to compute averages and draw new comparisons themselves. Major conclusions, like the mismatch between the English data and the stem-family household hypotheses in the simulations, do not seem to us very vulnerable to revision. An hypothesis that stem-family promoting practices were followed, but only by a fraction of a whole community, might well bring simulation figures and historical listings into line with each other, but the smaller the fraction, the less would such an hypothesis deserve the name of a stem-family household hypothesis and the less relevant to the present controversy would it become. Or at least so we claim, for our major conclusions. The finer points of our analysis, on the other hand, might be substantially revised by consideration of strata. Especially for researchers intrigued by hypotheses which link household composition to land tenure or inheritance custom, our assumption of homogeneity is one of the most important controlled conditions of our experiment to bear in mind.

Recapitulating, the demographic assumptions for our experiment described in this chapter raise a multitude of issues. The relevance of the rates to historical cases and the realism of the model are open to debate; for this debate we have tried to submit evidence. The conditions of experimental control that we have imposed—among them closed, homogeneous populations, absence of migration, fixed initial population, fixed and constant demographic rates, and fixed timespan of simulation—are likewise for challenge. In some cases they bring us up against limits to our current understanding of the randomness of historical events and open avenues that call for better exploration. Computer simulations force one to make decisions, and one must try to make them as judiciously as one can. Experiments require definite assumptions. Those of this chapter and Chapter 3 are the foundation underneath the conclusions of Chapter 4.

3

Household Hypotheses

Our experiment—adverting to the literal meaning of the word "experiment" in Wycliffe's Bible—is a test or trial. What is being put to the test are hypotheses about social practices with regard to household residence choice, the subject of this chapter. They are being tested by the fruits they bear, in the form of occurring types of households, when social practices are matched with demographic circumstances.

Our definitions in this chapter may recall the legalisms of a courtroom or the formalities of an examination hall. That is not for the sake of analogy with trials and tests, nor merely to satisfy demands of the computer, but rather for the advantages that household–kinship studies stand to gain from freedom from ambiguity. Burgeoning research in any subject creates pressure for refining the language of argument. Classification of households has elsewhere received deserved attention, and the formal structure of kinship benefits from a rich anthropological literature. Here we approach individual household decisions in the same spirit, offering our elaboration of a general stem-family idea into three detailed versions of household hypotheses as an illustration of the challenges of specification.

We pick the stem-family idea for its specifiability. Our interest, as Chapter 1 has insisted, lies not in the stem family as such, but in complex households, households accommodating coresident kin. Of the many types of complex households, households formed along stem-family lines have accumulated the largest previous literature and admit the easiest abstraction of guiding principles of organization. Thus they invite, before others, specification, in sharp explicit detail, in terms of rules for membership. Our sets of rules govern the transitions in the membership of households accompanying each demographic event of birth, marriage, or death. Like the demographic assumptions of our experiment, these social structural assumptions are stylized in various respects, to capture essential features of the stem-family household idea while permitting the firmest inferences about the relationships between variables in our model under controlled conditions.

Three dichotomies should be borne in mind throughout our presentation of household rules. The first is the distinction, at the heart of our whole experiment, between patterns of household membership decisions and patterns of household types occurring under the influence of demography. This distinction is discussed fully in Chapter 1, in terms of the notion of demographic filter, but we again emphasize that household hypotheses here mean hypotheses about input to the filter, not output from the filter, about decisions, conditional on circumstances, not about realized households, taking circumstances into account. The second dichotomy distinguishes behavior from preference or ideology and pertains to the conceptual status of our rules. We shall discuss this issue shortly. The third dichotomy is a question of detail versus general character. How much hinges on the fine points of specific versions, how much on the "stem-family" core of the hypotheses? From one perspective this question awaits our computer outputs discussed in Chapter 4, showing how different the consequences of different versions can be. From another perspective, we learn about the inner logic of the hypotheses by working them out into sets of rules, discovering in the process how central or peripheral the choices that remain arbitrary appear to be.

The inner logic of the rules can be analyzed further to trace probable effects of factors not incorporated in the computer model. In particular, allowances for migration suggest themselves. We treat this subject after expounding the rules themselves and before tackling the final subject for the chapter and precondition for all of our analysis, the scheme of classification of households into types by their patterns of coresident kin.

We have just alluded to the issue of behavior versus preference or ideology. Our rules themselves embody no assumptions about cultural, social, legal, or economic factors that might impel behavior. Sometimes we use the long phrases "individual decisions as to residence" or "social practices as to residence choice" for them. It is perfectly clear what these rules are in the context of a computer program; they are explicit instructions to change headship, to permit or impede marriage, to remove persons from and insert them into households, and to recompute kinship relationships. It is not immediately obvious what these rules mean outside the intricate game of the simulation model; to what events or processes in the real world are they relevant?

We might take the position that the rules in the computer program were the goals or motivations of individuals in an historical population, that is, that they were the same as the rules people had in their heads. This would be a dangerous position, for we have no direct way to verify whether people had such rules in their heads. Indeed, it is not clear what it means to have a rule in one's head. Furthermore, it should be obvious that such a position would be equally dangerous whether we were imputing psychological reality to the rules of a computer program, or to ideological statements in the myths or literature of a society, or to the statements made about behavior by natives of a society, or to the generalities constructed by historians out of their observations of documentary evidence.

We might fall back from this dangerous position and say that the rules of the computer program were akin to a description of discrete decisions taken by members of a society in the course of getting married and finding a place to live. Our rules would then be very like the ethnographer's description of how natives behaved, and we could ask, via our simulation, what the demographic and social organizational results of such decision making might be. We should have to be cautious about such statements, however, in view of our experimental stylization. Our computer program's decisions about household membership, unlike its demographic events, are quite mechanical. For any open decision in given circumstances, like inheritance of headship when a widow is younger than 45, there is only one outcome. There is no random component to our household decision rules. That is to say, they are not stochastic, even though we know that people in the same circumstances do not always behave in just the same way. We could alter our program to make these decisions stochastic. But our hypotheses are already more ramified than those usually put forward in historical debates. Randomized decision rules might complicate rather than enhance the application of our simulation results to present discussion of historical social structure.

If we regard our rules, however, as being on a par with ethnographer's notes on choices observed to predominate in fixed situations in a society, we may elude at least the most glaring misconceptions. A distinction between observable choices by natives and any interpretive scheme of the ethnographer's is natural. It is essential not to confound a description of behavior with some theory about its motives or origins. Whether practices promoting stem-family households can be explained by inheritance customs or a land tenure system, for instance, is a separate question from the one we are treating, namely, how do we recognize and rate the strength of such practices themselves?

Stem-family principles were enunciated by P. G. Frédéric Le Play (e.g., Le Play, 1864, Part 1, Chapter III, Section 30) and are widely known in the shape given, for example, on pages 124–128 of Zimmermann and Frampton (1936). Critiques of the historical evidence for their application as principles guiding the organization of coresident domestic groups appear in the introduction to Laslett and Wall (1972) and in Chapter 5 of this volume. Fundamental to the stem-family household, for our purposes, is "unigenitural coresidence": One and only one married child in each generation in a line of genealogical descent may coreside. Historians often identify two versions of unigeniture—primogeniture and ultimogeniture. In primogeniture the first-born surviving child or son, depending on the variant, brings a spouse into the parental household and raises a family there; in ultimogeniture, the last-born. Of course these terms are not restricted to residence and even more often pertain to inheritance of property. The principle governing inheritance of property may or may not govern residence, and vice versa. We reiterate that our rules are tied to no assumptions about property, nor do they exclude them.

Many other versions of unigeniture are conceivable. As Chapter 1 explains, the conclusions of simulations profit from sharp and stylized hypotheses, which give the clearest picture of relationships between variables. We are therefore interested among other things in the extreme forms of unigeniture. Now, a household can appear as a stem-family household only during the temporal overlap in the married lives of coresiding children and parents. Thus maximizing or minimizing this temporal overlap should nearly maximize or minimize the number of occurring stem-family households at any point in time. These extremes are achieved not by primogeniture or ultimogeniture, but by building the family stem through the first child or last child to marry, whether or not this child is the first- or last-born. We call such practices "Primonuptial" and "Ultimonuptial," abbreviating them to P and U. An earlier discussion of these practices and their implications, based on a previous simulation experiment, is published in Hammel and Wachter (1977).

The primonuptial and ultimonuptial rules aim explicitly to maximize and minimize, among unigenitural systems, the occurrences of households including parents coresiding with a married child. This aim settles most choices of detail. We would not pretend for a moment that any historical village would have had practices of this extreme and stylized mode. The primonuptial and ultimonuptial rules are artificial systems designed to yield upper and lower bounds on achievable proportions of households of stem-family type. The extremal character of the P-rules and the U-rules needs only slight qualification. If we compelled oldest children to marry early or youngest children to marry late, or if we depressed the death rates of members of the household stem, we could probably increase still further the stem-family proportions and perhaps not greatly distort the overall observed marriage rates or death rates. It is possible to imagine historical mechanisms with these effects. The more familiar practice, however, imitating old Laban in the Book of Genesis, of barring younger children from marriage before the marriage of the eldest, would decrease rather than increase the levels of stem organization which primonuptial rules achieve.

We seek not only upper and lower bounds on stem-family proportions, but a notion of how far inside the bounds some historically plausible system of rules might fall. Each historical case where stem-family household behavior has been hypothesized has its own twists and variants, its better supported and its more speculative features. Our third set of rules, the "primoreal" or R-rules, is a compromise system of male primogeniture which emerged from discussions with historians at the S.S.R.C. Cambridge Seminar of 1974.

We are concerned at each marriage, birth, and death with the ways in which persons move into and out of households, the way in which the headship of households changes, and the way kinship relationships within a household are rephrased when a change in headship occurs. No rules are included which alter household memberships except at the times of marriages, births, and deaths. There is no spontaneous migration or departure into service or retirement from household headship. As noted, our three rule systems are all varieties of unigeniture, as regards rights of household residence for married children. They differ in their conventions for selecting the child on whom these rights devolve. Only one of them, the primoreal, makes a stab at ethnographic reality, without of course claiming to mirror a particular ethnographic reality, colored as it would be in any case by subjective interpretation and sampling error. The other two, the primonuptial and ultimonuptial, are frankly artificial. Together, the P-, R-, and U-rules stake out a progression from strongest through moderate to weakest reasonable stem-family-household-promoting practices. The computer implementation of the primoreal rules is documented at length in Chapter 11 of the *SOCSIM Manual*. Here we discuss the logic, rather than the computer code, for all three rule systems. They are closely related to each other, distinguished by small but critical aspects of the decision process.

Central to the understanding of these rules is the notion of a line of designated heirs. This line is the *stem* that forms the core of stem-family organization over time. Every household must have a head. As soon as that head's successor can be identified according to the rule system in force, we call that successor a designated heir. The spouse of any designated heir is also a designated heir. So is any person who has been identified as the successor to a designated heir, supposing the heir became head. The stem is a line of heirs headed by the head. With one exception, succession is such that only biological children or spouses of either heads or designated heirs can become designated heirs. The exception is a widowed head over the age of 54 without coresident children or designated heirs, whose successor as determined by rules we give shortly, regardless of parentage, may become designated heir. The rules are designed to forestall lateral transfer of headship, except where a household would otherwise disappear.

The restriction of designated heirship to biological children of conjugal pairs of which one member is already head or designated heir involves certain subtleties for stepchildren. The son of a head can be heir. So can the son of the wife of a male head, that is, the male head's stepson. But the stepson through a former husband of a male head's wife, who may belong to the household, cannot be heir. Some consanguineal linkage must connect the parental conjugal pair with the offspring to permit transmission of headship. Of course we could change this rule in other simulations and include adoption. But adoption is not recognized in these simulations, because it is a rare event in the ethnographic situation we are modeling.

The designation of heirs takes place only at certain times in the evolution of a household, for instance at the first marriage in each generation. There are periods, then, when potential heirs are not yet designated heirs. Where possible, a designated heir is added only at the bottom of an existing line of designated heirs, so that a line of lineal descent connects each generation to the last one. It may happen, nonetheless, that designated heirs two generations apart are not related biologically, for a line may run from father to son, and then from son's wife to son's wife's son by another husband. The designated heirs are ordered by their seniority in the generational tree, with male designated heirs taking precedence over their spouses, who are also designated heirs in the same generation and are the only other designated heirs in the same generation. The junior designated heir is the heir with the lowest seniority. Usually generational seniority corresponds to seniority in age, although large age gaps between spouses can produce anomalies, and it is the generational ordering that prevails.

The inheritance of headship, upon the head's death, follows the same order in all three rule systems:

A sole survivor is de facto heir and head, else

A surviving widow less than 35 years old becomes head, else

The senior designated heir becomes head.

If the household contains no designated heir,

The head's widow over age 34 becomes head, else

The oldest ever-married male becomes head, else

The oldest ever-married female becomes head, else

The oldest male over 15 becomes head, else

The oldest female over 15 becomes head, else

The oldest male becomes head, else

The oldest female becomes head.

If there is no survivor, the household is extinguished. These rules give precedence to widows capable of continuing the family line, then to designated heirs by their generational seniority, with the stem maintained by including their spouses. If there are no designated heirs, rights revert to the aged widow, and then to successively younger and less sociologically mature kin, with preference to males only within each broader category. There will always be some new head unless the whole household dies out. Our programs do not arrange special treatment for orphans, so that in theory a single infant can find itself lone head of a solitary household, but such cases are so rare as not to merit extra attention for our purposes.

The crux of each rule system is the choice of household of residence for a newly married couple. Both bride and groom are subjected separately to a series of tests, described in later paragraphs, to determine whether each must remain in or must leave his or her present household. The two outcomes are combined into a single choice by the following scheme:

If both must remain, their marriage is prohibited, and the bride seeks a new prospective husband.

If both must leave, they establish a new nuclear household.

If the bride must leave and the groom must remain, the bride joins the groom in his household.

If the bride must remain and the groom must leave, the groom joins the bride in her household.

When a groom or bride moves, he or she brings along all of his or her children under the age of 15. If a head of household moves, the entire household accompanies the head. Such moves rarely occur, but they do produce some laterally extended households in any simulation.

Four impediments to marriage are common to all three rule systems:

Siblings and half-siblings may not marry.

Parents may not marry their own children.

Coresidents of the same household may not marry.

Two heads of households may not marry, unless the man is the only person in his household, and it is determined that the woman must remain in hers.

The first two rules are incest taboos. The third rule is consistent with our decision, discussed shortly, not to build into our model mechanisms for trading servants between households. The fourth rule prevents the merger of households except in extremity, in order to avoid increasing the numbers of non-stem-family households unnecessarily.

We come now to the criteria which ordain whether bride or groom must leave their households or remain. Consider first the *primonuptial* (P) system. A prospective bride who is head or designated heir must remain in her household. A biological daughter of the most junior designated heir in the ordering by generations, or of the head if there are no designated heirs, must remain and becomes upon marriage a designated heir (the new junior one). Such a child will not have any already-married surviving sister; otherwise the sister would have been designated an heir and would be more junior than the child's parent. If the head is a widow aged 54 or older without coresident children or designated heirs and if the bride is the head's successor under our previous rules for inheritance of headship, then the bride must remain. In all other cases she must leave the household. The same rules apply to bridegrooms, except that a groom who is sole member of his household (and therefore head) may leave to join a bride who must stay in hers. Thus the first marriage in the household in each generation triggers designation of the heir and the first child in each generation to marry becomes the designated heir for that generation and continues the stem.

Under the *ultimonuptial* rules a bride or groom who is not already head or designated heir and who has any coresident living siblings must leave and is not designated as an heir. After that check, all the rules for the primonuptial case apply in order. The effect of the extra check is to defer designation of an heir until the last child of a sibling set marries, and to continue the stem through that last child.

The *primoreal* rule system is more complex. It introduces preference rules based on age and sex. A head or designated heir must still remain. But if the bride's household contains a designated heir and the bride is a biological child of the junior heir and if she has a brother over age 15, she must leave. The oldest of her brothers is then designated heir for that generation, although the marriage to trigger the designation was not his own. If the bride has no brothers over age 15, her oldest sister over age 15 is tagged as designated heir and the bride must leave. If there is no designated heir but the bride is a biological child of the head, the same provisions apply. If she is not the biological child of the head or of a designated heir, she must leave. For the groom the same checks are carried out, too, with the same consequences, for his brothers, but not for his sisters. This rule system gives precedence to males over females and to older siblings over younger ones, in a version of primogeniture roughly patterned on European experience.

It is apparent, simply by contemplating the rule systems, that the primonuptial and ultimonuptial systems differ substantially. There are relatively few arbitrary choices embedded in them, for the stricture to maximize or minimize stem-family households dictates most details. On the other hand, the primoreal system, on the face of it, resembles the primonuptial closely, and it is filled with details that could as well be otherwise. Comparison of the simulation outputs from primoreal and primonuptial runs ought, therefore, to shed light on the question of the relative importance of general character versus detail in household rules.

We are now in a position to examine the rules with respect to the most serious substantive limitation of the SOCSIM simulations, the absence of migration. As we have said in Chapter 2, absence of migration is one of the controlled conditions of our experiment, and we are obligated to consider what adjustments to our conclusions it would entail. It is easiest to argue about migration under the primonuptial rules, where the first-marrying child of a household has rights to coreside with the parental couple and retains those rights even if widowed. Now, with slight qualification, it would make no difference to the organization of *that* household whether other persons emigrated while single, went into service, or (as our simulation provides) waited until marriage to leave. What difference would it make to other households? If children (contrary to our simulation model) went into service in other households in the same community, it would merely increase the number of persons unrelated to the head in other households. In our scheme, to be described shortly, the presence of such unrelated persons does not change any household classifications. If children emigrated, but the marriage rates in the community remained constant, the same proportion in any age group of the remaining siblings of the first-marrying child would marry and form new nuclear households in the same community. Thus, except insofar as the first-marrying child represented a larger fraction of the whole marrying sibling set, the proportion of nuclear and simple family households would not be depressed.

We must qualify these assertions slightly, for the migration of siblings more rapidly than they would have married could leave a household heirless in the occasional event of death without issue of the first-marrying child and spouse. Similarly, there are some marriage–age interactions that could affect nuclear household proportions. But by and large it appears that migration or departure into service of unattached persons, had we added it to our model, would not have greatly altered the proportions of complex households or nuclear households that we observe under the primonuptial rules.

Under primoreal rules, if we postulate that an oldest son or daughter, in expectation of inheritance, would not migrate or go into service, all the same considerations as in the primonuptial case obtain. Under ultimonuptial rules, migration might speed up the dispersion of siblings, making the last child an older child, marrying earlier, and so extending the time during which a household could appear in stem-family form. Or, migration might inflate the number of heirless households. The net effects are harder to foresee. Under all three rule systems, allowing departure into service would make it sensible to relax the prohibition against marriage of coresidents, but these couples unrelated to the head would then presumably start new nuclear households, so that the effects would cancel out.

Unlike the migration of unattached persons, migration of entire households is a Protean monster. If all complex households emigrated, a community could consist entirely of nuclear and solitary households, whereas if simple and complex households were equally likely to migrate or if immigration balanced emigration, nothing would change. By hypothesizing sufficiently perverse or regular migration, any observed pattern of household types could be explained. Moderate hypotheses about migration, however, probably do not carry surprising consequences. For instance, if we believe that Stuart England saw nuclear households on the move more frequently than complex households and that, on balance, migration flowed toward the mortality sink of London, then we would expect nuclear levels in outlying, migrant-contributing areas to be depressed.

We have presumed throughout our discussion the existence of a scheme for classifying households according to their kin composition. Classification is a delicate problem. But we need not dwell on it, for we are relying on a scheme already fully documented elsewhere and increasingly in common use among historians, the scheme given in Hammel and Laslett (1974) and slightly revised and implemented with computer routines in Hammel and Deuel (1977). The classification revolves around the concept of a conjugal family unit or nucleus. A nucleus consists either of a conjugal pair, or a conjugal pair and the child or children of one or both of them, or of an unmarried parent with child or children. Each person belongs to at most one nucleus, the person's family of procreation taking precedence over the person's family of birth. A household with a widowed head, his daughter, her husband, and their children contains one nucleus, made up of the daughter, husband, and children. The daughter is assigned to a nucleus with her husband, obviating the chance of the head–daughter pair to count as a nucleus. Not all persons belong to nuclei and not all households contain nuclei. Households with more than one nucleus have classifications containing the word "multiple" or the letter M. Households which contain persons who are themselves members of no nucleus but are still related to members of nuclei have classifications containing the word "extended" or the letter X. Households of any class may contain persons unrelated to the other members without altering their classification. The 10 classes appear in Exhibit 3.1.

Some households, like nuclear households, can only be classified in one way. Other households can be classified in several ways. For example, a household consisting of a married head and wife, his married son and wife, and his unmarried brother would be classified in three ways: first as multiple lineal (MLN) by virtue of the two conjugal pairs standing in lineal relationship; second, as extended lateral (XLT) by virtue of the link between the head and his bachelor brother; and third as extended lateral down (XLTD) by virtue of the avuncular-nepotic bond between the married son and his father's brother. The existence of households with several classifications entangles us into making two kinds of tabulations of households, not one. In one, the computer tabulates all the different combinations of classifications that occur, so that MLN–XLT–XLTD is a heading of its own just like MLN or XLT. We call these combinations "types." Each household has one type, so the numbers of each type add up to the total number of households. In the other scheme, the computer tabulates all the separate occurrences of a classification like MLN alone or in combination. MLN–MLT–MLTD is counted three times under each of the three "principles of organization." We call these categories "classes"; the numbers in each class add up to the total number of principles of organization, which exceeds the number of households by an "inflation ratio." The inflation ratio for each of our 15 batches, the total number of principles in all the replications of the batch divided by the total number of households, is found in Exhibit 4.1 and ranges from 1.009 to 1.171.

Although less intuitive, our 10 classes of household principles are more serviceable on the whole than our 50-odd types of households. Most types which are combinations like MLN–XLT–XLTD are too rare to be interesting. Nonetheless, if we had recourse to lumping types together, for

EXHIBIT 3.1.   Household Classifications

Abbre- viation	Name	Definition	Examples
NUC	Nuclear	Conjugal pair with or without children, parent with children.	Head plus wife, or head plus wife plus children, or head plus children.
MLN	Multiple lineal	Two or more nuclei in lineal ascendant-descendant relation.	Head, wife, son, son's wife.
MLT	Multiple lateral	Two or more nuclei in lateral non-descendant relation.	Head, wife, brother, brother's wife.
MLTD	Multiple lateral down	Two or more nuclei in lateral and descendant relation.	Head, wife, brother's son, brother's son's wife.
XLN	Extended lineal	One nucleus with a lineal relative not a member of any nucleus and in an ascendant or descendant relation.	Head, son, son's wife, or head, daughter, grandson.
XLT	Extended lateral	One nucleus with a collateral relative of the head in the same generation as the head and not a member of any nucleus.	Head, wife, brother.
XLTD	Extended lateral down	One nucleus with a collateral relative of the head not a member of any nucleus and in a different generation from the head.	Head, wife, brother's son.
SPEC	Special	Two or more related persons but no nuclei.	Head, brother, sister, granddaughter.
SOLE	Solitary	One or more persons with no kinship relation between any of them.	Head, unrelated lodgers.
INLAW	In-law	Two people present related through two or more affinal links.	Head, wife, wife's former husband's brother.

instance combining all the types in which MLN appears, we might prejudice the outcomes toward lineal, as opposed to lateral, complexity, or in some other way. The classes of principles record impartially the full diversity of complex household organization. But we must keep the meaning of the inflation ratios in mind. The proportion that all MLN households form out of the total number of households, which would interest us if we wanted to treat MLN as an inclusive category, preempting other categories, equals the inflation ratio multiplied by the proportion of principles in the class MLN, not the proportion MLN itself. For a breakdown of a community into exclusive categories of households, the tabulation by types is usually more appropriate than the tabulation by classes, since then each household, not each principle, ought to count once.

We base coarser classifications on the fine classification by types. Stem-family households are those in which lineal organization is visible, either multiple lineal households, MLN, when the conjugal units in two generations in a line of descent are both intact, or extended lineal households, XLN, when one of two lineally-related conjugal units survives only as a remnant rather than as a full nucleus. The stem-family households include most, though not all, of the compound types as well as MLN and XLN alone. We often quote a tripartite division of households into proportions stem, nuclear, and other, as in Chapter 4 of this volume in Exhibits 4.6, 4.7, and 4.10, or a four-way division into proportions stem, nuclear, solitary, and other, as in Exhibit 4.1.

The same household evolves from one type to another as time passes. Under the hypotheses of our simulation experiment, nearly every household should become a stem-family household at some point, although, depending on the rule system, it may be nuclear or solitary or laterally extended for greater or lesser stretches of time. Our system of classification treats the household as it appears at an instant, caught somewhere in the household life cycle, in the grip of demographic processes. It may be destined for other forms, but we classify it by appearance, not by destiny, for its appearance at a moment of time is all the historian in possession of a single listing can observe. The bulk of our historical data on precensus households consists of single listings. There are some consecutive listings of settlements, and from them we might hope to discern individual residence decisions, not just occurring household types. But we must not forget even with consecutive listings that demography only presents us at random with circumstances in which to observe individual decisions. Inferential problems about the influences of demography, similar to those we have been discussing, remain.

There is no single "stem-family hypothesis" any more than there is a single "extended family hypothesis" or "simple family hypothesis." Debates with such broad categories are bound to be vacuous. Hypotheses about the households of the past need to specify behavior in at least enough detail to capture the major distinctions that available data can reveal. In this chapter we have stated our hypotheses in full detail, believing that confusion would diminish in household studies generally if readers and not writers were allowed to be the judges of which details count as inconsequential. How far the details of our household hypotheses produce observable effects among patterns of occurring households is one of the questions we ask of our simulations in Chapter 4.

4

Experimental Results

The results from our simulation experiment come in the form of tables showing the number and proportion of households of each type in a listing of our artificial computer population made 150 years after the start of simulation for 15 batches containing 64 replications each. These numbers reflect the household composition which would characterize a medium-sized settlement subject to one of the sets of demographic rates described in Chapter 2 of this volume under the hypothesis that individuals choose their household of residence in accordance with one of the sets of rules described in Chapter 3. Because we repeat the simulation experiment 64 times with independent random numbers for each pairing of rates and rules, we actually obtain a statistical sample of household proportions from which we can estimate features of the random variability as well as the average levels.

We have already described at the end of Chapter 3 our system of classification of households by kin composition, along with our two ways of treating households classifiable in more than one way, which give rise to our two kinds of tabulations, those by type and those by class. Our first table, Exhibit 4.1, gathers under one heading all the types which correspond to stem-family households and shows the average proportion that these form out of all households, along with the average proportion whose

EXHIBIT 4.1. Mean Percentages of Types of Households in Simulation Batches

	Growth[a]	e[b]	bafm[c]	Stem[d]	Nuc[d]	Sole[d]	Other[d]	Inflate[e]	HH[f]
P1	+.00350	41	25	46%	43%	5%	6%	1.140	131.9
P2	+.00155	40	25	45	42	7	6	1.131	108.6
P3	−.00219	40	29	38	45	8	9	1.126	63.0
P4	−.00573	27	26	40	45	9	6	1.085	40.9
P5	−.00632	27	19	49	37	9	5	1.171	36.7
R1	+.00332	41	25	37	52	5	6	1.113	139.9
R2	+.00144	40	25	35	52	8	5	1.087	118.7
R3	+.00085	40	29	30	54	8	8	1.086	105.7
R4	−.00090	27	19	44	45	7	4	1.135	78.6
R5	−.00129	27	25	33	52	9	6	1.085	80.5
R6	−.00263	40	29	29	55	9	7	1.071	67.2
R7	−.00516	27	25	32	50	12	6	1.073	49.0
R8	−.00628	27	19	41	45	8	6	1.126	39.9
U1	+.00220	40	25	16	74	8	2	1.010	161.0
U2	−.00456	27	25	15	71	12	2	1.009	61.9

[a] Average crude growth rate in 64 simulations.
[b] Average female expectation of life at birth.
[c] Average age of brides at first marriage.
[d] Average percentage of all households of these types.
[e] Inflation ratio, average number of household principles divided by average number of households.
[f] Average number of households in a simulation.

type is nuclear or solitary or other. Each entry is an average of the 64 proportions for all the 64 replications in a batch. Proportions computed by pooling all replications (one household, one vote, as opposed to one simulation, one vote) differ only trivially from these averages. As in Chapter 2, batches are identified by P, R, or U for the primonuptial, primoreal, or ultimonuptial rule system. A full demographic profile of each batch is given in Chapter 2, Exhibit 2.1, but for convenience the average crude growth rate, female expectation of life at birth, and average age of brides at first marriage are quoted here. The last columns show the inflation ratio relating class to type totals described in Chapter 3 and the average number of housholds in each batch.

A more detailed breakdown is available in Exhibit 4.2, which shows the means of the proportions of household principles in each class based on a sample of 64 replications for each batch. Standard deviations for the more important classes are given later in Exhibit 4.9. They characterize the dispersion in the distribution of proportions, and they can be converted to standard errors of the means in Exhibit 4.2 by dividing by the square root

EXHIBIT 4.2.   Proportions of Household Principles Falling into Different Classes

	MLN	XLN	MLTD	MLT	XLT	XLTD	INLAW	SPEC	SOLE	NUC
P1	31.5	12.1	.2	.7	5.3	2.7	3.5	1.4	4.5	38.0
P2	29.3	14.0	.2	1.1	4.8	2.7	2.9	1.2	6.4	37.2
P3	24.9	11.0	.1	.8	7.5	3.2	3.2	2.2	7.6	39.2
P4	24.9	14.4	.1	.4	5.1	1.6	2.4	2.0	8.6	40.6
P5	28.8	18.7	.1	.2	4.2	2.9	3.6	1.7	8.0	31.7
R1	23.7	11.3	.4	1.1	4.8	2.1	4.1	1.7	4.1	46.7
R2	21.8	12.6	.1	.5	3.6	1.6	2.7	1.7	7.3	48.1
R3	19.1	9.9	.1	1.1	5.2	2.1	2.5	2.6	7.4	50.1
R4	26.5	16.8	.1	.2	3.0	1.8	4.3	2.2	5.6	39.5
R5	19.9	12.1	.1	.4	4.2	1.7	3.1	2.3	8.3	47.9
R6	19.0	8.7	.1	.7	4.4	1.9	2.5	3.5	8.6	50.4
R7	19.6	12.0	.1	.3	3.3	1.6	2.6	2.8	11.1	46.5
R8	24.8	16.1	.1	.1	2.2	1.1	3.8	3.3	8.2	40.2
U1	6.6	9.5	.0	.1	.9	.1	.7	1.1	8.4	72.7
U2	5.7	9.3	.0	.1	1.0	.1	.7	1.8	11.3	69.8

of 64, namely 8. As a rule, the estimation errors for the means are less than 1/30 of the means themselves.

In the ensuing analysis we lean heavily on the discussion in Chapter 1, which we refrain from repeating. It enunciates four ways in which the outputs of simulations can be read, and we proceed to read our computer outputs in these ways. The first addresses the general claim that demography does strictly constrain occurring household types, in other words, that the demographic filter has a strong distorting influence. Exhibits 4.1 and 4.2 demonstrate in an entirely unambiguous fashion that the constraints which demography imposes on stem-family household formation in the context we have investigated are very loose constraints. The patterns of individual decision-making which we have programmed into the experiment through the rules of household formation show up sharply in the achieved proportions of actually occurring household types. Our rules favor lineally-organized, stem households over all other modes of complex organization, and Exhibit 4.2 displays a preponderance of stem-family principles of organization, MLNs and XLNs, vis-à-vis other classes of complex kin composition. In every batch, the proportion of lineal extension is more than three times the proportion of lateral extension. The nature of the household rules shines through.

Compared, furthermore, with English and many European listings summarized in Chapter 5, the overall levels of stem-family and other complex households vis-à-vis nuclear households are high, though not overwhelming. The average proportions of stem-family types range between 38% and 49% for primonuptial rules, between 29% and 44% for primoreal rules, though only around 15% for ultimonuptial rules. The average proportions of all complex households (households other than NUC or SOLE) are, as we may expect, still higher, between 46% and 54% (P), 36% and 48% (R), and around 18% (U). When random variability is surveyed, we find cases among the 64 replications of some batches with complex family households amounting to as much as 68% of all households. The figures are substantially higher than any proportions yet found in European village listings outside of Russia and Latvia so far as we know. The other side of the coin is the relatively low proportion of nuclear family households in the primonuptial and primoreal simulations, averages from 37% to 45% (P) and from 45% to 55% (R). Although these figures leave room for naive wonder that decisions so oriented toward lineally complex households could lead even to as many nuclear households as this, they are so much lower than proportions in English listings as to appear puny by comparison. Had parishioners in England been choosing their households with anything like the stem-family propensities of our computer populace, three times as many of them or more on average would have been living with their kin.

Averages do not tell a full story, but in this case nothing in our examination later in this chapter of the random spread about the averages will revise our initial picture of mismatch between these theoretical outcomes and the English historical data of Chapter 5. No practices promoting stem-family households as strongly as our primoreal rules, much less as strongly as the stem-family-maximizing primonuptial rules, appear compatible with the data. Even the weak ultimonuptial rules produce average proportions of complex households exceeding the 15% mark below which most of the English listings fall. Any resort to demography for the sake of reconciling a theory of stem-family formation behavior with such low observed levels of occurring complex households appears unjustifiable. The proposed second line of defense for a stem-family hypothesis for England in this period which we have sketched in Chapter 1 is, in our view, demolished by the experimental evidence.

More generally, we deduce that the demographic filter which transforms individual residence decisions into occurring household types is a permeable filter for demographic regimes of the kind we are considering. When sharp patterns of decisions like the primonuptial rules are entered into it, sharp patterns of classes, like the upper left corner of Exhibit 4.2, emerge from it. Our experiment would seem to license inferences from household composition data to hypotheses of individual decision-making patterns, in the absence of good demographic estimates, more freely than might a priori have seemed safe.

The second item on our agenda of analysis outlined in Chapter 1 is the question of the leverage that specific choices in our model exercise over household types. Exhibits 4.3 through 4.5 display some contrasts in the distributions of classes of households, when one choice in the model is altered, all else remaining the same. The sizes of the slices of each bar represent the average fractions of household principles of organization falling in each class in a given batch. The demographic profiles for each batch, stating in detail what is similar and different between batches in the way of demographic rates, are found in Exhibits 2.1 and 2.2 of Chapter 2. These graphs are illustrative of the large number of contrasts that can be extracted from Exhibit 4.2.

The most dramatic of the graphs is surely Exhibit 4.3, representing the change from ultimonuptial to primoreal to primonuptial household rules, for three batches with identical demographic specifications including low mortality, medium-late marriage, and slow growth. The primonuptial and primoreal systems, two versions of decision patterns favoring stem-family households which might go under a single rubric of "stem-family hypothesis" in historical literature, are easily distinguished by their outcomes, and the much weaker stem-family promoting pattern, the ultimonuptial one, is entirely unlike the other patterns. The biggest shifts are

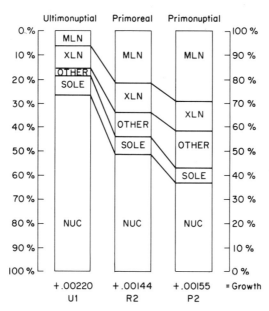

EXHIBIT 4.3. Different household formation rules for same demographic rates. Proportions of household principles falling into different classes. Averages based on runs of 64 simulations each.

in multiple lineal households, nuclear households, and other households (largely laterally extended ones), whereas the extended lineal households and the solitary ones are more immune to alteration.

These changes in averages are even more noteworthy when viewed against Exhibit 4.4 , which shows the effect of different growth rates, with the same (mild) mortality schedule and two pairs of marriage rate schedules, bride's mean age at first marriage around 28 on the left and around 25 on the right. Here there is some tendency toward greater stem-family prevalence on the right, where marriage is earlier and growth rate higher, but on the whole these changes in growth rate have little impact.

Surprisingly, quite drastic change in mortality, involving a jump in female life expectancy at birth from around 27 years to around 40 years, only barely increases household complexity, as the middle pair of bars in Exhibit 4.5 shows. A rise in bride's average age at first marriage, on the other hand, keeping mortality and growth the same, can reduce levels of complexity as much as a change in household rules can do. The left-hand

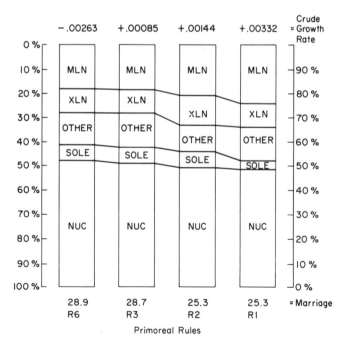

EXHIBIT 4.4. Effect of different growth rates under the same mortality and household rules. Proportions of household principles falling into different classes. Averages based on runs of 64 simulations each. ("Marriage" = bride's mean age at first marriage.)

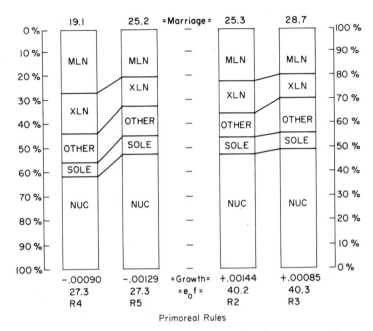

EXHIBIT 4.5. Effect of differing ages at marriage under the same mortality and household formation rules. Proportions of household principles falling into different classes. Averages based on runs of 64 simulations each. ("Marriage" = bride's mean age at first marriage.)

pair of bars in Exhibit 4.5 shows that under heavy mortality conditions a large rise of 6 years from 19 to 25 in the bride's age statistic has an effect comparable to the change from primonuptial to primoreal rules in Exhibit 4.3. Still, the right-hand pair of bars for the case of lighter mortality and a more modest 3-year increase in the average bride's age produces less impressive change.

We believe that one lesson to be drawn from these figures and others like them based on Exhibit 4.2 is that behavioral rules are more potent determinants of average household proportions than are demographic rates within the context we are studying. This assertion depends, as we have argued in Chapter 2, on whether changes like that from primonuptial to primoreal are justly comparable to changes like that from expectations of life around 27 to 40, when measured against the alternatives between which historians might reasonably waver for an English settlement of the 1600s or 1700s. No choice of cases can please everyone, but fortunately it is entirely feasible to create further batches of simulations in the future, so that our cases may at least provoke specific suggestions for cases on which claims like these would be better based.

A second observation from these figures is the preeminence of marriage age among variables. Mortality levels exercise much less leverage. Furthermore, as far as the evidence of Exhibit 4.5 goes, the drop in average proportion of stem-family households per year's increase in bride's average age at first marriage appears nearly the same whether the mortality is light or heavy. The rate of growth or decline (responding to fertility levels), so important for the shape of the age pyramid of a population, hardly alters household complexity. With only 15 batches of simulations we cannot trace refined effects like the relative impact of husband's age, age gap between spouses, remarriage rates, and so forth. But the overall importance of marriage age to attainable levels of stem-family household prevalence is particularly interesting in view of the findings of Wrigley (1966) of wide and rapid variations in the mean ages of women at marriage in Colyton, England before 1800. Not merely from the point of view of social fertility limitation mechanisms, but from the point of view of interpreting levels of household complexity, we conclude that knowledge of marriage ages merits top priority.

We come now to the third point of Chapter 1 of this volume, the setting of benchmark levels of household complexity to enable us to say how much is much. A glance at Exhibit 4.1 reveals that a pattern of behavior strongly favoring stem-family formation ought to produce percentages of such households in the high 30s and 40s, with complex households of any form reaching percentages in the high 40s and 50s. Ratios of lineally extended to laterally extended households computable from Exhibit 4.2 should be well above 3. These percentages are a good deal higher than the guesses usually made. None of the known English cases begin to approach these levels, nor do any of the European cases in Exhibit 6.1 of Chapter 6 except 1795 Grossenmeer, Germany, and 1792 Alsónyék and 1816 Kölked, Hungary.

A fuller standard of comparison is provided by the "triangle plot" in Exhibit 4.6. A triangle plot is a trick for graphing three variables on only two axes when the three variables are proportions that sum to unity. The principle is illustrated by the point labeled U2. The length of the vertical line dropping from U2 to make a right angle with the base of the triangle represents the proportion of stem households. The length of the line stretching left, perpendicular to the left side of the triangle, represents the proportion nuclear. The length of the third, right-hand, line represents the proportion other. The plot capitalizes on the property of an equilateral triangle that the sum of the three perpendiculars to the sides from any point is always the same, just as the sum of proportions equals unity. If we had an equilateral triangular plate and hung three masses from the corners, masses whose weights were the numbers of households of stem,

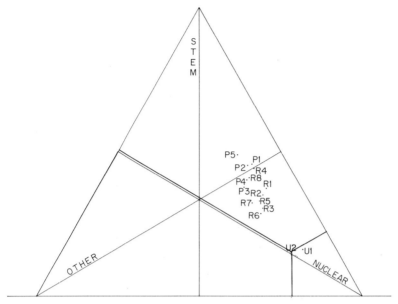

EXHIBIT 4.6. Triangle plot. Proportions of stem, nuclear, and other household types. Batch averages of 64 simulations each.

nuclear, and other type, the center of gravity of the masses would fall on the point we should plot for the settlement.

For convenience, three axes are drawn perpendicular to the sides through the center of the triangle, so we can measure off parallel to them the lengths of the perpendiculars through any other point. Notice that all points along a line at 30° clockwise from vertical have the same proportion nuclear. All points along a horizontal line have the same proportion stem.

The 15 points on Exhibit 4.6 show the average proportions of all households of stem, nuclear, or other type for the 15 batches. Exhibit 4.7 shows a close-up of the region of the triangle where the 13 primonuptial and primoreal batch averages lie. Into the plotting symbols we have encoded information about the average values of demographic parameters for the batches, so that scrutiny of the plot can reveal the directions of influence of demographic gradients on household proportions. The circles stand for primoreal batches, the inverted deltas for primonuptial batches. The size of circles and deltas increases with increasing mean age of brides at first marriage. Circles or deltas with four spikes on top denote batches with female life expectancy at birth around 40; those without spikes, those with life expectancy at birth in the upper twenties. The number below the symbol is the batch number; since the batches are

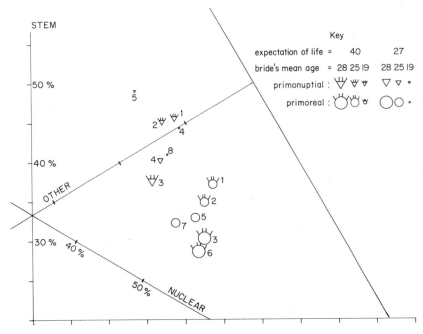

EXHIBIT 4.7.   Triangle plot closeup of primonuptial and primoreal batch means.

ordered in order of decreasing growth rate, these numbers reflect (for batches with the same rule system) the relative growth or decline.

We see clearly how lowering marriage ages raises the standard of how much stem predominance counts as a lot. Furthermore, for the same rule system and the same average ages at marriage, points with different mortality and growth are deployed along lines with constant proportion nuclear, trading off stem for other households. P4 is an exception to this pattern. The shift in rule systems from primoreal to primonuptial, interestingly enough, appears to cut nuclear and raise stem fractions equally, preserving the proportions of other households and shifting points to north–northwest on the graph.

Suppose we have some historical listings all with about 40% stem, 45% nuclear, and 15% other (falling near the R8 point, the tiny dot, on Exhibit 4.7). Then our experimental results tell us that knowledge of marriage ages will be useful for distinguishing between an hypothesis of strong stem-family household maximizing behavior and an hypothesis of moderate stem-family household promoting behavior, since the marriage age parameter distinguishes the primonuptial from the primoreal points in this vicinity. By the same token, the whole range of possible stem percentages from the high 20s to the high 30s for nuclear proportions just above 50% could be typical of the same individual household decision patterns of a primoreal variety.

Thus Exhibit 4.7 gives us clues, in the language of Chapter 1, to inverting the demographic filter. In situations where the possibility of stem-family household tendencies is interesting, we can calibrate observed proportions in historical listings by plotting them relative to our theoretical points. For instance, the breakdown of the 141 households of Grossenmeer in 1795 produces a point very near the point R5, the spikeless middlesize circle; that of the 120 households of Alsónyék in 1792, a point very near the point R8, the tiny dot near the small delta. Straight comparison with the simulated points indicates that if brides on the average married 5 years younger in Alsónyék than in Grossenmeer, all else being equal, the seeming contrast in stem-family levels could be wholly accounted for. On the other hand, if brides in their early twenties were the rule in Grossenmeer, we have some rationale for judging any tendencies toward stem-family households in Grossenmeer much weaker than those in the Hungarian settlement. Notice, furthermore, that our simulations warn us away from framing the same argument in terms of mortality or growth rates instead of marriage age. We might have thought that we could discount the observed household differences between Grossenmeer and Alsónyék if we posited severer death rates in Grossenmeer, or population decline. But we find that our theoretical evidence militates against doing so. These are the sort of questions that inevitably arise in the interpretation of any historical listing. Plotting on a triangle plot a three-number summary of household proportions from a listing to compare against Exhibit 4.7 is a convenient procedure for tackling them, although comparisons with the more detailed but less easily graphed breakdowns of Exhibit 4.2 are also helpful.

Having ventured this concrete example of the use of simulation with historical data, we must emphasize and reemphasize that such a comparison gives no more than suggestions grounded in theory, which must be weighed against, corrected by, and cited in the light of all the other information a researcher has about a village. We are offering a piece or two of evidence to be merged with all the other evidence about Grossenmeer and Alsónyék by those who know the villages and the data better than we. Retirement and dowry and inheritance customs, street plans, house designs and land tenure systems, migration rates, crops and crafts, and a dozen other factors must dictate the relevance or irrelevance of the simulation comparisons.

We come finally to the fourth point of Chapter 1, the notion our simulations give of the minimum amounts of randomness to be allowed for the proportions of household types for villages of around 200–800 inhabitants. The contrasts we have been discussing are contrasts between average proportions or central tendencies, but the simulations in each batch spread out around these averages, just as the proportions for historical villages with the same long-term demographic rates and household tendencies would spread out around the typical levels. With historical data there is always the hope that the observed pattern is typical of the basic structure and there is always the task of characterizing the structural differences we would hypothesize if we took the data as typical. Nonetheless, inferences from data to structure must be graded on a scale of increasing caution, the larger the effects that could be produced by chance alone. Usually when assumptions of statistical independence fail, as they do for households in the same village, we have no way of telling how much random variability to assume, but here we can read off this information from our simulation outputs.

The results are, in one word, chastening. Exhibit 4.8 contains stem-and-leaf plots like those described in Chapter 2 for the proportions of households of nuclear type in the 64 simulations in each of two batches, R4 and P4. For R4 the median proportion nuclear is 44%, yet there are many cases as low as the middle 30s and as high as the 50s. The majority of the cases are as far away from the center of the distribution as the means of other batches. For P4 the spread is even greater. That is no surprise, since we expect larger random variability when there are fewer people and fewer households, and the populations of the P4 batch decline on the average from the original 409. The picture for all batches emerges in Exhibit 4.9. The first columns give the median terminal population and the percentages nuclear between which each succeeding quarter of the 64 cases of each batch lie. The last columns pertain to classes of household principles instead of types of households and give standard deviations for proportions in some of the major classes. These are standard deviations of the quantities whose means appear in Exhibit 4.2.

EXHIBIT 4.8.   Proportions of Households of Nuclear Type in Batches R4 and P4

	R4		P4
2+		2+	7577
3	1	3	444
3+	9887985977	3+	885567597857
4	44213423101122020 3340	4	2441424233040
4+	5756767799988556885	4+	858986557686867
5	12242331100	5	1211203203234
5+	65	5+	6596

EXHIBIT 4.9. Quartiles and Standard Deviations of Household Proportions

	Median population	% Nuclear type					Standard deviations			
		min	¼	med	¾	max	MLN	XLN	SOLE	NUC
P1	710	31	40	43	46	53	4.3	2.5	2.0	4.7
P2	514	34	37	42	46	53	4.6	3.4	3.1	5.0
P3	287	26	39	44	49	64	5.4	4.0	3.8	7.2
P4	175	15	31	38	43	59	6.9	5.6	4.8	7.8
P5	159	25	38	44	50	59	7.5	5.6	5.2	8.5
R1	669	43	49	52	55	61	3.7	2.6	1.9	3.8
R2	531	42	50	52	54	60	3.6	2.8	3.2	3.8
R3	452	44	51	54	57	64	3.2	2.4	3.4	4.0
R4	353	31	41	44	48	56	4.1	3.8	2.6	5.4
R5	371	37	48	51	57	61	4.4	4.0	3.9	6.3
R6	279	36	48	54	59	70	5.2	4.2	4.5	7.8
R7	190	33	45	50	56	69	5.7	4.7	5.3	8.1
R8	174	26	39	45	51	60	8.2	5.6	4.4	8.1
U1	572	66	70	74	76	81	2.3	2.5	2.5	3.5
U2	211	51	67	71	75	91	3.7	3.8	4.5	7.2

These univariate statistics tell only part of the story, for they ignore the correlations between the sizes of different classes. More comprehensive implications for historical data analysis present themselves when we revert to the three-number summaries of proportions of stem, nuclear, and other households on triangle plots like Exhibits 4.6 and 4.7. The xs in the triangle plot Exhibit 4.10 denote the 64 independent simulations in the single batch R3 with primoreal rules, light mortality, slow growth and late marriage. Compare this cluster with Exhibit 4.7. The spread of separate simulations within a single batch is larger than the whole spread of means for all the primoreal and primonuptial batches.

We must not build a case on small differences observed between settlements. That is the general lesson of Exhibits 4.8 to 4.10. But we can learn more specific lessons from our outputs. We can put together tools for dealing with listings, for saying how high are the risks of mistaking noise for structure, if we require differences of some minimum size before we build a case on them. Our presentation here has to be statistical, but we keep in mind our goal of tools that are usable, mentioning the main statistical issues at the end.

Our first concern is the probability of making one particular kind of error, the error of supposing that an observed difference in household proportions between listings reflects a systematic difference when in fact the observed difference arises from chance alone. Recall the 64 points on

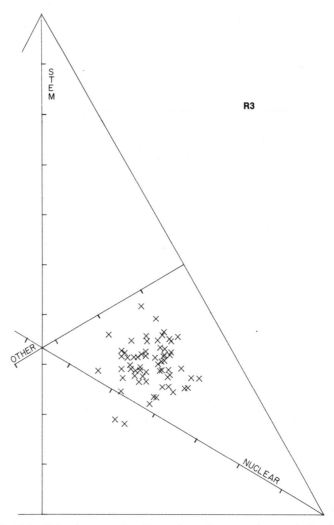

EXHIBIT 4.10.   Triangle scatterplot. Proportions of stem, nuclear, and other household types for the 64 simulations in batch R3.

Exhibit 4.10. Some are close and some far from each other, though the spread is due entirely to chance. Taking all 2016 pairs of these 64 points, measuring the distances between them, and counting what proportion y of the distances are less than each fixed amount x gives us the curve in Exhibit 4.11. The curve is called the "empirical distribution" of the interpoint distances for R3.

Consider the consequences of a policy of affirming a systematic differ-

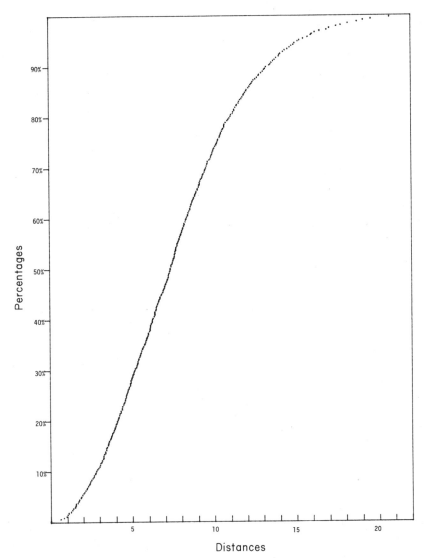

EXHIBIT 4.11.   Empirical distribution of interpoint distances on the triangle plot for R3.

ence between two settlements when and only when the observed distance between points plotted for them on a triangle plot exceeds some fixed number of units, say 5 percentage units. If the settlements actually do not differ systematically but both reflect household formation practices and demographic conditions like those modeled in our batch *R3*, then under this policy we should be right only 28% of the time. This score of 28% is the height of the curve at the x-value of 5 on Exhibit 4.11. Although none of the points in Exhibit 4.10 differ systematically, 72% of the distances between them are larger than our critical value of 5 units, so a policy that 5 units of distance spells systematic difference would make us wrong here 72% of the time.

If we took as our critical value 15 units instead of 5 units, we should be right 95% of the time when we were dealing with settlements that were all really, although we might not know it, like R3. In order to be wrong less than one-third of the time, we should take our critical value around 9 units. Because there are components of randomness in historical processes not incorporated in our computer model, as we have said in Chapter 2, these critical values are likely to be a little low rather than a little high. In practice, a margin of a unit or two plus or minus the critical values is also advisable, in recognition that our models never exactly match an historical situation. Still, approximate as they are, these critical values bring us surprising and important news: A 5 percentage unit allowance for randomness is puny. Allowances as large as 10 to 15 units are the price of safety.

Of course the larger an observed difference we demand before we affirm a systematic difference, the more liable we make ourselves to another kind of error, the error of overlooking a difference when one does exist. Probabilities of this second kind of error are more elusive, since they depend very much on what the actual differences are and since they may be somewhat sensitive to the components of randomness absent from our model. Some feeling for them comes, however, from comparing Exhibit 4.10 with Exhibit 4.12, which is a triangle plot of the 64 simulations in each of two other batches, P2 toward the top and U1 toward the lower right. Most of the points for P2 or for R3 are closer to each other than to any point for U1. With a critical value of 15, we would miss a difference between a settlement like the P2 model and one like the U1 model less than 1% of the time. The comparable error rate for R3 versus U1 is 17%. P2 and R3 are harder to distinguish, but again the error probability with a critical value of 15 for this second kind of error is only 37%.

These are cheering results, for they mean that historians may hope to distinguish patterns of household organization on the basis of numerical data from household listings not only in spite of demographic influences but also in spite of randomness. However, as Exhibit 4.11 shows, only large observed differences may safely be taken at face value. What probabilities of error one is willing to tolerate is a personal matter. Undoubtedly historians, up against the imperfections of historical data, are prepared to be wrong when denying chance full credit more often than the 5% allowance traditional in statistical significance tests. On the other

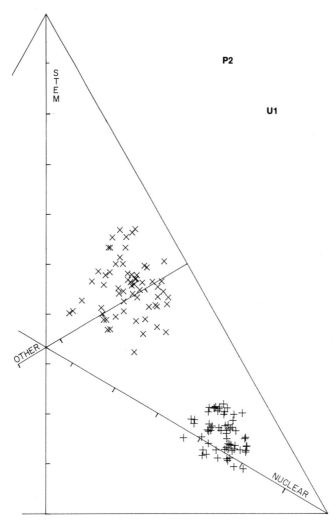

EXHIBIT 4.12. Triangle scatterplot. Proportions of stem, nuclear, and other household types. Crosses indicate the 64 simulations in batch *P*2 and plus signs indicate the 64 simulations in batch *U*1.

hand, it is pointless to indulge in explanations of differences between settlements where the odds are heavy that chance produced them. For villages of the sizes we have been simulating, which match the sizes of most precensus listings, these odds go up more rapidly than writers on household organization seem to have appreciated.

We offer three examples of how these allowances for randomness might be applied to actual data, subject to the same caveats as our similar examples for the allowances for demography. For the first two examples, we may use a handy formula for distance measured on triangle plots, so that we do not need to draw a plot before we can determine the distance. For two listings whose proportions of stem, nuclear, and other households are s_1, n_1, o_1 and s_2, n_2, o_2 respectively, the distance between them on a triangle plot equals:

$$[\tfrac{1}{3}\{3(s_1 - s_2)^2 + (n_1 - n_2)^2 + (o_1 - o_2)^2 - 2(n_1 - n_2)(o_1 - o_2)\}]^{\frac{1}{2}}$$

Using this formula, we see that the two continental settlements included in Exhibit 6.1 in Chapter 6 whose listings date from 1792–1793, Oestersheps in Germany and Alsónyék in Hungary, fall a full 16 units apart on a triangle plot, even though the proportions of stem-family households are very close. Those proportions are 37% and 40%, both in the middle of primoreal levels. Exhibit 4.11 shows an error rate of less than 4% if we always take distances as large as 16 units to imply structural differences. At that rate we could hardly quarrel with anyone contrasting household organization in Oestersheps against that in Alsónyék on the basis of this evidence.

Our second example involves a French and an Italian settlement around 1780, Longuenesse in 1778 and Colorno in 1782, both in Exhibit 6.1. The contrast between 20% stem-family households in Colorno and 12% stem-family households in Longuenesse looks less impressive when we recognize that the distance between them on a triangle plot, 8.1 units, is smaller than the median of the distribution of wholly random distances in Exhibit 4.11.

Our third example involves the two English samples to be discussed at length in Chapter 5. Exhibit 4.13 is a triangle plot for these 64 English places, where the xs represent settlements in the main sample in Exhibit 5.1 and the dots represent settlements in the reserve sample in Exhibit 5.2. Comparing these points against Exhibits 4.10 and 4.12, it is apparent that the spread of the English data is somewhat larger but by no means very much larger than spreads achievable in the simulations from chance alone. Some 30% of the interpoint distances are larger than 15. The cluster of points is less nearly circular than the simulated clusters, a property no doubt related to the closeness of the English data to the lower boundary of the triangle plot. The spread is just great enough for us to suspect the presence of mild systematic differences between settlements, but not enough greater than the simulated spreads for us to expect many such systematic effects to stand out clearly above the randomness in the data. All these issues will be our theme in Chapter 5.

In the discussion so far we have been suppressing most of the statistical

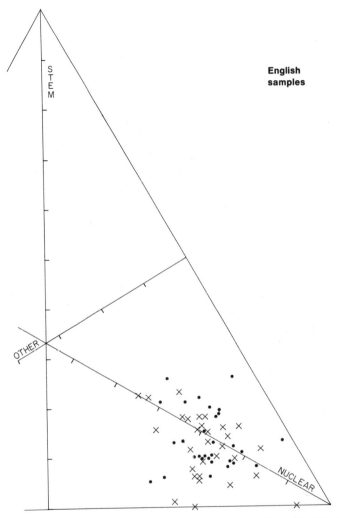

English samples

EXHIBIT 4.13. Triangle scatterplot. Proportions of stem, nuclear, and other household types. Crosses indicate the English main sample of Exhibit 5.1 and filled-in circles indicate the English reserve sample of Exhibit 5.2.

arguments which support using Exhibit 4.11 as a yardstick for random-ness in household proportions in the way we propose. Readers may well wonder how many corners have been cut along the way for the sake of directness of presentation. To answer them, we devote a few paragraphs now to the technical statistical issues, before summarizing the lessons of our outputs.

The critical values in Exhibit 4.11 depend to some extent on the choice of the batch $R3$ for the plot. Empirical distributions like Exhibit 4.11 for interpoint distances from other batches rise more steeply or less steeply, largely depending on whether the number of households in the batch is larger or smaller on average. The more households altogether, the less randomness in the batch of simulations, the smaller the interpoint distances, the steeper their empirical distribution, and the smaller the critical value that corresponds to a fixed probability of mistaking randomness for structure. The mean number of households for the batch we have used, $R3$, is 105.7, which is very close to the average number of households in the settlements of the main English sample of Chapter 5, found in Exhibit 5.1. That mean is 110, which is also, coincidentally, the mean for the Continental settlements in Exhibit 6.1. If we are willing to regard the sizes of the settlements to which we apply our method as themselves manifesting a random distribution centered around 100 households, then it makes sense to rely on Exhibit 4.11 despite the dependence of error rates on size.

If we want to apply our results to collections of settlements with sizes rather different from those of the tables in Chapter 5, further information is needed. A crude but handy formula for adjusting the critical values is to divide them by the square root of the average number of households and multiply by 10, which is around the square root of the average number for $R3$. Predicting critical values based on $U1$, with 161 households on average, from the $R3$ values in this way gives errors less than half a percentage unit over all but the top half percent tail of the distribution.

This rough rule for adjusting by the square root of the number of households has its logical defects. Their story is a whole subject in itself, which we title the "Root N Rule." The rationale for the rule lies in a misapplication of statistical sampling theory to our context. If the households in a settlement were an independent sample of some infinitely large collection of households all produced by the same random mechanisms and behavior patterns, then the randomness in household proportions would be covered by the multinomial probability law. In that case, the standard deviations of the proportions would decrease like the reciprocal of the square root of the number of households. Within certain ranges, so would statistics like our critical values. Of course the households in a small settlement are not independent, because of the marital ties and lines of descent between individuals, so we have no good reason to expect the standard deviations to follow this square root. Nonetheless, we can ask how large the number of households must be before the dependencies cancel each other out and the deviations mimic the independent case. The generally bell-shaped distributions in Exhibit 4.8 are consistent with multinomial probabilities. The standard deviations in Exhibit 4.9 are also of the right order of magnitude for a near-universal Root N Rule. But when we make a comparison within a batch between numbers of households in individual simulations and the amount that proportions of household types stray from the mean values, the relationship predicted by a multinomial model is violated, even for batches with many households on average like $P1$. Here lurks an intriguing statistical problem, which we reserve for separate treatment.

Most of our discussion of randomness has focused on distances measured on triangle plots, and it is natural to wonder what is special about triangle plots. Would similar methods work, say, for plots of proportion stem versus proportion nuclear on rectangular axes? The answer is no. Triangle plots are in fact special. They treat each category—stem, nuclear, and other—on an equal footing, instead of giving precedence to two categories over a third, and a happy byproduct of this equal treatment is the roughly circular shape of the clusters of points within each batch, as in Exhibits 4.10 and 4.12. In statistical jargon, we say that the transformation to triangle coordinates tends to equalize the variances of the principal components for each batch. Were this not so, our account would be enormously more complicated, for we should have to allow for different amounts of randomness in different directions, and the directions would depend on the batch. Of course, even on triangle plots the clusters are not exactly circular and their shape depends somewhat on the demographic rates and household rules. But this dependence is pleasingly slight. If departures from circularity were great enough to matter much, they would show up as unusual patterns in empirical distributions like Exhibit 4.11. Actually, our empirical distributions of interpoint distances are very close to what we should predict from a standard probability model, a chi square distribution on two degrees of freedom.

The simulations in a batch vary not only in their household types, producing the random sets of points on triangle plots that we have been discussing. They vary also in their demographic measurements, which cluster around their average values for the batch just like the household proportions. In a batch with stationary average population, some villages are growing and some declining. Is the household structure correlated within batches with the realized demographic rates? By and large this appears not to be the case. The random differences within batches in demographic rates are enough smaller than the systematic between-batch differences that they exercise little apparent influence over proportions.

All these considerations encourage us to think that the pattern of randomness in a batch of household proportions is not very dependent on the rule systems and other details of the model we have programmed. As a first approximation, pending further experiments with other models of household formation, we would be willing to recommend the standards we have given for allowances for randomness even where stem-family tendencies are not the tendencies at issue.

This concludes our technical statistical discussion. We may now recapitulate the highlights of our simulation outcomes as we have discussed them in terms of the four points of Chapter 1. First, our results support a general claim that the constraints which demography imposes on household structure are loose constraints. In particular they discourage any effort to explain the low observed levels of stem and complex family households in English precensus village listings as an artifact of the demographic circumstances. Second, they show that details of a pattern of individual residence decisions have more effect on household types than most demographic parameters, bride's age at marriage being the only obvious exception. Third, they provide a whole collection of benchmarks against which to gauge whether levels of complexity, allowing for demography, are large or small relative to attainable levels. Fourth, they show that allowances for randomness in household proportions should be larger than has been previously assumed, but not so large as to preclude interesting inferences from household listings. Chapters 5 and 6 of this volume take up the relationship of these findings to the current data on English and European settlements from another point of view.

In summary, our simulations provide us with a picture of the levels and variations in proportions of households by kin-composition that would occur under special controlled conditions. Our particular work addresses constraints of demography on the formation of households of stem-family type. How far dare we generalize from these outputs to demographic conditions less like the English 1600s and 1700s as they affect complex household formation less like the stem-family model we have chosen? Partly that is a matter for intuition. Partly also it is a matter of how long until simulation outputs dealing with other conditions and other hypotheses about household structure become available. These four chapters have given an account of tools and approaches now available to the working social historian.

Some of the labor in a simulation experiment is technical labor. But the greater part of our discussion has focused on conceptual issues. Formulating the problems of historical demography and social structure so that experimental evidence can be brought to bear and so that the effects of randomness are given their just due is not a task that technical cunning can resolve. Simulation merely brings to the fore issues that lurk in the background of any historical thinking on these subjects. Alongside any use that researchers with historical listings may be able to make of our concrete results, we hope to have opened essential issues to debate.

5

The English Evidence on Household Structure Compared with the Outcomes of Microsimulation

The understanding of household structure in preindustrial times depends for its evidence on surviving lists of inhabitants of communities or settlements. The largest existing collection[1] of such listings at the present time is held in Cambridge, and is drawn from English records, some of them stretching back to the late 1500s. Such records become rather more plentiful from the late 1600s on until 1821, when we take the wholly preindustrial era to have ended. Some 500 documents of this kind are held in the files of the Cambridge Group for the History of Population and Social Structure, and the English tables which illustrate this chapter

---

[1] To belong to this collection a listing has to include (or claim to include) every inhabitant of the settlement named: For a first description of this file and the original programme of research, see Laslett (1966) and for further discussions Laslett (1971, page 257), and Laslett (1977, Chapter 1). Partial listings exist in much larger numbers, that is listings which, like those made for taxation purposes, ordinarily include only people of a particular type. We collect copies of such documents at Cambridge when they have special points of interest, as for example when they are earlier in date than those in our master file. Some of these partial listings go back to the 1200s and 1300s: See Laslett and Wall (1972, pages 47–48), for serf lists of some East Anglian manors in 1268–1269 and Laslett (1977, Chapter 1), for the work of Richard Michael Smith on Poll Tax Lists of the later 1300s. A small collection of listings from overseas is being assembled, such as those in Exhibit 6.1. Some are original documents, others ideographic transcriptions.

present numerical indications of household structure in the 30 best and the 34 second-best of these listings, ranked by a criterion which we shall shortly explain.

A. THE CAMBRIDGE COLLECTION OF LISTINGS OF SETTLEMENTS

The great friend of the historical sociologist interested in households and families has always been the busybody. Neither the state, the church, nor the landowner was interested in the composition of the household for its own sake. Nevertheless all three authorities occasionally had lists of inhabitants drawn up in earlier times. It is when one of the individuals acting on these orders went beyond the requirements of the authorities concerned that we find ourselves provided with fine detail of the living arrangements of our ancestors. Some of these busybodies have become eminent in the history of the social sciences, and of these Gregory King is the most famous. But most of them were obscure, anonymous persons.

The second of our tables (Exhibit 5.2), for instance, contains a real prize in number 32, the listing of Ealing in Middlesex drawn up as early as 1599 by a constable asked to provide information about the poor. This lowly but highly literate official went so far as to annotate his list with the occupations of household heads, and even with the ages of all individuals, including among them "her majestie's mowltaker," the functionary in charge of keeping Queen Elizabeth's lawns and gardens free from molehills. It is the first age listing of an English speaking community so far known and the only one before 1600.[2] In 1684 the eccentric squire of Chilvers Coton in Warwickshire ordered that all and every one of the households and individuals present in that village, even domestic animals and trees, should be listed by his steward, thus creating a remarkable record of the community into which, a century later, the novelist George Eliot was to be born. Except during the 1690s when a taxation ordinance of the government in London gave rise to a considerable body of complete English listings and presented Gregory King with his opportunities, a majority of those who wrote out such documents were probably clergymen.

It must be recognized that what was produced by such recorders was

[2] Mols (1956, volume III, page 204), publishes ages from listings of Pozzuoli in 1489, Sorrento in 1571, and Carpi in 1591 and makes it clear that by the end of the 1500s such listings were fairly common in Italy. Only one age listing earlier than that for Ealing has been noticed for any other Northern European country, however; that for Wittenberg in 1591 (Mols, 1956, volume I, page 36).

very various in purposes, exhaustiveness, and reliability. Only those list-ings which divide the whole population unequivocally into what we call coresident domestic groups are admitted into the Cambridge master file, and of these only the ones which give consistent information as to kin relations within households have been used for our tables. Any discussion of household composition which is to have rigor and precision, therefore, has to be based on a very small selection from the body of available materials, itself an arbitrary and imperfect sample of what we should like to have to hand.

The English collection, as we have said, represents the one substantial body of evidence of this kind yet assembled. Complete listings continue to be discovered in our country, but their quality seldom permits detailed analysis of household structure. It is already known, however, that other western European preindustrial societies of a high level of literacy, and particularly France, Germany, and Italy, possess materials of this type on a much more extensive scale and probably of higher quality in respect of such details as recordings of ages (see Laslett, 1977, Chapter 1). Neverthe-less, the issues of contrast between complex and simple households, between random and systematic variation, and between behavioral pat-terns and demographic constraints originally arose out of examination of the English file. Furthermore, since England was the first country to undergo industrialization and the only country to undergo it spontane-ously, and since this process has always been seen as intimately bound up with the transformation of domestic arrangements and of the structure of the domestic group, the English file for all its imperfections will always continue to command attention.

B. CRITIQUE OF THE ENGLISH DATA

The origins of present international interest in comparative household structure in history are to be found in a meeting held in Cambridge in 1969 which gave rise to the volume published by the Cambridge Group in 1972 under the title *Household and Family in Past Time*. The predomi-nance of nuclear families, especially in England, reported there came as a considerable surprise in view of the very widely held conviction that preindustrial Europe was everywhere marked by a peasantry living in large and complex households. The townsfolk were likewise assumed to have had a similar domestic system, though it has always been supposed that their households were usually smaller and simpler than in the coun-tryside. The outcomes made public in 1969 failed to confirm this belief for England, and it has not been possible to demonstrate marked urban–rural differences in the work done since that time. But there have been three developments since 1972 which have changed the situation and which contribute the three interlocking themes of this chapter and of the one which follows.

First, as might have been expected, there has been a tendency to reject the implications of the English evidence. Researchers have brought to light Continental cases very different from the English and have fallen back on modified versions of predominant complexity in European household structure, including what we call here the stem-family hypothesis. The second development faces up to the difficulty, already recognized at the 1969 meeting, of allowing for the effects of demographic rates and of the domestic cycle when inferences are to be drawn about the behavior of people in forming households in various circumstances and at various periods, using as evidence records of households actually occurring at points in time. The series of experiments with computer microsimulation reported in detail in Chapters 1 to 4 of this volume were mounted to provide an analytic framework against which to interpret just such sets of data. The third development has been the winning of the much larger English sample here presented, along with a small installment of accurate measures of the household structure in other areas of Europe, which will be found in Exhibit 6.1 in the following chapter. To this must be added the close study of stem-family households in areas of Germany, considered there.

The special interest which attaches to the coresident domestic group and its internal kinship structure is affirmed in the introduction to *Household and Family in Past Time*. The kin composition of households in 10 English communities at various dates from the 1500s to the 1800s were presented there in very summary form, along with similar rough figures for five settlements on the European continent and three from outside Europe.[3] The greatly extended body of closely analysed English evidence of the same kind is set out in Exhibits 5.1 and 5.2 and summary statistics for this material will be found in Exhibit 5.3. Exhibit 6.1 contains similar figures, but not quite so detailed, for 15 places elsewhere in Europe, our Continental sample. The figures in these four tables are strictly comparable with the outputs of the simulations described and discussed in Chapters 1 to 4. We are in a position, therefore, to contrast these simulation outputs with outputs from 64 English settlements dating from 1574 to 1821

---

[3] See Table 1.3 of Laslett and Wall (1972): One Scottish settlement was included, and sets of figures for later dates in the mid-1800s for some of the English places. This information is repeated in Table 1.1 of Laslett (1977) *Family Life and Illicit Love in Earlier Generations* where a sample from Ireland in 1821 is added. In Table 1.2 of that book the Continental sample is considerably extended as discussed subsequently.

and with those from 15 Continental places. We can decide how far what we have called the primonuptial, primoreal, and ultimonuptial stem-family models correspond with these examples from the past.

We begin with the English settlements, the evidence for which will have to be discussed in some detail. This is because it is no easy task to elicit such things as proportions of lineally extended or lineally multiple households from lists of persons inhabiting English settlements up to four centuries ago. To attain the level of rigor necessary for the strictest possible comparison with our computer outputs, a series of decisions has had to be made, which we shall describe. But let us first insist on the straightforward message of Exhibits 5.1 to 5.3.

As has already been said in our previous chapters, the figures in these tables rule out any possibility of explaining English household structure in the past on the stem-family hypothesis. We can see from Exhibit 5.3 that the mean of multiple lineal households (MLN) is only 2.9% in the first sample and 3.8% in the second. This is lower than any of the figures under MLN in Exhibit 4.2, including the two for ultimonuptial rules. As for lineal extension, at 9.1% and 10.4% XLN the English figures are lower than all but two of the means for primonuptial and primoreal simulations, though the second English figure just exceeds the two for ultimonuptial. We must repeat that it is the shortfall of multiple households of all kinds that defeats the stem-family hypothesis for English evidence, although extended households can sometimes reach modestly high levels. And in individual places, of course, English figures for complex households and even for multiple ones can reach those typical of areas where household organization was very different, so marked is the variability between small settlements in such social structural variables.

The listings appear in our tables in order of date, with a figure for the population in each settlement and for the number of households into which the community was divided by the list-maker. The succeeding columns, with headings from SOLE to IND, give the percentages of each type of household composing the settlement. The classification scheme is the one adapted from Hammel and Laslett (1974) and Hammel and Deuel (1977), which is described at the end of Chapter 3 of this volume and is employed also for the simulation experiments. The percentages in Exhibits 5.1 and 5.2 are calculated to give the maximum levels for the extended and multiple categories compatible with the information in the listings, in order to display the strongest case that can be made with these English data for the prevalence of complex household forms. Following rules which are explained in detail in the Appendix to this chapter we have added definitely classifiable households to provisionally classifiable households so as to reach the figures.

EXHIBIT 5.1.   English Main Sample of 30 Settlements

	Date	Settlement	Population	Total households	Percentage of households lacking structure SOLE (1) Solitaries	(2) No known structure	Percentage of nuclear households NUC (3)
1	1622	Stafford, Staffordshire	1549	384	13.0	.5	80.2
2	1674	Stoke Edith, Herefordshire	183	39	7.5	2.5	61.5
3	1688	Clayworth, Nottinghamshire	411	91	7	1	84
4	1689	Renhold, Bedfordshire	157	37	16	0	76
5	1697	Southampton St. John, Hampshire	147	40	7	3	65
6	1699	Harefield, Middlesex	567	122	8.2	4.1	68.9
7	1700	Wroughton, Wiltshire	478	134	18	4	72
8	1701	Lyddington, Wiltshire	253	66	14	0	74
9	1705	Wootton, Kent	85	20	15	0	75
10	1724	Puddletown, Dorset	612	153	12.4	4.6	71.9
11	1760	West Wycombe, Buckinghamshire	1141	255	5.9	3.9	71.0
12	1767	Darlington, County Durham	1482	396	15.9	2.3	74.2
13	1770	Steeple Ashton, Wiltshire	474	111	9.0	10.8	55.0
14	1771	Lower Heford & Caldecot, Oxon.	253	56	5	4	75
15	1780	Wembworthy, Devon	222	41	0	2	68
16	1787	Morley, Derbyshire	234	48	10	4	73
17	1787	Bampton, Westmorland	678	148	11.5	2.7	66.2
18	1787	Hilton, Westmorland	159	40	10	3	62
19	1787	Kaber, Westmorland	156	34	3	3	94
20	1787	Murton, Westmorland	125	16	0	12	69
21	1787	Newby, Westmorland	212	49	8	6	73
22	1787	Stainmore, Westmorland	621	125	7.2	2.4	78.4
23	1787	Great Strickland, Westms.	187	40	7	3	72
24	1796	Ardleigh, Essex	1126	207	4.3	1.0	82.1
25	17—	Nether Winchinson, Oxon.	240	51	4	14	57
26	1801	Binfield, Berkshire	800	184	10.3	4.3	69.6
27	1801	Barkway & Reed, Herts.	1021	206	4.9	3.9	73.3
28	1811	Littleover, Derbyshire	347	65	8	2	75
29	1811	Mickleover, Derbyshire	582	114	8.8	1.8	69.3
30	1821	Digswell, Hertfordshire	202	37	5	3	76

Note: Capitalized headings like MLN are those described in Chapter 3. Figure–letter pairs like 4a or 5b accord with *Household and Family in Past Time*, Table 1.1, page 31.

Since households clearly classifiable in more than one way are extremely rare in our materials, we need not concern ourselves with the distinction between types and classes discussed in Chapter 3, except to mention that households with both lineal and lateral structure enter the lineal categories. This order of precedence among categories has been adopted in accordance with our declared intention to maximize levels of complexity. The actual totals of extended and especially multiple households in many of the places in our lists were no doubt lower than those we have displayed.

The first two columns following the number of households in Exhibits 5.1 and 5.2 subdivide the category SOLE into one column for completely solitary persons and one column for households with no evident family structure. The figures in the columns are percentages. The next column, headed NUCLEAR (NUC), shows simple family households, and after it come two columns with extended family households, those extended vertically (XLN) and those extended laterally (XLT). Next come multiple

Percentage of households extended lineally XLN 4a,b,d	Percentage of households extended laterally XLT 4c	Percentage of multiple households with lineal disposition MLN 5a,b,e	Percentage of multiple households with lateral disposition MLT 5c,d	Percentage of indeterminate households IND	Percentage of households extended or multiple (% complex) index A	index B	Criterion ratio	Percentage of all households definitely assigned	
3.7	1.7	.5	0	0.3	5.4	6.2	7	99.5	1
13	13	2.5	0	0	20	28	1.75	90	2
5	3	1	0	0	8	9	8	99	3
0	8	0	0	0	5	8	2	97	4
18	0	0	0	7	15	17.5	6	90	5
12.1	3.5	3.3	0	0	18.1	18.9	22	99.2	6
1	5	0	0	0	6	7	3	99	7
6	4	0	0	2	8	11	2.5	95	8
10	0	0	0	0	10	10	∞	100	9
6.5	2.6	1.0	1.0	0	10	11	16	99	10
12.3	3.4	2.7	0	0.8	14.1	18.8	3	94.9	11
4.6	2.0	.6	0	0.5	6.1	7.7	4	98.4	12
15.2	2.8	7.2	0	0	17.8	25.2	1.8	91	13
12	4	0	0	0	14	16	8	98	14
11	6	7	0	5	22	24	9	93	15
6	2	0	0	4	8	12	2	96	16
14.2	2.0	3.4	0	0	19.6	19.6	∞	100	17
20	0	3	3	0	25	25	∞	100	18
0	0	0	0	0	0	0	∞	100	19
12	0	6	0	0	18	18	∞	100	20
5	3	4	0	0	10	12	5	98	21
6.4	2.4	3.2	0	0	11.2	12.0	14	99.2	22
8	5	5	0	0	18	18	∞	100	23
9.1	1.1	2.4	0	0	11.6	12.6	12	99	24
14	0	8	0	4	16	22	2.7	90	25
9.6	2.4	1.8	0.9	1.1	14.4	15.7	5.7	97.8	26
14.2	1.4	1.6	0.8	0	12.7	18.0	2.4	94.7	27
8	2	6	0	0	12	15	4	97	28
9.2	3.1	7.0	0	0.9	14.1	19.4	2.7	93.9	29
8	0	8	0	0	13	16	5	97	30

family households, those disposed lineally (MLN), then those disposed laterally (MLT). The residual column INDETERMINATE (IND), not part of the scheme in Chapter 3, includes the few households for which classification by kin relationship is impossible, although it is clear that some persons are related to each other in the groups concerned. The next two columns give two estimates of the overall proportion of complication. The difference between them is bound up with our criteria for the admission of lists to our sample which we discuss in the Appendix, and which are represented in the figures in the last two columns of our tables.

The 30 complete listings of English preindustrial places in Exhibit 5.1 are documents of high quality from the point of view of household analysis. The 34 complete listings in Exhibit 5.2 are documents of slightly lower quality. The combined sample of 64 includes all those in the master file of 500 English listings in which all or the vast majority of the individuals have some designation of household status, either child, kin, servant, lodger, visitor, etc. In all the rest this information is given with a consistency too low for fine analysis. These designations of household status in

EXHIBIT 5.2.　English Reserve Sample of 34 Settlements

	Date	Settlement	Population	Total households	Percentage of households lacking structure SOLE (1) Solitaries	(2) No known structure	Percentage of nuclear households NUC (3)
31	1574	Poole, Dorset	1330	242	2.5	0.8	67.8
32	1599	Ealing, Middlesex	400	86	12	2	71
33	1676	Broughton, Lancashire	636	193	9.3	3.6	74.1
34	1676	Clayworth, Nottinghamshire	401	98	8	1	78
35	1684	Chilvers Coton, Warwickshire	780	176	7.4	2.3	59.7
36	1689	Ludlow, Shropshire	1289	375	16.5	4.8	67.7
37	1690	Dersingham, Norfolk	175	41	15	0	73
38	1694	Norwich St. Peter Mancroft, Norfolk	1055	255	11.0	4.7	76.1
39	1695	London, 8 parishes	4850	1010	5.7	3.1	72.7
40	1696	Southampton, Hampshire, 4 parishes	1153	277	8.3	2.5	74.7
41	1697	Southampton, Hampshire, 3 parishes	635	150	8.0	2.7	72.0
42	1697	Swindon, Wiltshire	752	180	8.3	3.9	73.9
43	1697	Clipston, Northamptonshire	380	98	9	0	73
44	1697	Hasebeck, Northamptonshire	150	27	0	4	70
45	1697	Kelmarsh, Northamptonshire	118	26	12	0	69
46	1697	Loddington, Northamptonshire	140	32	16	6	53
47	1700	Wroughton Tythings, Wiltshire	256	50	0	6	64
48	1700	New Romney, Kent	434	134	26.9	0	65.7
49	1701	Wanborough, Wiltshire	549	146	14	2	66
50	1701	Stoke-on-Trent, Stoke, Staffs	1624	367	6.0	4.1	70.2
51	1752	Forthampton & Swinly, Gloucester	288	54	2	0	85
52	1757	Tunstall, Kent	115	16	12	0	56
53	1762	Leverton, Lincolnshire	262	57	11	0	79
54	1773	Renhold, Bedfordshire	300	54	7	2	83
55	1787	Askham, Westmorland	294	62	5	5	71
56	1787	Barton Constablewick, Westms	237	51	12	6	76
57	1787	Kings Meaburn, Westms	160	36	8	3	66
58	1787	Morland, Westms	233	57	4	7	77
59	1787	Newbiggen, Westms	124	28	7	4	71
60	1787	Barton: Hartsop & Patterdale, Westms	317	65	6	5	51
61	1790	Corfe Castle, Dorset	1239	262	9.5	4.6	58.4
62	1801	Shalley, Derbyshire	618	111	5.4	0.9	71.2
63	1805	Bibury, Gloucester	281	73	10	3	78
64	1821	Braintree, Essex	2983	640	6.9	3.9	78.6

the listings we have selected need not take the form of explicit descriptions in all cases; some inference from surname or placement in the list is allowed. However, a listing is generally excluded if there are many ambiguities, or if one or other category or description is absent, or so conspicuously rare as to imply inconsistent recording. Notwithstanding, highly meticulous listings with great detail about lodgers, boarders, and visitors, for instance, are accepted, even if no servants or no kin appear. For example, the list of Kaber in Westmoreland (19), rich in descriptive detail, enters our main sample of 30 though no kin are found in the population.

Our insistence on explicit descriptions for individuals rules out listings which, if more guesswork were to be tolerated, might produce cases very different from those we have come to regard as likely. One reading of a document from the little country town of Kirby Lonsdale in 1696 would yield unparalleled levels of complexity, but a more probable resolution of the many ambiguities would leave it unremarkable. While for other pur-

Percentage of households extended lineally XLN 4a,b,d	Percentage of households extended laterally XLT 4c	Percentage of multiple households with lineal disposition MLN 5a,b,e	Percentage of multiple households with lateral disposition MLT 5c,d	Percentage of indeterminate households IND	Percentage of households extended or multiple (% complex) index A	index B	Criterion ratio	Percentage of all households definitely assigned	
4.6	4.0	8.3	9.1	0	2.9	26	1.3	85.9	31
8	5	2	0	0	0	15	1.2	93	32
5.5	2.8	4.7	0	0	0	13	0.8	92.8	33
8	5	0	0	1	0	14	1.6	95	34
18.2	4.5	2.8	0	0.6	4.5	26.1	0.3	75.6	35
4.8	1.6	1.1	0	0	3.5	7.5	0.3	90.7	36
10	0	0	0	0	2	10	0	88	37
4.7	0	1.2	0	0.8	1.6	6.7	0.2	95.3	38
6.9	4.1	2.6	0	3.1	1.9	16.7	0.5	86.7	39
8.6	4.0	0.4	0	0.4	1.1	13.4	1.5	93.4	40
9.2	3.5	0.7	0	0.7	3.3	14.1	1.1	90.0	41
6.8	4.3	2.8	0	0	0	13.9	1.5	94.4	42
11	0	2	0	0	4	13	0.1	84	43
15	0	11	0	0	0	26	0.7	86	44
12	0	8	0	0	0	20	0.2	84	45
6	0	0	0	3	16	9	0	75	46
13	7	8	0	0	2	28	0.4	78	47
3.5	1.7	1.5	0	0	0.7	6.7	0.5	94.8	48
9	0	4	0	0	4	13	0.3	86	49
13.9	2.0	1.4	0.5	0	1.9	17.8	0.8	88.0	50
7	0	6	0	0	0	13	0.7	93	51
13	0	19	0	0	0	32	0.2	75	52
9	0	2	0	0	0	11	0.2	81	53
6	0	2	0	0	0	8	1.0	96	54
19	0	0	0	0	0	19	0.5	87	55
6	0	0	0	0	0	6	0.5	96	56
14	0	8	0	0	0	22	1.0	89	57
10	0	2	0	0	0	12	1.3	95	58
18	0	0	0	0	0	18	1.5	93	59
25	0	14	0	0	0	39	0.7	77	60
23.5	0.9	2.3	0	0.4	0.4	27.1	0.7	83.2	61
9.5	1.4	9.0	0	1.8	0.9	21.7	1.2	89.2	62
8	0	1	0	0	0	9	1.3	96	63
7.6	0.8	1.1	0.6	0.2	0.3	10.3	1.1	94.7	64

poses it is an important listing, it fails to find a place in our English series, as does the enormous but intractable list of the inhabitants of the city of Lichfield in 1695, written, in part at least, in the hand of Gregory King himself.

Further details about the criteria used to select these lists and to assign them to our two English tables, are presented in the Appendix. Let it simply be said here that a difference between the two indices in the columns sharing the heading "complex" is a sign that there is uncertainty about the exact proportions of households of the types concerned in the listing at issue, and the greater the difference the greater the uncertainty. Low figures in the next two columns are warnings of the same kind.

The dates of the listings in Exhibits 5.1 and 5.2 range from 1574 to 1821 and the regions represented stretch from Devonshire to Durham and Westmorland to Kent. It would be idle to expect 64 settlements to be representative of the whole of England, or to be effective for indicating change over time. Nevertheless, 25 of the 40 counties of the country

EXHIBIT 5.3. Summary Statistics of Household Proportions in English Samples

	Sole		Nuclear	Extended		Multiple		Indeterminate
	Solitary	No family	NUC	XLN	XLT	MLN	MLT	IND
Main Sample of 30 English Settlements (most reliable data)								
Mean	8.5	3.6	72.1	9.1	2.8	2.9	0.2	0.9
St. dev.	4.5	3.3	7.8	5.0	2.7	2.7	0.6	1.8
St. err. $(\bar{x})$	0.8	0.6	1.4	0.9	0.5	0.5	0.1	0.3
Median	7.9	3.2	72.1	9.2	2.4	2.6	0	0
Minimum	0	0	55.0	0	0	0	0	0
Maximum	18.0	14.0	94.0	20.0	13.0	8.0	3.0	7.0
Reserve Sample of 34 English Settlements (next most reliable data)								
Mean	8.7	2.9	70.4	10.4	1.5	3.8	0.3	0.4
St. dev.	5.2	2.1	7.9	5.3	2.0	4.5	1.6	0.8
St. err. $(\bar{x})$	0.9	0.4	1.2	0.9	0.3	0.7	0.3	0.1
Median	8.1	2.9	72.0	8.9	0	2.0	0	0
Minimum	0	0	51.0	3.5	0	0	0	0
Maximum	26.9	7.0	85.0	25.0	7.0	19	9.1	3.1

appear with one or more settlements, and only 1 county, Westmorland, in 1787, can be said to occur much too frequently for its relative importance. Industrialization of the power-driven kind may be assumed not to have taken place in these localities at the times of the listings, but what certainly did intervene over the period covered by our samples is sharp demographic change. In the 1500s and early 1600s many localities must have experienced rapid increases in population, giving way in the mid-1600s to decreasing fertility and stagnation, even decline, in total levels, and re-entering by the mid-1700s a cycle of rising fertility, with some decline in mortality along with substantial growth. The demographic regimes in different places as well as at different times must, therefore, have varied considerably, so that the sensitivity of household types to different demographic rates is of importance in analyzing our samples.

A fair guess at a median size for English settlements in preindustrial times might be as low as 200 to 250 persons living in 40 to 60 households (cf. Laslett, 1971, pages 56, 57, 274). It will be seen that the settlements in our samples, with the exception of Tunstall in Kent (52) and a few others, are rather larger than this size, and some are quite big by the standards of that era. Corfe Castle (61) with 1239 inhabitants was a substantial rural center and Poole (31) in Dorset with 1330 inhabitants was a sizeable port town. Stoke-on-Trent (50) in Staffordshire, where the listing covers only part of the whole settlement, was in 1701 an incipient manufacturing center about to become the famous pottery town. Our main sample of 30 includes 8 listings with fewer than 200 people, 7 with between 200 and 300, 10 with between 300 and 1000, and 5 with over 1000, and the sizes in our reserve sample of 34 listings are similar. The median sizes of the places represented in the two samples are 253 and 380. In some of these places, like Clayworth, (3) and (34), for which we have two listings separated by a dozen years, the parish is the unit, and it covers a whole distinct settlement, typically divided in this instance into two hamlets. In other places, such as Barton (56) in Westmorland, a constablewick or civil area otherwise named is at issue, and these were generally parts of a settlement rather than the whole. In yet other cases, such as Norwich (38) and London (39), the documents themselves only very partially cover the entire community. It must not be imagined, therefore, that these settlements are all self-contained or natural units, and comparison between them must be judged accordingly.

But these two samples of English listings possess a virtue which sets them apart from all other such collections as far as they exist at all at the present time. The criterion for their selection for analysis from the 500 such documents which we possess has been in no way connected with an interest in one particular form or pattern of types of household. All that we have in mind is the potentiality of a particular document to yield exact information on points of social structure, of which household composition is only one. The two English samples can be sharply contrasted in this respect with the smaller Continental sample of Exhibit 6.1, where the criterion of selection adopted by the researchers from whom these results are taken has very frequently been an interest in the more complicated household forms. The rather special bodies of data from German areas discussed in Chapter 6 were also sought out with particular types of household composition in mind.

It might not be unfair, in fact, to describe our Continental collection as a congeries of special cases. There is at least some hope, however, that a true random sample of the 10,000 English parishes present on the preindustrial map would throw up a set of proportions of household characteristics roughly similar to those recorded in our tables for that country.

C. HOMOGENEITY IN THE COMPOSITION OF ENGLISH HOUSEHOLDS

Since demography is of importance to us in relation to household structure, it is necessary to decide whether our tables show any tendency for complexity in household composition to grow or decline over time in England as population changed. At first flush, there does seem to be some evidence of an increase. Only 2 of the 13 places with more than 5% multiple lineal households—Poole (31) in 1574 and Kelmarsh (45) in 1697—have listings dated before 1700, even though 22 out of the 64 listings are this early. The listings in Exhibit 5.1 are distributed as follows in respect of date and proportions of multiple lineal households:

	Before 1750	After 1750
0% MLN	5	3
Less than 5% MLN	5	9
More than 5% MLN	0	8

A chi square test of the hypothesis of no association between time and proportion of MLN would reject the hypothesis at the 3% significance level. The chi square test might be suspect since one cell of the table is zero. However, a Kruskal–Wallis test also shows association between dates of listings and these three levels of MLN significant at the same 3% level. Although in the reserve sample in Exhibit 5.2 there is no such statistically significant association, these results for the main sample at least make out a prima facie case that multiple lineal organization increased over time.

A pattern of increasing complexity over time is not borne out, however, by our two overall indices of complexity. We may use a Spearman rank–order test of the correlation between the date columns and the columns headed "% complex" in Exhibits 5.1 and 5.2 to test the null hypothesis that there is no trend at all over time. For either the principal or the reserve sample and for either the A or the B index of complexity, this test fails to reject the hypothesis of no trend, even at significance levels as lax as 20%. Furthermore, the pattern of change for multiple lineal households is not reproduced among the extended households. A glance at the relevant columns in Exhibits 5.1 and 5.2 shows that the proportion of extended households showed no discernible tendency to increase over time in these settlements. This outcome is somewhat surprising, for there are other sources of evidence which do record a rise in the proportion of resident relatives in the population and of households containing resident relatives over the later part of the period covered by our tables. In subsequent decades, moreover, in the middle of the 1800s when urbanization and industrialization really got underway, numbers of households with resident individuals making them extended on our definitions grew quite markedly and remained high until such matters pass out of observation entirely in 1871.[4]

Our observations about change over time, therefore, are equivocal. An increase of multiple households of the lineal kind is not accompanied by an increase in extended households, at least in our carefully selected and tested sample. Under these circumstances we may turn back to the simulation results of Chapter 4 to find out how large or small we should judge these differences in multiple lineal organization. In every 1 of 15 batches of simulations reported upon there, each of which is a random sample of 64 identically-distributed cases, the range of multiple lineal proportions is larger than 11%. In the 64 English cases in Exhibits 5.1 and 5.2 the range is from 0–19% and if the three highest figures are disregarded,[5] it falls to 0–9%. Thus at its very maximum the whole observed range in multiple lineal proportions is only half again as great as the smallest range found in the simulations, and a realistic estimate might be that the range of multiple lineal households in preindustrial England was not likely to have been larger than the smallest figure yielded by our simulation experiments. Now the ranges in the simulations represent variability from chance factors alone where there are no structural differences in household formation practices. The differences over time which are in question here, therefore, fall well within the span that might be expected to occur entirely at random. To the extent that we are willing to regard the rates and rules described in Chapters 2 and 3 of this volume as relevant to English preindustrial settlements, we find ourselves discouraged from regarding any but the largest differences in the MLN proportions in the listings, much less the slight shift we see over time, as evidence for structural as opposed to random differences.

This is information that we could never have gathered from our listings themselves. For we could not have told beforehand whether to ascribe

[4] In a sample of 30 settlements from the years 1650–1749 the proportion of resident relatives in the population was 3.2% and the proportion of households with resident relatives was 10.3%. In a further sample of 40, 1750–1821, these figures were 4.2% and 12.9%. As for later developments, we have indications that these higher levels of extension continued until the end of the 1800s (see Laslett, 1972) and Michael Anderson, who has worked extensively on household structure in mid-Victorian England, has stated that "The urban–industrial revolution, then, seems, contrary to all expectation ten years ago, to have been associated with a considerable increase in the co-residence of parents and married children [Laslett and Wall, 1972, page 223]."

[5] Tunstall (52) at 19%; Barton, etc. (60) at 14% and Haseback (44) at 11%, all three settlements forming part of the reserve sample and all containing a fair proportion of provisionally assigned households. The medians and interquartile ranges are as follows: for all 64 places 2.0% and 0–3.2%; for the main sample 2.4% and 0–4%; for the reserve sample, 2.0% and 1.0–8.0%.

differences between settlements to systematic or to random effects. The simulations, however, advise us quite clearly to discount the increase with date of multiple lineal households, and to decide that there is no convincing evidence in our English samples of structural changes in households towards greater or lesser complexity over time, within the period which concerns us.

If it cannot be confidently claimed that English household structure changed with the passage of time in the period before the census, neither can it be shown that there was any marked variation between urban and rural communities. The parish of St. Peter Mancroft (38) at the heart of the city of Norwich in 1694, the eight London parishes (39) representing the central area of the richest city in the preindustrial world, and the Southampton parishes listed in the same decade (40–41), show little detectable difference from the dozens of more rural settlements, like Puddletown in Dorset in 1725 (10), or Broughton in Lancashire in 1676 (33), or Leverton in Lincolnshire in 1762 (53). It must be remembered that these urban examples all date from the 1690s, a time of war and inflation, and that central parishes may not be representative of the whole area of cities. Although it may be against expectation to find so little difference in urban and rural lists in our two closely refined samples, an exactly similar circumstance has been established for a much larger body of evidence dating from about 1700 and necessarily of lower quality. In work done by Margaret Jones at the Cambridge Group in 1976, the household compositions of seven London parishes, five Southampton parishes, and three Shrewsbury parishes have been compared with 11 settlements in East Kent and 6 in Wiltshire. Discussing these three urban areas and two rural areas, Richard Wall (1977) concludes as follows:

> Nowhere did kin constitute an important element in the household. . . . The small numbers make it difficult to determine whether there were important differences between the five areas, particularly in relation to the various categories of kin. All that can be said is that it would be very difficult to argue in favor of variation from these figures. Instead it is the similarities which are noteworthy [pages 277–278].

The full evidence from which our abstract is drawn suggests that ecological variation was not entirely absent from English household structure, nevertheless. Extended households in Southampton, for example, tended to contain more laterally related persons, such as sisters of the wife, than were present elsewhere, and this is detectable in London, too. A detailed comparison of all the materials from Kent in 1705 and Westmorland in 1787, including those documents which fall below the standard qualifying them for our tables, hints that there was greater complexity of households on the sheep grazing hills of that northern county than there was in the mixed farming plain of the southeastern corner of England, and that the structure differed in subtle ways.

Some systematic variability between areas may therefore have been a feature of traditional English household structure both in time and space. Compared to the random variability we expect on the basis of the simulations, however, the systematic variability appears slight and so, perhaps, numerically undemonstrable from such hard evidence as we are likely to possess. Homogeneity is the message of Exhibits 5.1 and 5.2. The most notable respect in which the English listings appear homogeneous, especially contrasted with the Continental sample in Exhibit 6.1, is the paucity of multiple households of any kind. We do not mean that there are no settlements with many multiple households. In Tunstall (52) in Kent we find no less than 19% of all households to be of multiple lineal familial form, well up to levels on the Continent, though Tunstall is a small village, it is true, and one in which a full 25% of all households are provisionally rather than definitely assigned. In our samples the exceptional settlements are so few as to reinforce the impression of homogeneity.

The relative uniformity of English household composition over the whole area of that country should not lead us to suppose a similar want of variation throughout all the three British countries. The Scottish Isles are known not to be likely to have conformed as closely to the English pattern as lowland Scotland seems to have done (see Laslett, 1977, Table 1.1, for household composition at Aross-in-Mull in 1779). Early in 1978 evidence came to light from the area of Waterford in Ireland implying that, in two villages at the time of the 1821 Census, households there might have attained a level of complexity far higher than we have yet observed for England. These contrasts from the Celtic extremes serve in their turn to emphasize the peculiarity of historic England itself, its peculiar homogeneity.

If we came to our English listings without any prior background, we might well ask ourselves just what the status of such an assertion about homogeneity could possibly be. Who could tell what scale of variation would be surprising, if homogeneity was the underlying fact? Or how far an individual variant would have to go in order to convince us that it constituted an exception? Or at what point a number of extreme examples ought to persuade us to abandon the idea of homogeneity altogether? The way at present open to us to decide these questions is microsimulation. The full story of what has been accomplished with this technique is set forth in the first four chapters of this volume. No doubt this experimental aid to understanding social structure, however, will be new to many historians and social scientists. For this reason we shall here refer to what is there set out and summarize what we believe we are learning of a substantive historical character from these experiments.

D. LESSONS OF MICROSIMULATION EXERCISES FOR ENGLISH HOUSEHOLD STRUCTURE

The first simulation experiment on historical household structure was conceived in 1971, and young though this technique still is, we have a good 6 years of experience which we can review. Seven statements about English household structure and about the so-called stem-family controversy seem to us to arise out of the experimental sequence:

1. That the population of England in traditional times, at least after the end of the 1500s, was not behaving in such a way as to bring into being nearly as many complex households as they could have engendered whether of the stem-family type or, by inference, of other types.
2. That any given set of household formation principles is likely to be robust to demographic variation. Since the English are found to have been living so predominantly in nuclear family households, we can conclude that they were not prevented from realizing more complicated forms of household composition by the constraints of birth rates, death rates, or even marriage rates.
3. That the number of extended and multiple forms observed in England are no basis for postulating successive phases of a stem-family cycle occurring in most, some, or even a small proportion of households. Whatever effect the family cycle had on household composition, it does not seem to have been of this character.
4. That regularity and homogeneity in household composition from place to place and time to time among the English population are indicated by comparing the variance determined from simulation runs with that arising from our observed samples.
5. That there existed on the Continent of Europe individual places, and probably particular areas, where the principles of household formation were clearly different from those which obtained in England, and were such as to bring into being distinctly higher levels of complication. It follows from Statement 2 that this difference was most unlikely to have arisen entirely from random variation or from the constraints of differential demography.
6. That countries on the Continent of Europe cannot be supposed to have displayed a homogeneity in respect of household composition

similar to that observed for England. Complexity could rise to high levels in some localities in some countries, high that is when judged on the scale suggested by our microsimulation exercises. But it is certainly not the case that the Continent as a whole had a uniformly high level of complexity, always higher than in England. Contrasts between small areas and between individual places close together in time and space can be found in Western and Central Continental Europe (though not necessarily in Great Russia, as we shall see in Chapter 6). These contrasts seem to imply structural differences which likewise cannot have arisen solely from random effects or demographic variation.

7. That though we may never know what principles of household formation the English had in their heads when they made their coresidential choices, we do have an expedient to hand for pursuing the logic of their behavior further. This expedient is a set of simulation experiments taking the nuclear family as a model and modulating it with exceptions to provide against the obvious hardships that a universal rule of nuclear family living would impose on any population. We call this the nuclear hardship model, and we believe that the devising and testing of it will be an important step towards understanding the family composition characteristics of England for a long way back in time.

Such then is an outline of what we have learned about household structure during half a decade of microsimulation experiments, experiments discussed in the first four chapters of this book. We hope that experiments with the nuclear hardship model will give rise in due course to outcomes of the same kind as are reported in Chapter 4 for testing models of complex household formation. Will these experiments show that a nuclear hardship model accounts no better for the English data than a stem-family hypothesis? Or will it turn out that our sample of listings is compatible with the supposition that the English favored no family–household form other than the nuclear? Will it be shown, that is, that the occasions on which extended and multiple households did occur in England, as is indicated by the small but nonzero proportions in Exhibits 5.1 and 5.2, can in fact be explained by the exigencies of special hardship cases? We must wait for answers.

We have insisted that the seven assertions which we have ventured to make could not have been arrived at without the results of microsimulation experiments. An illustration may help to persuade the reader of the force of this statement. Assertion 3, about the family cycle in relation to English household structure, rests on a comparison of the proportions of lineally extended (XLN) households and lineally multiple (MLN) households as they are to be observed in the outcomes of microsimulation on the one hand and in the English data of Exhibits 5.1 and 5.2 on the other hand. In our main sample, Exhibit 5.1, there is a rank–order correlation of .41 between the proportion of multiple lineal households and the proportion of extended lineal households. This correlation is significantly different from zero at the 4% level. A natural interpretation of such an outcome would be to ascribe it to the operation of a domestic group cycle in which many households passed through successive structural phases of which lineal multiplicity and lineal extension were two. That is, XLN households would be appearing as remnants of MLN households after the death of a spouse in one of the lineally related conjugal family units. Circumstances which permit more lineal multiplicity would be assumed to permit along with it, as part of the cycle, more lineal extension. To see whether a domestic group cycle would produce in this way the effects that we are tempted to explain by postulating it, we turn once more to our simulations. We have programmed just such a domestic cycle: This was indeed one of the objects of the exercise.

Among the batches of simulation output for a given set of household rules and differing demographic rates we certainly do find a correlation between the average proportions MLN and XLN in a batch, as can be seen from Exhibit 4.2. For the eight primoreal batches, the rank order correlation between these proportions is .86, which is significantly different from zero at the 1% level. But we can go beyond summary statistics like correlation and look at the pattern of association which gives rise to it. In the historical data set out in Exhibits 5.1 and 5.2, it is rare to find English settlements where multiplicity is relatively high and extension low or absent, but the reverse is not true. A relatively high degree of lineal extension is no indication whatever of a relatively high degree of lineal multiplicity or any other multiple household form. The observed correlation arises in fact from a special relationship: There are no instances of high lineal multiplicity accompanied by low lineal extension. Among the simulation batches, however, just the opposite is true. There the special relationship which gives rise to the correlation is the complete absence of low MLN with high XLN batches, whereas batch R1 among the primoreal batches and P1, P2, and P3 among the primonuptial batches are all examples of relatively high MLN with low XLN levels.

The discrepancy between the pattern in the data and the pattern in the simulations cannot but discourage us from espousing an explanation of the MLN and XLN proportions in our English samples by reference to a developmental cycle of the stem-family kind. We might be able to account for this discrepancy as an artifact of some feature of domestic group cycles which we have omitted from our computer model. But until such an explanation is forthcoming we cannot maintain the initially tempting interpretation of the relationship between proportions MLN and proportions XLN. Such a conclusion as this would not have been possible, of course, without the aid of microsimulation.

Two other points deserve mention on the XLN versus MLN patterns. It makes a difference whether we look at the average proportions of XLN and MLN for different batches of simulations, or look instead at the proportions of XLN and MLN for the different simulations within a single batch. Variations in these proportions between batches should arise from differing demographic circumstances, and these circumstances might well give rise systematically to more multiplicity and more extension in such a way as to bring about a relationship between them even when household formation rules are kept the same. Random variability is all that should lie behind differences in these proportions within any given batch of simulation results, which would be less likely to give rise to any association between multiplicity and extension. And this is indeed what we find to occur. We have seen how strong the correlation between proportions XLN and MLN can be between batches, while within the batch of simulations labeled $P2$, for example, described in Chapter 4, the rank–order correlation is a mere $-.11$, not even significantly different from zero at the 28% level. Thus, whether we should expect to find association between MLN and XLN proportions in collections of listings like those we have for England depends on whether we are prepared to regard them as differing systematically in their demographic circumstances or whether we are more inclined to regard them as differing only randomly from each other, exemplifying a common set of conditions tempered by random effects.

E. VALUE OF THE SIMULATION EXERCISES

It would be unwise to exaggerate the value of microsimulation experiments if it encouraged us to neglect the paramount importance of seeking out more evidence and analyzing it comparatively. None of our statements here should be taken to deny that contrasts as informative as those between English data and microsimulation outputs could be drawn between English data and Continental European data or data from the rest of the world, if the latter were available in satisfactory scope and form. If, for example, we were presented with data from a group of places where we had good reason to suppose the family cycle did give rise to successive phases of extension and multiplicity in household composition, and it did turn out that proportions XLN and proportions MLN were correlated in the same way as the simulations, this would provide confirmation of our third assertion, the assertion which questions a connection between extension and multiplicity for the English household system. We shall investigate such a body of materials and its analysis in Chapter 6.

A case might well be made for some at least of the other propositions in our list of seven on the basis of close and imaginative comparisons of the English figures with those we already have from the Continent in the light of the whole body of evidence, some of it, as we shall see, comparable figure for figure with our tables. To be convincing, we must remember, such arguments from these data would have to be quite intricate, more intricate than historical arguments usually are. This is so because of two circumstances. First is the character of most such evidence, its having been selected with an interest in certain types of household to the exclusion of others. Second is the difficulty of distinguishing systematic variability due to demography or to behavioral differences from random variability, which we now know is bound to be so sizable.

Of course, the more data we come to have, and the better these data are, the more we shall be able to say, even without benefit of microsimulation. A critic might perhaps be disposed to wonder, therefore, whether the difficulty and expense of mounting our microsimulation experiments have in fact been justified.

Several considerations may be argued in reply to observations of this kind. Some of them have a relevance which goes beyond the issue of household structure or of microsimulation and bear on the relationship of mathematics and numerical techniques in relation to historical sociology generally. It may, therefore, be worth our while to take them one by one.

It would, in the first place, be an extraordinary thing to depreciate the value of a set of outcomes on the ground that they might possibly have become available in the ordinary course of the advance of historical knowledge. To have an idea of what may be going to be found out, which will give meaning to what is already known, is an enormous advantage. There is no need to labor the point that an isolated fact, a fact without a frame of reference, does not of itself constitute knowledge at all, in order to appreciate how important it has been to us to be able to place the new and unexpected items of information which have suddenly been discovered about English household structure into an ordered context almost as soon as they have appeared.

What is more, although the model, rules, and rates of any particular simulation may not match exactly the historical reality that any particular historian might argue for, it simply is not true that the technique of microsimulation is inexact or speculative; rather the reverse. Simulations tell us what would be true if certain rules were consistently obeyed and were modified first by randomness and second by such regularities as rates of births, marriages, and deaths. This is just the sort of thing that historians want to know, or ought to want to know.

Third comes the conventional consideration as to hindsight. Nothing is more tempting than to pronounce, when faced with an indication of something which was in fact unexpected, that you knew it all already. It is always easier to find reasons for accepting, even accounting for, a novelty than to arrive at the novelty in the first place. These are by no means trivial distortive tendencies on the outlook of social scientists, historical or otherwise.

Finally, it must be emphasized again that the outcomes of simulation are in no sense offered as substitutes for empirical knowledge but as aids to judging the empirical knowledge that we do possess. Some of the information which simulation brings into being, such as that pertaining to variance, might never have become available at all from investigation of the conventional kind. To take up simulation is to invite yourself to proceed further with your data than you have already done, to pursue the suggestions which the outcomes put before you, outcomes which are often unexpected, always illuminating, and sometimes devastating.

APPENDIX: SELECTION AND COMPLETENESS CRITERIA FOR ENGLISH LISTINGS

To explain the division of our usable material into a main sample of 30 and a reserve sample of 34, we must first explain how ambiguous cases in generally good listings are handled, and how our two different estimates of overall complexity of households are derived. In a perfect list like that from Bampton (17) there is no individual whose relationship to a household head is not specified. As poorer and particularly earlier material is surveyed, so-called unspecified individuals appear along with the well-described ones. We are left with some households of indeterminable structure. Many unspecified persons were undoubtedly lodgers or servants whose status, though not noted by the listmaker, would make no difference to the classification of the groups in which they appear. But their presence has led us to prepare the two indices of complexity rather than a single one.

The first index aims at a maximum ascribable complexity in household structure, and so assumes that all unspecified individuals are kin according to rules which we now set forth. The second index omits all households in a settlement which contain unspecified individuals, individuals, that is to say, whose relationships to the heads of their households might, if they were known, alter the composition of the households to which they belong.

Most of the indeterminate households have the structure of one conjugal family unit together with an apparently unrelated individual. This form of domestic group can only be complex by being an extended household, not a multiple one, though we cannot tell what form of extension it might have had. That is true except under the very unlikely circumstances that the unspecified extra individual was in fact the spouse of one of the children in the conjugal family unit, his or her child or even parent. In any of these three situations a second conjugal family unit would be present and the household would indeed be multiple, not extended. We have disregarded those remote possibilities, but it must always be remembered that the occasional physical defect in a list, a tear in the paper, a blot, an illegibility, is a possible cause of such important relationships not being recoverable even in our 64 highly select English documents, where personal descriptions are consistently good.

On our worksheets we call these households with one conjugal family unit and one undesignated individual "provisionally extended." This category includes households where the extra person shares the head's surname but where the nature of the relationship is not explicit. In our tables we have assigned the provisionally extended households to the columns for XLN and XLT, in the same ratio as the ratio of determinate households which are XLN to those which are XLT. Where there are no determinate extended households, all provisional extended households are given as XLN. This arrangement seeks to preserve the ratios between lineal and lateral extension so far as we can estimate them, while presenting maximum levels of complexity consistent with the information we have.

We follow a similar procedure with provisional multiple households. Households with two or more conjugal family units linked by no evident relationship are occasionally found. If such a household was complex, it must have been multiple rather than extended. Households with more than a single extra person but only one conjugal unit could have been either extended or multiple; we include them among the provisionally multiple, unless ages or other information rule out the possibility that they could have composed another conjugal family unit. Assignment of the provisionally multiple households to the columns MLN and MLT parallels the provisionally extended case. Only the households which elude even provisional categorization remain indeterminate, while those provisional households which could only be simple in structure are given as nuclear.

The worst lists yield no households of determinate structure more complex than nuclear households but are replete with provisional households. The best lists have only determinate households. The ratio of determinate complex households to provisional complex households plus indeterminate households serves as our criterion for the quality of lists, and such a ratio is given for each listing in the penultimate column of Exhibits 5.1 and 5.2. The 28 listings where this ratio exceeds 2.0 plus the 2 listings of Steeple Ashton (13) for 1770 and Renhold for 1689 (4), where the ratios equal 1.8 and 1.7 respectively, make up our main English sample, Exhibit 5.1. The 34 listings with the ratio falling between 1.6 and 0 make up our reserve sample, Exhibit 5.2.

The A index of complexity in these tables is the ratio of the number of households known to be extended or multiple over the number of households of known composition. The B index is the ratio of the number of households either provisionally or definitely extended or multiple over the total number of households. The last column shows the proportion of all households which have been definitely rather than provisionally classified. Low values in the last columns admonish caution in building a case on the corresponding lists.

6

The Stem-Family Hypothesis and Its Privileged Position

We have made it plain in the course of our discussion so far that nothing could now encourage the sociological historian to adopt the stem-family household hypothesis as an explanation of the patterns of residence of our English ancestors. The reason why this particular model of familial behavior has taken up so much of our attention in these chapters on the microsimulation of household composition in relation to demographic variability is its privileged position. For there can be no doubt that the stem family has exercised a peculiar fascination over the minds of those who have previously concerned themselves with the history of household and family, and with the social structural development of England and of Europe. This position of privilege has by no means yet been abandoned.

So strong in fact is the attachment to this familial form that there is a disposition to look upon every example of household formation as betraying the presence of the stem-family pattern. Such an attitude not only makes the English evidence very difficult to comprehend, but might stand in the way of the appreciation of the known facts about variation in household composition over the area of the European Continent as a whole. For, interesting evidence is beginning to appear which might end by convincing us that in historic Europe most recognized forms of household composition have been represented and may have coexisted over long periods of time. It is becoming possible in fact to distinguish polar opposites in the European familial pattern, with simple family households dominating the homogeneous British and Northwest European area at one pole, and with highly complex households, although not of the stem-family type, manifesting themselves amongst Russian serfs at the other pole, but with a remarkable intermixture coming in between, spread over most of the Continent. A first, tentative discussion of this European family geography has already been published, "Characteristics of Western Family Considered Over Time," in Laslett (1977). The form of the coresident domestic group is only one of a number of distinguishable characteristics which are there suggested as forming an integrated pattern; others are late age at marriage for women, brief age gap between spouses, high proportion of what are called life cycle servants, all of which tend to covary over the European area. Here we must confine ourselves to the specific comparison of English household composition with those examples of household composition on the continent of Europe which could be colorably claimed as showing forth the stem family.

A. EVIDENCE FROM THE CONTINENT OF EUROPE

Some of the settlements on the European Continent which appear in Exhibit 6.1 may perhaps have had populations which conformed to stem-family rules of household formation. The analysis of these listings has been carried out in the same way as for the English settlements in Exhibits 5.1 and 5.2, and the results set out so as to make strict comparison possible between these sets of data and the outcomes of microsimulation. We have not, however, worked out indices of reliability for the Continental proportions because in some cases (as for the Hungarian and Estonian settlements) the originals are in languages unknown to us and their substance has been communicated by the ideographic system set out on pages 41–42 of the introduction to Laslett and Wall (1972). Original listings, even in French and German, present formidable difficulties for the nonnative when it comes to such exacting analysis, which draws attention once again to the necessity of each language file being studied locally if really close comparison is to be carried out.

It must be repeated that the listings in Exhibit 6.1 make up a biased sample, biased toward complexity of household composition. Restricted as their coverage is, and distorted as they must be as a collection in view of the way they have been chosen, comparative examination of these 15 sets of figures bears out the assertions we have already made: that the peculiarity of English settlements is the paucity of multiple households; that in Northwest Europe [illustrated here by Lisswege (1), Hallines (4),

Longuenesse (5)] the pattern was close to the English; that this was also true at individual places elsewhere on the Continent, as at Vehrenbach (7), or even Lesnica (13) in Poland in 1720; that lineal multiplicity was much more common in other continental places, like Montplaisant (2), Alsónyék (10), or Vändra (14), and certainly high enough to allow of the stem-family pattern to have been present. The median figure for multilineality in ten of these places [excluding (1), (4), (5), (7), and (9)] is 18.0%, six times as high as in England (2.6% for our main sample, 2.0% for the reserve sample). This is not quite within the range of the primonuptial simulation outputs (19.0–26.5%, see Exhibit 4.2), but almost three times as high as for the outputs for ultimonuptial rules (6.6% and 6.7%).

In these 10 Continental places, moreover, multilineal proportions are significantly correlated with extended lineal proportions (at the .05 level). This set of scattered figures, therefore, is adequate to provide a positive contrast to the negative statements we have made about English household composition: that in our English materials the stem-family pattern cannot be shown to have been present, and that such complex households as are found there are unlikely to be adequately explained by the domestic group cycle. On the Continent the stem family certainly could have existed, at these select places at these particular times, and could certainly have been affecting the life cycle. Other traditions of household formation could have been present as well. And all this, as microsimulation has shown, could have been the case quite independently of the effects of differing fertility and mortality.

A much more dramatic comparison can be drawn for the English household if we include figures for certain settlements which do not appear in Exhibit 6.1 because the original data have not been analyzed in the same way. It has been shown that in certain villages in Southern France in the 1600s and 1700s the proportions of complex households could exceed 40%, and that it might rise almost as high in a settlement in Brittany in 1773. In villages in the area surrounding Florence, Italy it might exceed 50% at the same time. In Latvia the corresponding figure (unfortunately rather problematic in its calculation) is above 60% for a settlement in 1797, and a very clearly defined result for a Russian serf community at the same period is well above 80%. Over three-quarters of all households, that is to say, were in some way complex.[1]

---

[1] See Laslett (1977, Chapter 1, Tables 1.2 and 1.3) with reference and acknowledgments. The Russian serf community, Mishino in Great Russia in 1814, according to research of Peter Czap, has 11.7% extended, 72.6% multiple. This wider sample confirms the coexistence in extensive areas of Europe of communities with complex households alongside of communities with simple ones, as at Kassa and Sziget in the 1550s, places now in Czechoslovakia. (Unfortunately in the first impression of Laslett [1977] the figure of 4.4% for extended households at Sziget in 1551 in Table 1.2 is misprinted as 44%.)

EXHIBIT 6.1.   Continental Sample, 15 Settlements

Date and settlement	Population	Total house-holds	Percentage of households lacking structure (SOLE)		Percentage of nuclear (NUC) house-holds (3)
			(1) Solitaries	(2) Known structure	
1 1739 Lisswege, Belgium	796	156	1.9	1.3	85.3
2 1644 Montplaisant, France	338	63	11	2	44
3 1697 Rognonas, France	117	26	8	4	50
4 1773 Hallines, France	241	54	6	4	81
5 1778 Longuenesse, France	333	66	2	6	76
6 1687 Löffingen, Germany	697	125	.8	.8	82.4
7 1705 Vehrenbach, Germany	177	40	5	5	80
8 1793 Östersheps, Germany	341	65	3	0	60
9 1795 Grossenmeer, Germany	882	141	1.4	.7	52.5
10 1792 Alsónyék, Hungary	685	120	2.5	0	45.0
11 1816 Kölked, Hungary	643	111	0	0	46.8
12 1782 Colorno, Italy	308	66	8	0	73
13 1720 Lesnica, Poland	1637	311	1.0	1.0	92.3
14 1683 Vändra, Estonia	976	132	3.8	.8	64.4
15 1733 Belgrade, Serbia	1350	176	3.4	2.8	54.5

Once figures of this order are reached, and when the actual composition of households like those found in Russia and in the Baltic areas are contemplated, three further statements can be made. First, much higher levels of household complexity existed in places in historic Europe than are created by our simulation exercises on the stem family, even when what we have called primonuptial rules are used. Some of the patterns of coresidence were apparently very unlike the stem-family model. Second, although these examples of communities which actually existed may have had ages at marriage for women, and rates of marriage too, different, perhaps markedly different, from those simulated in our exercises, or those which obtained in England and in those Continental places where simple family households predominated, their birth and death rates are unlikely to have been of a different order. Third, however we construe the contrast between the English family system and those prevailing on the Continent, it cannot have been a straightforward one, decidedly not a contrast between the relatively homogeneous simple family regime covering England and the British Isles, and a Continent uniformly subject to the stem family.

An attempt to place English household composition in a comparative European context, therefore, soon raises questions which transcend the issue of the stem family. We cannot pursue these questions here, but we

Percentage of households extended lineally (XLN) (4a,b,d)	Percentage of households extended laterally (XLT) (4c)	Percentage of multiple households with lineal disposition (MLN) (5a,b,e)	Percentage of multiple households with lateral disposition (MLT) (5c,d)	Percentage of indeterminate households (IND)	Percentage of households either extended or multiple (% complex)	
2.6	7.7	1.3	0	0	11.5	1
16	7	21	0	0	43	2
12	0	18	5	4	35	3
6	2	2	0	0	9	4
9	5	3	0	0	17	5
4.0	.8	4.0	.8	6.4	16.0	6
3	3	0	0	5	10	7
18	0	19	0	0	37	8
16.0	3.2	16.7	9.5	0	45.4	9
13.3	3.3	26.7	9.2	0	52.5	10
13.5	.9	31.5	7.2	0	53.2	11
9	0	11	0	0	20	12
5.5	0	0	0.3	0	5.8	13
3.8	3.0	21.2	3.0	0	31.1	14
9.1	5.1	12.5	5.1	7.4	39.2	15

can learn a great deal more about the stem-family hypothesis, and about the English system, too, if we confront the English evidence and the outcomes of our simulations with the work recently undertaken on particular regions of Europe where the stem family is claimed to have been a recognized and established tradition. Before we do this, we ought to remark upon the possibility that weaker, perhaps much weaker, residual forms of the stem-family tendency could have existed in England, a possibility which cannot be disposed of simply by noting how much lower levels of household complexity were in that country than they are in the outcomes of our microsimulation. Alternatively, a strong form of the principle could have been present, but affecting only a small proportion of the population.

Final demonstration of a negative is never possible. We have seen how peculiarly difficult this would be for the matters in hand, because only quite gross differences will stand out above random variability. It may become possible to decide whether a particular group, the gentry, say, who are known to have had resident kin in their households more frequently than others, lived so often under the stem-family principle that they accounted by themselves for all, or most, of the complexity in household composition which is found in England. Even if, as seems very likely, this should turn out to be untrue, it could yet be suggested that very weak forms of the same principle were to be found in the society. Or it might be insisted, as has been done by Lutz Berkner, the acknowledged authority on the stem family, that at a time previous to that for which evidence is available this privileged type of the domestic group could have been dominant, or prevalent,[2] and that what we observe in our tables for England are its scattered remnants, still at large in the social universe like the persisting fragments of an exploded stellar object.

Even if it should turn out that the simulation of what has been called the nuclear hardship model fits the English data, this would still not finally negate a suggestion of this kind. But what is the point of insisting on a conjecture about a minority, perhaps a small or very small minority, when what was happening to all the rest of the society has still to be explained? Persistent attachment to the original thesis of the great pioneer of familial sociology, P. G. Frédéric Le Play, should not be allowed to lead historians of European social, familial and property arrangements to overlook the proper object of their own enquiry, which is the position of the mass of the people in these respects. How long will it be before the privileged position of the stem-family hypothesis is abandoned?

B. INHERITANCE, PARTIBLE AND IMPARTIBLE, IN RELATION TO HOUSEHOLD COMPOSITION

The most recent, the best documented, and the most illuminating discussion of the stem-family pattern is certainly of an entirely different character. In comparing two areas of Northern Germany in the year 1689, Berkner finds the stem-family form of the household to be prevalent, perhaps dominant in one area, and rare, almost entirely absent, in the other.[3] Where, and when, impartible inheritance was customary,

---

[2] See Berkner (1972) and for an earlier comment on England in the same vein, Laslett and Wall (1972) pages 150–151, and Tables 4–16 on page 154 for the greater proportion of households of gentry containing resident kin. In Laslett (1977, Chapter 1), work in progress by Richard Michael Smith is cited which points toward the predominance of simple households in England as early as the 1300s, or even the 1200s, when the country must surely be counted as having had a peasant population, if ever it did so.

[3] See Berkner (1976), "Inheritance, Land Tenure and Peasant Family Structure." The volume in which this study appears, *Family and Inheritance*, edited by J. Goody, J. Thirsk, and E. P. Thompson, contains general discussions of household composition, and much relevant material. It is the relationship between inheritance custom, property distribution and the form of the household which interests many of the contributors. A subsequent study of the same materials is contained in another interesting article by Berkner (1977), "Peasant household structure and demographic change in Lower Saxony (1689–1786)," published in *Population Patterns in the Past*, edited by Lee (1977) and occasional references will be made here to that essay also.

extended and multiple forms which can be associated with the stem-family pattern are found in a substantial proportion of households, and it can be persuasively argued that the developmental cycle of the domestic group was displaying the effects of this set of residential conventions. When, and where, partible inheritance was the norm, all forms of complex domestic group become insignificant. The study is based on published materials, and the results are presented numerically.

Here then is an opportunity to make comparisons with the analysis of our English data, and to check against the benchmarks provided by our simulations a real-world example of the stem-family pattern in the past. It is in fact the first such opportunity because other studies, including an impressive discussion of a set of Austrian villages made by Berkner himself[4] have not cast their results in a form which can be compared at all closely with other numerical studies and have been based on unpublished and inaccessible evidence.

Notwithstanding the opportunity provided for us by Berkner's essay of 1976, it must be admitted at the outset that a number of barriers hinder really rigorous comparison between his figures and our own. Some of these barriers may be due chiefly to differences in intention and emphasis, others to the intrinsic character of the German data. Four points of warning seem to deserve special mention before we proceed to our comparisons.

First of all, we do not know from Berkner's article how his sample of material has been chosen out of the vastly larger corpus in the printed *Kopfsteuerbeschreibung*. If his principles of selection have been very different from the criteria based solely on completeness of kin descriptions and quality of recorded detail employed in selecting our English sample, comparisons may be vitiated. Berkner's (1976) statement that "the data below are based on a sample of about two thousand households in 75 villages drawn from administrative districts grouped by geographical region within the two territories [page 85]" does not carry us far enough. It appears to leave open the possibility that households of certain types or villages with a large share of households of certain types have found themselves systematically included or excluded from the sample, by virtue of an association with some unspecified selection criterion.

This is a question of great importance. One of the surprises in Berkner's

---

[4] See Berkner (1972) and compare Laslett in Laslett and Wall (1972, pages 20–21 and 150–151). In his studies of 1976 and 1977, Berkner makes no reference to his Austrian work of 1972: The criteria for the stem-family pattern are different in all three cases, and the results do not appear to be strictly comparable. The printed version of the tax lists on which Berkner (1976) is based is *Die Kopfsteuerbeschreibung der Fürstentümer Calenberg-Göttingen and Grubenhagen von 1689*, edited by Max Burchard and Herbert Mundhenke, published in 13 parts at Hanover and then Hildesheim, 1940–1972.

tables, as we shall see, is the low proportion of solitaries and no-family households in his partible areas. It is easy, however, to locate in the published lists an abundance of single-person entries for a number of the settlements where he tells us that partibility was the rule in 1689. These entries are evidently not finding their way into the tables. The same may be true of other categories which are harder to inspect. Depending on the principles of sample selection and their consequences for the representation of various types of households, it may be that it is wrong to take Berkner's tables directly as tables of household structure for settlements comparable to our tables for England and the Continent.

A second point to bear in mind is that Berkner is not confident that the fiscal units of his analysis were in fact families, households, housefuls, or any form of coresident domestic group. "We cannot assume that the seventeenth century officials who drew up the tax lists had any consistent notion of what constituted a household [Berkner, 1976, page 93]." Some tax units can be found in the printed lists which patently did not consist of people living together. A sceptic might parody Berkner's stem-family pattern as a tendency for parents (married or widowed), their children (unmarried, married, and with or without their own children), and their siblings to appear together in tax units in particular combinations and with particular ages. Nonetheless, it does seem highly probable that the tax units were ordinarily households or at least housefuls. Examination of the printed volumes supports this view.

Third, however, the quality of detail in the published lists of taxpayers is extremely uneven. Although this evidence must be described as the most extensive yet discovered for the purpose of investigating the forms of the domestic group in a particular region in historic Europe numerically, and is revelatory of family patterns, much of it is coarse and of problematic completeness: In the partible inheritance area it is quite inferior. Parts of it are much richer in information about ages and occupations than the English material. Other parts are very sketchy. In view of the doubts about the nature of the units, few of the lists for particular villages would satisfy the criteria required for entry into the Cambridge Group collection or qualify for Exhibits 5.1 or 5.2. Hence we must proceed with caution in placing too much weight upon comparisons.

In the fourth place, Berkner's scheme for the classification of households is not spelled out in detail. His categories do not cover all the possibilities and he does not indicate how ambiguous cases are resolved. He nowhere refers to other systems of classification nor does he make any comparison whatever with the results of numerical examinations of household composition previously undertaken. A considerable effort of deciphering and reconstruction has been necessary for the approximate comparisons that we put forward. In the end, a reader cannot avoid guesswork which a more detailed discussion of the classification or the use of a standard system of classification would have forestalled.[5]

Nevertheless Berkner does present us with figures for the prevalence of stem-family forms, figures that he uses for his own comparative purposes, and which he presumably intends others to use as well, where there is an appropriate opportunity. We think it is important, therefore, to learn what we can by setting his results alongside our own, despite the difficulties we have listed. In his studies the existence of a stem-family tendency in the relevant area and its connection with impartible inheritance are convincingly established. The case for the domestic group cycle being modified by stem-family patterns in that area is cogently argued. We are at last in the presence of a European peasant community which quite evidently respected to a considerable extent that "organization of the families which," so Le Play maintained in the title of his famous work, was "the true model shown forth by the history of all races of mankind throughout all time [Le Play, 1871]." But let it be said at once that Berkner's authoritative examination of a particular case in no way justifies the privileged position of the stem-family hypothesis as to the usual composition of European peasant households—quite the contrary.

The grounds for this conclusion are many and various. The following propositions, also four in number, can be set out about these researches in relation to the general question of the definition, analysis and social importance of the stem-family pattern. Taken together they seem to dispose by themselves of this pattern as the expected residential norm in traditional Europe. Each of them, moreover, suggests that an instructive comparison could be drawn with our simulation outputs and with our English figures.

First, the point of Berkner's exercise is precisely to show that the stem-family pattern was *not* universal in the rural life of historic Europe, but an accompaniment of impartible inheritance. He maintains that nuclear families were associated in a similar way with partible inheritance, but not that they were always so associated, nor that these two familial forms were the only ones which could be found.

Second, his researches accordingly bear out the suggestion that over

---

[5] Some puzzles have resisted solution. We are told, for example, that the description *Leibzüchter* indicated retired persons and it is implied in the text and tables that persons so described were retired heads of households or their spouses, persons who had surrendered the *Hof* to their heirs. But persons given this title can be found in the printed evidence whose names or ages seem to preclude their having retired. It would be helpful to know whether the title *Leibzüchter* has been taken to imply a kin relationship for the purpose of classification when other designations are absent.

most of the European Continent, apart from the British Isles, forms of the domestic group were mixed. Here an area showing one form to a noticeable degree is contiguous with an area dominated by another form.

Third, he does not undertake to prove directly that the stem-family pattern characterized the domestic group cycle of one of his localities, to prove it that is to say by following a set of "families" (here meaning lines of succession, or patrilines) as far as possible through their developmental cycles. Although his sources[6] might have allowed him to link nominal data on numbers of individuals, he has confined himself to one listing only made on one occasion, and to inferences from aggregates. This is also true for our English and Continental observations, but not, of course, for our simulations.

Fourth, Berkner's notion of the stem family is wider than that of strict coresidence and need not demand coresidence as part of it. We take his model of the stem family in its wider sense to go something like this. Succession to the *Hof*, that is the farm, farmhouse, and appurtenances belonging to a particular peasant family line, often leads to coresidence between possessor and successor, or possessor and predecessor, especially when impartible inheritance prevails. This in turn gives rise, when it occurs, to the characteristic stem-family forms of the household, those we have called extended lineal and multiple lineal, and an identifiable developmental cycle through which the household (houseful) passes. The domestic group goes from multiple household on the marriage of the resident heir, to extended on the death of the heir's father, to simple or nuclear when no member of the preceding generation is left, and back to multiple when the next heir marries. But there are many variations involving siblings of possessors, predecessors, and so on. Moreover, no characteristic stem-family form of household need necessarily appear at all within the lifetime of any one holder of the *Hof*. This is not only because of demographic vicissitudes, such as the possessor dying before the marriage of his heir, but also because of choice. The heir may decide not to bring his wife into the *Hof* on marriage, for example, and may even perhaps reside elsewhere after his succession, leaving his predecessors as inhabitants of the *Hof*.

The stem-family pattern as thus defined could accordingly be present as

[6] *Die Kopfsteuerbeschreibung* contains references to earlier unpublished tax lists obviously of a similar character. In Parts 5 and 6, for example, it would seem that every name has been painstakingly cross-referenced by the two original editors back to a tax list of 1686, 3 years previously. Use of this research (or an independent comparison between the two listings) would permit in many instances direct observation of the succession of heir to holder, and so on. Berkner makes no reference to this unique research opportunity, although he has evidently done a great deal of analysis of the unpublished materials for other purposes.

an attribute of peasant patrilines without the peculiar coresidential arrangements manifesting themselves over a series of successions to any particular *Hof*. Under these circumstances the stem-family trait could be called recessive, present in a descent line but not manifest in any family grouping at a particular point in time.[7]

C. CLOSE COMPARISON WITH GERMAN FIGURES

It follows from all this, if Berkner has been correctly understood, that the stem-family forms of the coresident domestic group, and even the stem-family cycle itself, are only contingently related to the stem-family tradition itself. Such a view is of obvious importance to the general issue of the nature and existence of the stem family as an institution and its relation to inheritance customs. We shall have to return to these matters in the conclusion of this chapter. But in practice Berkner himself, as we have said, shows no hesitation in referring to the fiscal units in his evidence as "households," nor about taking coresidence, its forms and their relative prevalence, as indications of the presence or absence of his stem-family tradition. Let us accept this procedure and compare as closely as we can what he finds about proportions of households assuming various forms with the proportions we have worked out from our samples and from our simulation exercises.

We can do this in two ways, by taking Berkner's criteria for the stem-family pattern and by taking our own. The difference between them is the

---

[7] It could even exist among a whole society consisting of such patrilines for prolonged periods, although no marked tendency towards extended or multiple family living appeared, as for example amongst the English nobility. See Laslett, in Laslett and Wall (1972, page 23, footnote 40). Several of the contributors to Goody, Thirsk, and Thompson (1977) refer to peers and great landowners as having stem-family attributes of this kind (e.g., the chapter by J. P. Cooper), but are vague as to its relation with coresidence, which nevertheless seems usually to be assumed. The same is true of the only recent attempt to suggest that the stem-family pattern existed in New England communities. See an article by Waters (1976), "Patrimony, succession, and social stability: Guilford, Connecticut in the 18th century." This interesting study seems to me to be an apt illustration of the wish to believe in the stem family wherever evidence of some kind pointing generally in that direction makes its appearance.

The wider definition of the stem family set out in the text is exactly that used in *Household and Family in Past Time*, though the metaphorical notion of recessiveness has been introduced here. It is puzzling therefore, to read Berkner's (1976) statement on page 85 of the Goody, Thirsk, and Thompson volume about coresidence under one roof being the only criterion for its existence allowed for in *Household and Family*, and suggesting by implication in his review of that work (Berkner, 1975) that to talk in terms of rigorous definition in this way is to misuse census data for the historical analysis of household structure.

treatment of laterally extended or multiple households which show no lineal extension or multiplicity. Berkner takes these to be stem households, while we do not. On his definition, he reckons (Berkner 1976, pages 87–88 and Table 3) that, in 1689, 28% of all peasant households showed stem-family characteristics in his impartible area and 6% in his partible one. This can be set against some 15% (on his, not our, definition) for our first English sample (Exhibit 5.1), 16% for our second (Exhibit 5.2), and roughly 31% for the 10 high-MLN Continental settlements of our Exhibit 6.1.

It seems reasonable to conclude from the contrast in these figures that German peasant villages with impartible customs had considerably stronger tendencies toward the stem family than English settlements. These tendencies were, however, rather lower than the average for the rather arbitrary selection of Continental places we have had to accept for the purposes of contrast. But German peasant villages with partible inheritance apparently had markedly inferior proportions of the required household characteristics, inferior even to the English, and below any Continental settlement yet encountered. If we bring in figures from our simulation exercises modulated so as to correspond to Berkner's conventions, the comparative proportions can be scanned in the first column of Exhibit 6.2.

When judged from Berkner's perspective, then, impartible inheritance is associated with a pattern of coresidence intermediate between the levels produced by the systems we call primoreal and ultimonuptial. Of course it does not follow that these German peasants were acting in accordance with a system which would be a recognizable hybrid between our ultimonuptial and primoreal systems. The scale is slightly factitious.

EXHIBIT 6.2.   Comparative Household Proportions

	Stem (1)[a]	MLN[b]	Stem(2)[c]
German impartible area 1689	28	c.13	c.22
German partible area 1689	6	c. 2	c. 5
English main sample in 5.1	15	2.9	12
English reserve sample in 5.2	16	3.8	14
European full sample in 6.1	27	12.5	20
Ten "high MLN" places in 6.1	31	18.0	28
Primonuptial simulations	48–59	28.8	38–49
Primoreal simulations	38–44	20.8	29–44
Ultimonuptial simulations	17	6.1	15

[a] Mean percentages of stem-family households of all types on Berkner's definitions.

[b] Mean percentages of households of multiple lineal type.

[c] Mean percentages of stem-family households of all types on our definitions.

But to find, in the area which he nominates as most favorable to the stem family, proportions of households of that form which fall between ultimonuptial and primoreal levels, rather than between primoreal and primonuptial levels, is sobering enough.[8] It is certainly no dramatic vindication of the view that impartible inheritance has a powerful effect in bringing about stem-family households. What is more, the proportion of stem-family forms in his partible area seems too low when we set it against our English and Continental tables, so low indeed that it looks as if the data may be faulty. We shall return to this point. Here it may make the contrast between partible and impartible look sharper than it might have been in fact.

The failure of proportions of stem-family households, when defined as Berkner chooses, to reach even primoreal levels in his impartible areas is disconcerting in view of the expectations attached to impartible inheritance. This is usually thought of as allotting the whole inheritance to the eldest son, who brings his wife into the household and has his children there. Such an arrangement would resemble our primonuptial model, the strongest of the stem-family tendencies we have programmed, and would require proportions of coresident groups of the stem-family type far in excess of those found in this German area.

When we change perspective and look at these German figures with our own classifications in mind, comparison remains complex and uncertain. One or two fairly straightforward statements can be ventured, however. We may begin with the prevalence of stem-family households themselves as defined by us, that is the proportions of domestic groups known to have contained two conjugal family units descended the one from the other.

Highly approximate calculations from Table 3 of Berkner (1976, page 87) show that stem-family households as thus defined—domestic groups actually marked by lineal multiplicity (MLN) existent in 1689—made up some 13% of all those in the impartible area, and about 2% of those in the partible area. We set out the comparison with multilineal proportions in our other sources in the second column of Exhibit 6.2.

Such figures could be said to place the stem-family tradition associated with impartibility in the same relative position as before, that is between primoreal and ultimonuptial, and so to confirm that tentative judgment. The impartible area certainly had many, many more households of the MLN type than England did, but not all that large a number in compari-

<hr>

[8] Berkner presents no evidence on variation in proportions of households of various types between villages, and seems indifferent to the importance of measuring variance whenever statistics of this kind are worked out. We cannot, therefore, compare his results in respect of covariation between XLN and MLN, and thus apply the indicator we have used for the existence of the stem family as an affect of the domestic group cycle.

son with the few places on the European Continent which we know about. Indeed in our Continental sample (Exhibit 6.1) nearly half of the settlements exceed the primoreal proportion of MLN households, which is never approached in these German figures, and one, Kölked (11), even exceeds the primonuptial level. It begins to look as if the German impartible areas had fairly pronounced but by no means very pronounced proclivities towards multiple households when viewed comparatively, but as if England was particularly free of them. It is also true that the English figures for multilineal households as such appear to have been somewhat higher than those for the German partible area. But this, as we have hinted, may have no significance.

Our definition of the stem-family pattern as such, as distinct from the stem-family household as a coresident group, includes lineal extension (XLN) and lineal multiplicity (MLN), but excludes lateral extension and lateral multiplicity. Unlike our classification, Berkner accepts such extension as a qualification for believing that a household can be counted as situated at a particular stage of the stem-family cycle. If the figures are reduced on both sides by subtraction of these statistics, then 28% of households having stem-family forms as he defines them become 22% or thereabouts in his impartible area and about 5% in his partible area. The figures for comparison look like those in the third column of Exhibit 6.2, though the conversion from Berkner's basis being even more approximate, we have rounded all the others. The effect is to confirm the level of stem-family proportions in the impartible area as lying about midway between primoreal and ultimonuptial and to bring it down a little closer to the English figures.[9] The shortfall in the partible area seems even more conspicuous, but nothing else is changed by these calculations.

When the critique we have used for analyzing our English documents and their data is brought to bear on the German materials, however, and when the German figures are looked at in the light of our simulation experiences, the claims made for the extent of stem-family residence look somewhat strained. In the simulation process the one reason why a married heir should live in the same household with a parent or parents is

---

[9] It is possible that landholders only in the impartible villages might have been following residential rules considerably closer to the primoreal (see Berkner, 1976, Table 4 on page 88). A calculation of the same kind on the figures of this table but allowing for omitted categories yields a proportion of stem family households as judged on our criteria of some 27%. It is surprising that no other separate analyses were made for such households, since it is on them that inheritance practices would have operated most strongly. In these households alone does the number of young children being socialized into households complex in structure seem to have been high enough to make complexity a majoritarian experience (compare Laslett and Wall, 1972, Introduction, Section IV).

succession, the formation of a stem. Coresidence for other reasons, for companionship, for welfare, is excluded. Of course the German and English figures include all such coresidence, whatever the reasons that promote it.

Without knowledge of the previous history of each group represented in the tax units, it is impossible to say how many cases of the presence of the wife's parents, or father, or mother were in fact due to the inheritance of property through these individuals. Berkner counts all such groups as belonging to the stem-family model, even when it is only the mother-in-law who coresides, and it must always be remembered that "it is not clear whether they were living in the same house or on the same property [page 85]." It has to be assumed, because it cannot be demonstrated, that the stem-family tradition is the reason for the connection. It also has to be assumed that this tradition either excludes the motives of companionship and welfare, or represents the form which such motives take under the system. This begins to look like a privileged position for the stem family all over again, and the same is true of the decision to count all residing unmarried siblings of a household head as instances of the stem family in operation. These are not trivial objections, for it is the inclusion of siblings in Berkner's figures which gives the impression of over a quarter of all households being affected, instead of a little over a fifth.

If allowance is made for the presence of parents which cannot be shown to have been due to inheritance, and this has to be done for an attempt at realistic comparison with our simulation outputs, then the 22% for stem-family households of all types on our definitions as presented previously would certainly fall below 20%, perhaps quite markedly. The English figures would fall slightly too, slightly because they are small in any case. The strongest general statement which could now be made, then, is that rules like ultimonuptial rules were being followed in the impartible area. This is the weakest form of stem-family principle and one not very far removed from the nuclear. If, therefore, our practice and principles are followed for the German materials, as far as that is possible, the effect of impartible inheritance on household structure there can scarcely be called impressive.

The comparison with the German area of partible inheritance may not be at all decisive because, as we have repeatedly hinted, figures from that direction can be called into question. The level of simple family households there associated with partibility is certainly high, as might be expected with such very low proportions of complexity. At about 90%, as against 65% going with impartibility, the percentage nuclear is the highest ever reported to us at Cambridge from any country or region for an area, as distinct from a particular settlement. Only one individual place in

England has more than 85% simple households, Kaber in 1787 (19 in Exhibit 5.1), small in size and with a proportion of 94%. Lesnica in Poland (13 in Exhibit 6.1) and Bristol, Rhode Island, in America in 1689 (Laslett and Wall, 1972, Table 13) are known to reach 90%, but no region or microregion has figures of the same order.

Now to have nine-tenths of all households of nuclear form over an area about the size of an English county looks improbable. It is even less acceptable in the absence of households adapted to those who could not be accommodated in the simple family, the widowed, the unmarriable, and so on. It is noticeable that households of this kind are also conspicuously lacking in Berkner's figures from this area. There appear to be only about 4% SOLE and about 5% XLN and XLT as against 11–12% and 10.5–12.8% in England. If these proportions are based on a representative sample of households from his partible area, it would seem that there was simply nowhere to go for the rejects from the nuclear family living in these villages.[10] In spite of these obscurities there can be no doubt that if the comparative exercises were to be undertaken exclusively between German households under impartibility and English households, then the effect of impartibility in the stem-family direction would look weighty and conclusive. It would remain, of course, an entirely open question whether the absence of the stem family in these English settlements (not all of them rural, as will be remembered) was associated with widespread or universal partible custom. And in this situation, without other sets of figures to refer to and above all without the simulation outputs, we would be in no position to guess how strong was the stem-family tendency in the impartible areas, certainly not to recognize that it was relatively weak.

We can press this examination of the one well-documented example of the stem family in operation in historic Europe no further here. We shall not try to assess the force of its most persuasive and ingenious argument, from ages of household heads and their children to stages in a domestic cycle which can only have been of the stem-family type.[11] We must turn

---

[10] These are some of the considerations taken into account by the nuclear hardship model we hope to experiment with. Where simple family households are the general rule, those lacking spouses or parental homes (i.e., hardship) are likely to form their own households, live with others in nonnuclear arrangements or live as relatives in nuclear families thus forming nearly all of what complication is found. That this may fit the facts in England is clear from Exhibits 5.1 and 5.2, though it is not quite so clear at Lisswege (1) and at Lesnica (13 in Exhibit 6.1). The variance between individual places was high, however, and it can be seen from Exhibits 5.1 and 5.2 that some places could have no solitaries at all.

[11] See Berkner's Tables 4 and 5 and the discussion in his text. His position is weakened here also by his ignorance as to whether the persons whose ages are averaged actually coresided, and by his decision not to proceed nominally, which accounts for inability to

in conclusion to what this study has to teach us about the stem-family hypothesis itself, particularly in its relation to the customs of inheritance of land.

D. CONCLUSION

Adding an examination of the stem family as a real-world entity to the study of English households, and to our simulation exercises, is certainly revealing. It might be thought discouraging too, especially for the would-be believer in the stem-family household as an institution widespread amongst the European peasantry. The doubts which have arisen in the course of the analysis as to the status and nature of the stem-family pattern itself make the task of the familial historian even more demanding. If the structure of the household is not properly revelatory of the phenomenon we are trying to understand, not an adequate indicator, then we shall have to go further afield in order to reach a conclusion. A feature of the two German areas which a believer in the stability and continuity of peasant social structure may find somewhat surprising is the impermanence both of the form of the household and of inheritance practices. Berkner (1976, page 95) tells us that stem-family households showed a considerable increase in his impartible area within two or three generations. There was also a dramatic increase over the same span in complex family living in his partible area. Indeed, in Berkner's second essay (1977), he asserts that "a new kind of household developed between the 1690s and 1760s [page 64]." He even talks of a change to impartibility in his second area. It would seem, therefore, that all these features of peasant life could vary, presumably usually varying together, but no doubt also responding individually to economic and technical change, and even to demographic pressures.

For, we must not misconstrue what we have learned from our simulations about demographic change and household structure. Household structure may be surprisingly resistant to fluctuations in birth and death rates acting by themselves, but this does not mean that choices about coresidence could not be modified in accordance with demographic

---

follow their behavior over time.

His study is remarkably informative about tenurial arrangements and estate administration. He provides a lucid guide to the complexities of the stem-family issue and describes the data with care. The uncertainties about the criteria for selection of his sample which we have mentioned in the text are, however, serious. The numbers of households in his different tables add up to different totals in most cases, suggesting that different subsamples are being used to enforce different points. The seeker after the most exact possible comparisons is bound to find these problems discouraging.

exigencies, and so in turn alter the membership of households. We have shown that a rise in the age at marriage under all the stem-family patterns we have tested would be likely to lead to a fall in the proportion of stem-family households, and a rise in the age at marriage for women is a classic response to the threat of numbers. An alternative response might be to modify postmarital residency rules in the belief that keeping the children at home after marriage would ensure that they had few children of their own. This reaction has been suggested for Hungary in the 1700s and 1800s; it would have ensured that the household structure would change in relation to population change, and might do so dramatically.[12]

In his second study of 1977, Berkner shows how the population of both impartible and partible areas rose between 1689 and 1766. In the first area households became even more complex, but population expanded more slowly than in the second, his partible area. There as we have seen, complex households also became much more common, and there was apparently a change towards impartibility in inheritance custom. In both areas new household formation rather than growth in household size was the major form of expansion. In the German example, therefore, we find inheritance systems, population levels, forms of coresident group, and of course economic factors, especially techniques of production, all varying together. It is not yet clear how each influenced the others and whether one of them should be taken as antecedent and primary. It is certainly not true that everything flows from the inheritance custom, or that the form of the household is in constant relationship with such custom.

This being the case, it is not surprising that a particular pattern of

---

[12] See Andorka (1975) and further unpublished essays by him, including one presented at a conference in Budapest in September 1976. We are indebted to him for copies of these papers and for translating his 1975 article into English for us. His suggestion is that as land ran out in newly recovered Transdanubian Hungary in the late 1700s, rising population reduced household formation, but did not reduce the marriage rate: Children stayed at home after marrying. This led, under parental supervision, to what he calls the one-child family as a means of checking expansion, and may help to explain the very high level of household complexity in such places as Kölked in 1816. An increase in household complexity has been observed in Estonia between 1816 and 1834, when population was likewise rising (from 44% to 47% multiple in one place, from 9% to no less than 43% in another: work of J. Kahk and H. Uibu kindly communicated by H. Palli of Tallinn). Taken together with the German evidence, these facts suggest the possibility that where a tradition allowing household complexity existed, this variable may have been liable to change as demography changed, but that the process took place to a large extent through a change in postmarital residence choices. If this was the case, the notorious stability in English household size and structure over the whole period despite the population rise and all the economic changes of the 1700s and 1800s become easier to understand, considering that English households had apparently been simple in structure for a very long time. But, even in that country, as has been stated previously, there was some increase in the proportion of complex households during this period, although we could not allow it to have been significant until the middle of the 1800s.

household structure, the stem-family pattern, should appear to have the recessive character we have identified, and that its relationship with impartibility should prove to be rather weak and perhaps vacillating. In *Household and Family in Past Time* (Introduction, Section IV, "Family ideology and family experience") it was insisted that forms of the household were rarely values in the cultural areas there under study. The vocabulary for types of household was largely lacking and references to coresidence as a duty, indeed any reference at all, were difficult to find. In spite of the value traditionally attached to *das ganze Haus* in Germany, in spite of the intriguing cultural evidence about large family living from Austria (Berkner, 1972), this seems to be true of the German areas we have considered here.

We have noticed the indifference of those who drew up the German lists to the definition of the household. So little did the kin relations within the household which create its structure interest these taxation officials that they only occasionally mention whether the extra resident was a relative, or even whether he or she was the parent of the household head. These facts have to be inferred from name matching. The stem family is very unlikely to have been a behavioral norm in the impartible area. Norms about household structure do not seem to have had much substance anywhere, except perhaps where joint family traditions existed.

The stem family, therefore, can scarcely have been an institution of the German peasantry at the time in the areas under consideration. It was not widespread enough, even where impartible inheritance and economic influences generally were in its favor, nor did it have the required ideological and social structural status. How then can the stem family be defined?

We cannot make our way through all the reasons why peasants should adopt complex household living. Evidently such developments had numbers of predisposing circumstances, and each instance has to be understood in view of the whole social context. In this context inheritance customs, retirement customs, and economic circumstances, including the policy of landlords, estate stewards, and political officials, interplay with traditions of cooperation between siblings or more distant relatives, and with attitudes of affection and responsibility towards parents and ancestors, children and descendants. But if a behavioral trait had to be singled out as the final mover in the direction of the stem-family pattern, then it is identification with a descent line which we should select. By identification is meant not simply the sentiment which a landholding peasant family held for its ancestors and descendants, especially in the male line, but also the feeling for the family name, the family land, the family house, the family rights in the village community, the whole of the *Hof* in fact in the German context.

It was this sense of identification with the family possessions which itself made impartibility acceptable, or even required its existence. In order for the family *Hof* to continue, it had to be kept as a unity while father gave way to son and son to grandson, or when the patriline was broken and females or more distant heirs had to be brought in. This same sentiment presumably persuaded a possessor to retire, just as it persuaded the brothers and sisters of designated successors to be content with less as a portion than a piece of the family land. When the peasant landholders were serfs, of course, the serf owner had an interest in maintaining the integrity of the peasant plot. In the case of tenants, like the copyhold tenants for three lives in Southern England, the landlord would pursue the same policy.

But it must have been family feeling which ensured that a lineal heir should always if possible succeed. The sense of family was at play when an heir decided to live in his predecessor's house, not always that of his parents, after he had married, and when he felt obliged, or was in fact obliged by agreement, to keep his predecessors or predecessor in the household after succession had taken place. These things, of course, imply early marriage, and relatively early marriage, at least of heirs, must be regarded as an enabling condition for the stem family to exist, as well as perhaps a predisposing circumstance.[13]

In these ways, therefore, identification with the patriline was prior to the set of conditions, all the conditions, including impartibility, which gave rise to the stem-family pattern of coresidence. But in order to understand how the two, that is patriline identification and proportions of stem-family households, were related, it is essential to recognize three things.

First, that the degree of identification with a patriline was not a constant over the face of Europe. It varied, from place to place, and, presumably, from time to time as well. Second, that the extent to which this identification with the patriline was associated with a disposition on the part of possessors, successors, and predecessors to live together in the

---

[13] When there is disastrous mortality and the population is threatened unless all marriages take place at the earliest possible moment, then survival requires very immature marriage partners. Child bridegrooms and brides are obviously more likely than adult ones to live with parents after marriage, and in this way demography could be a final "cause" of complexity in households, but acting once more through the marriage age. It seems very unlikely that such conditions were approached in any of the regions and places discussed here, and the huge mortalities of early 1700s Iceland certainly did not have this effect. A requirement that all successors marry earlier than others would point to a marked stem-family tendency, as would an insistence on possessors retiring while still active. Early retirement may possibly have been characteristic of the 1700s Austrian example (Berkner, 1972), but we have seen no demonstration that heirs were anywhere generally younger at marriage than the rest, though this circumstance is often hinted at.

same household or houseful also varied, no doubt in time and place as well. Third, that identification with the patriline was not the only reason for coresidence, anywhere or at any time.

It follows that for stem-family household patterns to appear, for reasons of patriline identification, two conditions, not one, had to be simultaneously satisfied. The identification with the patriline had to exist, and presumably to be quite strong, and it had to be accompanied by the further disposition to coreside. If the first was a constant, and the second varied, then the recessive characteristics we have noticed would have been in evidence. It also follows that it is an error to presume that the presence of a relative within a domestic group which could conceivably be a result of patriline identification necessarily testifies that patriline identification was at issue. This presumption overlooks those motives for coresidence, such as welfare, duty, or affection which may have had little or nothing to do with patriline identification.

Furthermore, to make this assumption about resident relatives obscures the possibility that a tradition of a rather different kind, a joint family tradition, may have been at work when one or more married sons shared the household, before or after the death of the father.[14] All three of these reasons, and probably more, for living together must be taken into account if simulation can be extended so as to cover the structure of those European households in our Exhibit 6.1 which so much exceed in complexity those from German impartible areas. We have already had some experience with the much-discussed *Zadruga* of the Serbian peasantry, and the *Zadruga* was a joint family of the type often called *frerèche*. The joint family, as opposed to the stem family, might perhaps have a tendency to elevate the form of the household to the status of a desirable social norm. Nevertheless it is a notable fact that the attractive and influential word *Zadruga* was not used by the Southeast European peasantry. It has been given currency by subsequent scholars.

In attempting to describe how patriline identification is related to proportions of households of particular structure, we may even now have overlooked the possible complications. For economic and demographic processes, events and situations may themselves have intervened to weaken or to strengthen patriline identification or the disposition to express such identification by taking up coresidence. They may even have brought about coresidence when such identification was not particularly

---

[14] This tendency towards laterally disposed multiplicity is particularly evident in the Russian serf communities studied by Peter Czap, to which reference has already been made. In a further unpublished study, Berkner has himself analyzed coresidence of this kind in communities which preserved the much discussed tradition of *affrairement* in certain areas of South Central France (see Berkner, 1978).

strong, as has been hinted. We find ourselves caught in that intricate complex of causal connections and correlations which is so common in the analysis of social structure, even when, as in the present case, the attempt is to find a final point of reference.

We must not, therefore, lose sight of the one regularity of behavior which seems so far to have survived all the exceptions and the complications. In England patriline identification certainly existed during the period represented in Exhibits 5.1 and 5.2. We do not have to suppose that, as they contemplated the simple family households thronged with servants in which they lived, the substantial yeomanry of Stuart times, and the great reformist farmers of Hanoverian times, were without family pride and without the hope that their names and estates would be perpetuated into a distant future. Indeed, many of them have been perpetuated. There were certainly economic and political influences at work in England in these generations which might be thought to favor impartible inheritance as well.

England by the 1800s was a land where large, leasehold farms were very widespread. The great landowners of His Britannic Majesty, who was also the Elector of Hanover where both Berkner's impartible and partible areas lay, had powerful motives to keep their tenants farming in a big way. But in England as far as we know, patriline identification led to stem-family coresidence only very, very rarely. No other manifestation of complex household living is so far detectable in our country either, during the period and within the regions we have been able to examine.

The determined preserver of the stem-family hypothesis might be tempted to say of England since the later 1500s that the pattern existed, but was perpetually recessive. This is certainly permissible, given the terms of the argument we ourselves have pursued. We are back, however, in the position where this hypothesis has to be privileged at all costs in this country, even if no discernible portion of the actual familial experience of the entire population is known to have been affected by it. In our view it would be more profitable to wonder what it was in the structure of society which ensured that the forces which led to complex coresident groups elsewhere in the world should not do so in England. Perhaps after all there could be said to have been a normative regulation amongst English landholders which was obeyed with surprising regularity, and uniformly over the whole country—a negative sanction against living in domestic groups arranged in a multiple fashion, in the stem-family way or in any other.

England cannot have been the only European area where such a sanction limited residency choices, since there were so many places, localities, and regions where living in simple households was entirely predominant for such long periods of time. The mechanism which brought these things about demands investigation, as we have asserted when referring to what we have called the nuclear hardship model. It may seem a wearisome road we have had to trudge so as to reach such a destination, but one which could not have been avoided, given the elusive, even baffling character of the stem-family hypothesis itself, and given its purchase over the minds of scholars for almost a century.

We end with a final judgment on the stem-family hypothesis, as distinct from the stem family as the name for a particular family form. Interesting, useful and fascinating as the hypothesis undoubtedly is—for this is the way we have had to describe its attraction for students of the family group—it is not quite what it seems to be. For the stem-family tradition does not turn out to have constituted a desired, respected, even obligatory form of living together in households, widespread throughout the countries of Europe and with claims to having once been the universal rule. This tradition, in fact, cannot be shown ever to have been a general feature of the social structure of the European peasantry, and even where it existed, it was likely to have been in a weaker rather than a stronger version. Its claims to the status of an institution in the areas where it can be traced are equivocal, and this is not because demographic factors prevented its realization. Considerations of the family cycle do not go far towards persuading the insistent investigator that the stem family was in fact much commoner and more influential than it seems to be at first sight.

The further we probe the hypothesis the more equivocal it becomes; the less instructive, the less advantageous as a point of departure for investigating domestic groups and their structure, and the actual familial experience of earlier Europeans. Doubts arise as to whether the stem-family tradition is to be taken as a thing in itself, rather than as a loosely connected set of associated relationships, even as a coincidence of circumstances. If the present work should succeed in driving the stem family from the center of the stage, it will have been a bright beginning.

7

Measuring Patriline Extinction for Modeling Social Mobility in the Past

Our aim in this chapter is to exploit some readily accessible numbers which bear on the task of distinguishing exceptional from ordinary rates of social mobility in preindustrial England. These numbers only gain their relevance, necessarily, within the framework of certain models of the social system in this traditional society and of the demographic and social processes which generated the numbers, and so this chapter will be an excursion into modeling. More accurately, it will be a series of excursions into model building at different levels of generality and precision, some historical and some statistical.

We shall begin with a sketch of the elite in the society and the meaning of patriline extinction and patriline repair. We propose a framework within which patriline extinction has consequences for social mobility, and we then try to pin down one element of our picture by undertaking the estimation of a normal rate of patriline extinction, facing up to statistical issues raised by the data that we have. Drawing at this last stage on formal models from probability theory, we shall be illustrating a role for probabilistic models even where their traditional justification in terms of controlled experiments or statistical samples capable of replication become—because the context is historical—meaningless or far-fetched. We shall, in other words, be exploring ways in which the disciplines of history and statistics interlock, in the course of examining and emphasizing social continuities and intrinsic processes within one traditional society.

A. BACKGROUND TO THE QUESTIONS

England in the 1500s to the 1700s is our concern here, a society, like all European societies of that era, dominated by an elite. A particular sort of social mobility within such a social structure is what we shall try to define, to isolate and do our best to measure, what we shall call "replacement mobility." Though elite domination and replacement mobility are especially characteristic of such social structures, they do not seem to be entirely absent from others, even from the structure of the high industrial society established in England and elsewhere in our own day. Behind our more formal models, there is a conception of an elite which, when viewed over time, appears as a collection of patrilines occupying more or less fixed slots in the social structure.

We shall expand in due course on our use of the words "elite," "patriline," and "slot," and we shall have to admit that that framework has certain difficulties. But within it the idea of "replacement mobility" is an obvious one. When patrilines die out because of the failure of heirs, and when a slot in the elite persists in some sense beyond the disappearance of its occupants and requires filling if the elite is to keep its strength, then there will ordinarily be promotion into the elite to fill such a vacant position. Furthermore, the rate of such promotion will be partly demographically determined. Hence it will be possible to speak of an "intrinsic" rate of mobility, meaning by that a rate of patriline promotion for which the social system would have to provide in the long run to maintain itself in the face of the long-term effects of demography. Rates of promotion below or above such an intrinsic rate can be thought of as composed of two elements. One is the random fluctuation implicit in the demographic processes and in the response of the social system to them. The other is the effect of special historical processes, things that might ultimately be expected to strain the system, to have special historical consequences, and so to deserve special historical explanation. One example might be the "rise of the gentry," that so preoccupied historians of English society writing in the 1940s and the 1950s. Our exercise might help to decide whether the rise of the gentry was indeed a special historical process, or whether it was a part of this intrinsic rate of what might be called normal replacement mobility. The same decision might finally come to be made about a much wider and still fashionable expression, "the rise of the middle class."

The important feature of this schema, the feature that makes it worth entertaining, is that the "intrinsic" rate of replacement mobility which is postulated by it is a variable subject to quantitative measurement. There is evidence from which we can estimate how rapidly, on the whole, patrilines in the elite became extinct in England in the 1600s and 1700s. There is also sufficient mathematical understanding of the extinction process to predict, at least approximately, the size of random fluctuations due to demography for which one should allow.

It may perhaps be asked, what is gained from a situation like this one in which one of the components can be tied down and assigned numerical value? We gain a standard against which to calibrate all other related effects and so can begin to be able to answer questions of the following kind: How much promotion or how little promotion must a historian observe before he should express surprise? How much of the anecdotal evidence for upward social mobility is it fair to ascribe to the ordinary functioning of the social system and how much to exceptional and special developments and to the epidemiology of revolution and transition? How large must historical changes turn out to be in order to rank above the random ups and downs inherent in the fabric of society in the mobility of patrilines? How grossly wrong must the assumptions of our picture be to invalidate the distinctions it suggests between the exception and the rule? One set of answers to these questions, a first set of answers at least, emerges from building a model in which we can define our intrinsic promotion rate and use available data to estimate it.

We shall now sketch briefly what we use the words "elite," "patriline," and "slot" to mean, and dwell a little on "mobility," if only because it draws attention to features of the architecture of the elite in traditional society, perhaps indeed to some extent in all societies, which do not seem to have been much noticed by historians or social scientists. As far as "elite" is concerned, we are thinking in the first instance of an elite defined by status. In England, males belonging to it can be identified in documents by designations accompanying their names, which range from "Mister" (Mr.) and "Esquire" (Esq.) at the lower boundary of the elite up to "Sir" and "Lord" at its top. The womenfolk were called "Lady" among the elite, at least above the level of baronet. At that level they were properly called Dame rather than Lady; so also was the wife of a Knight, an Esquire, or a plain gentleman. These titles and descriptions and the social functions of their holders are discussed, among other sources, in Chapter 2 of Laslett (1971). The issues we explore in this chapter are raised there briefly on page 201 and footnote 189 on page 308. The explicit marking of status in this society is of great convenience to us, because it enables us to obtain a well-defined, although entirely nonrandom, sample of the elite by picking out the holders of a given high-status designation granted by the king. Our particular sample consists of the baronets in lines elevated by King James I. The sample group is small, but it is far from minute in comparison to the elite as a whole. According to figures of the contemporary herald Gregory King for 1688, which may serve as a rough guide, the families of all baronets accounted for 5% of the some 16,000 families which in his estimate composed the English elite as a whole, that is, whose heads styled themselves Gent., Mr., Esq., or held more distinguished titles. One-quarter of all the baronetcies extant in 1688 are lines in our sample group, lines originally promoted by James I. Thus we are including in our sample about 1 out of every 100 elite families defined in this way. This elite as a whole represented just over 1% of the 1,300,000 or so families which King estimated to have been present in England at that time.

We must hasten to say, however, that family, as in Gregory King's usage, is not the right word for the social unit that interests us, though if it were expanded into family over time, or family over generations, it might suit better. It is appropriate for some purposes to treat the elite at any one moment as a collection of individuals for the most part living together as families. Yet it is more appropriate, when observing it over time, to regard it as an association of patrilines. This is not the place to expound the notion of patriline at length, as has been done, for instance, in the introduction to Laslett and Wall (1972) page 19ff. Even those unfamiliar with such discussions will have in their minds a stereotyped picture of an English gentleman seated in his manor house. He and his children are within the patriline, as was his father, as will be the succeeding family of his eldest son or of the son who turns out to succeed him. The wives of successive "representatives of the line" can be regarded as belonging to the patriline though not born into it. The brothers and sisters of the gentleman himself though not actually living with him are within it for some purposes, like matters of succession or what we shall call "patriline repair," and are outside the patriline for other purposes. The same will be true of the brothers and sisters of the heir who succeeds.

It could happen, of course, that the gentleman in a manor house recognized as "head of the family" was not himself born within the patriline, although his wife was. This would be the case where "patriline repair" had been effected by the son of another family, preferably a family of kin, marrying in. If neither the husband nor the wife were direct descendants of the last person to preside in the manor house, then there had been patriline replacement, rather than repair. But in either case there had been mobility, and it is to mobility that we now turn. It may help to clarify the issues and also to give them substance if we take an example of mobility of this kind which effected repair in a patriline which has since become world-famous in its way.

The family of Knight in the late 1700s had, like many English landed families, two seats, one in Kent, the grand one, and one in Hampshire, a lesser one. In our terminology, one slot in the elite had fallen vacant but had not been filled up. Rather it had been taken over by a patriline which already filled another slot. But in the 1780s the patriline of Knight found itself heirless, and for the second time in its known history it showed clear signs of dying out. Hence some complex genealogical maneuvers which we shall try to describe because they illuminate the process we are interested in.

The head of the house of Knight in the 1780s was Thomas Knight, Esquire, whom we shall call Thomas Knight II. His father, Thomas Knight I, had married into the Knight family, as husband of one of the two daughters and coheirs of the last of the Knights. Thomas Knight I had in fact changed his name twice for purposes of patriline repair, for he had been born Thomas Brodnax, a genteel Kentish name, became May, and on his taking over the Knight patriline became Knight. He died in 1781. His son, Thomas Knight II, held the two seats of Godmersham Park in Kent and Chawton House in Hampshire for only a dozen years or so, but all his children—four sons and five daughters—seem to have died well before he did. In order to ensure that the line should continue in some way or other he adopted his paternal grandmother's brother's great grandson Edward Austen (Berry, 1833, pages 46–48). Edward was the son of George Austen, who held one of the Knight family livings and was well connected but without an estate of his own. Edward, an attractive child and then a well-mannered young man, was in the position most likely to threaten demotion, and to be adopted by his rich relatives in this way was a stroke of good fortune indeed. After the transmogrification he married a baronet's daughter.

There were other brothers and two sisters: Two of the brothers found themselves having to seek their fortunes in the Navy, a familiar expedient at that time for those on the way down, but one which turned out well since both of them became admirals. Eighteen years after he took over the Knight estates and houses in 1794, the lucky Edward changed his name to Knight, and in the 1970s his direct descendents still live at the Knight family seat at Chawton in Hampshire. But this is not the reason why the village is much-visited, and the house in the park is not the one which people go to see.

In 1809 Edward Austen (Knight) was able to offer his widowed mother and his sisters Cassandra and Jane a cottage at Chawton to live in. This is why so many people find themselves looking at Chawton cottage, and staring at the Knight memorials in Chawton church where mother and daughters went every Sunday. For, the younger sister was Jane Austen the novelist who created for that surname a reputation which will never attach to the surname of Knight. During much of the 1800s, however, the Knights were much grander than the Austens, and some of them seem to have thought Jane Austen not quite well enough bred for polite company. In the county pedigree book Jane's entry under the Austen family simply reads "Jane, born 1775 at Steventon, died ummarried."

We classify here the action of Edward Austen (later Knight) as upward mobility. We do so because he might otherwise have been demoted from the elite, demoted as a single individual perhaps, because he might under those circumstances never have married. We also classify the line which descended from him as a new patriline, and regard the change of name as a device. From our point of view the original Knight patriline died out when Thomas May took it over, name and all, and the second "Knight" patriline similarly disappeared when Edward Austen succeeded. It seems likely, although we do not yet have the evidence to decide, that most patriline replacement went on like this, by what might be called sideways movement rather than by the promotion of a patriline from below the elite, that is, from the society at large. Once this is recognized it will be obvious that the stereotype of patriline promotion, where a man who made money and acquired power was born beneath the elite, but went up wife, children and all to found a replacement patriline in a vacant slot, was probably not the normal case. Such pure upward mobility would presumably only occur when sideways movement of the Austen kind could not be effected, and take place more often when the number of slots was expanding, either because of a general growth of the size of the society, or because of a process which made more resources available to the elite so that it could become bigger as a proportion of the population. In the late eighteenth century both English population and English resources were in fact growing very rapidly. Edward's admiral brothers may not have filled vacant slots at all, but have brought new patrilines into being, which added to the number of slots available.

This is only a beginning of a description of the mechanisms of elite maintenance in a traditional society and we have only space here to point out two of its important features. First, any differential between the demography of the elite and the demography of society at large is crucial. If the elite expanded faster than society, then demotion would be inevitable in the long run, demotion primarily of individuals in the way already described. If the growth rate of the elite resulting from its fertility, mortality, and so on was less than that of society as a whole, then it would tend to shrink over time, more slots would fall vacant, and if its relationship with the total population was to be maintained, more upward promotion would take place.

The second feature of this complex but interesting process which we should like to stress is the importance of the market. If Mr. Knight had not been acquainted with his "cousin" he would not have been able to appreciate Edward Austen's qualities as a potential successor. Edward Austen did not happen to marry into the family of Knight as Thomas May, born Brodnax, had done. But marriage was a much more frequent case of patriline repair, and it must be obvious how anxious he, his father, and the whole Austen family would have been to locate an heiress he could marry and so save himself from social demotion. When these facts are recognized the operations of the London season, the balls and Bath Assemblies, the social gossip in the newspapers, the endless discussion in the correspondence of who had married whom, who was widowed, how many sons and daughters any particular couple had had, all became more understandable. They functioned as parts of the mechanism of maintaining the social supremacy of the network of elite patrilines. We have emphasized the role of the males in this machinery because they are less often discussed. Everyone knows what went on among the English elite of that age in respect of the marriage of daughters. It is the chief theme of the imaginative and epistolary literature of traditional society.

Our interest here fixes on continuity and turnover in the group of elite patrilines over time, on succession, promotion, demotion, and extinction of the kind that are involved in the history of the Knights and Austens. It fixes on patrilines rather than individuals. For, it is much harder to isolate long-term, stable factors which might be subject to measurement and which would govern levels of individual mobility. For patrilines, the connotations of promotion and demotion of course varied according to the rank of the patrilines concerned. At the lower boundary of gentility, promotion from below (as distinct from sideways movement effecting patriline repair) meant the acquisition of land, a manor or manors, application for the grant of a coat of arms from the College of Heralds; a member of the family would rise enough in the eyes of the world to write the letters "Esq." after his name. Higher up the elite, promotion meant the achievement of a formal hereditary honorific status from the king, of which after 1611 a baronetcy was the lowest order. Above baronets came the titled nobility, barons, viscounts, earls, marquesses, and dukes. In the opposite direction, primarily at the lower boundary of the elite, demotion of patrilines also certainly occurred although demotion of individuals was no doubt more common.

The land and property held by a patriline could become insufficient for economic reasons to maintain a gentleman. He or his son might have to drop the appellation esquire or mister and adapt themselves to yeoman status. For patrilines with baronetcies or noble titles, however, the threat of demotion must surely have been eclipsed by the threat of extinction. In the 1600s titles did not commonly disappear because families ran out of money. Their inherited status itself was generally sufficient to attract the means to continue the house, if only the patriline could be kept in being by the uninterrupted succession of heirs. But if a gentleman's eldest son failed to marry or to father children, and his other sons died, for instance, in the wars or at sea, and no cousin put in an appearance with a rightful claim to succeed, even if what we have called patriline repair was effected, then the patriline would die out. The lands and manors would pass into hands other than those of the patriline heir, and the social responsibilities associated with the gentleman's position in the community would devolve upon another patriline.

This brings us to the most fragile concept in our general picture of replacement mobility, the idea of a "slot" which would persist and require filling after the extinction of a patriline. The concept of a slot is most satisfactory when it can be equated with an estate and its appurtenances, such, for instance, as the single manor house in a rural village whose owner from time immemorial had held the office of Justice of the Peace. Many cases fit such a description, but in many others the social role of the local gentleman was more nebulously defined. What we wish to call slots could be elastic, and might sometimes be split among several patrilines and sometimes consolidated under one powerful house. Within bounds, however, this elasticity need not negate the assertion of an intrinsic rate of replacement mobility. A measurement of extinction rates still indicates the frequency of a kind of natural dislocation for which the social structure had to compensate either by mechanisms of role expansion or by promotion. Thus such a measurement still provides calibration for the level of continuity within the elite of the 1600s and 1700s.

An extinction rate clearly depends upon demographic parameters which affect the chances of a gentleman dying without heirs. It also depends on economics and politics, to the extent that they affect mortality and birth and family-planning strategies. Furthermore, it is a function of conventions as to who shall count as heirs, and thus on the pool of people eligible to inherit by law, by custom, and in practice. This brings us to an intricate question, for we are proposing to use data on extinctions of baronetcies to anticipate levels of ordinary replacement mobility more generally throughout the elite. But extinction of a baronetcy is subject to sharper legal specification than extinction of a mere gentleman's patriline. For this reason study of baronetcies threatens to give a distorted picture of extinction rates in other sectors of the elite.

Three aspects of the differences between baronets and other gentlemen are worth noting in this connection. First, baronetcies could descend only through male lines, while for gentry without male heirs, as we have seen, it was not unusual for an heiress to marry a man in a position to take over the estates and family standing, and so "repair" the patriline. The husband in such a match might or might not assume the wife's name as Thomas May, originally Brodnax, had assumed the name of Knight. The social readjustments occasioned by such a transfer of status between patrilines might be minimal. On the other hand, such patriline repair functioned as one of the classic avenues by which men of lower status rose through the elite in traditional society or by which younger sons of gentlemen, otherwise destined to fall in status, were able to found their own new patrilines within the elite. Thus it is still desirable to count the failure of male heirs as extinction, for gentlemen as much as for baronets, when we are concerned with levels of upward replacement mobility. Second, the demographic experience of baronets may have differed from the demographic experience of lower-status gentlemen, just as we believe, on the basis of Hollingsworth (1964), that the demography of the peerage and their families may have differed to some extent from that of England as a whole. But the elite was small and homogeneous compared to the country; there is no reason to suspect demographic differences within the elite so great as to affect our conclusions at all seriously. Third, there are special legal provisions which governed the inheritance of baronetcies, but not the inheritance of gentlemen's estates. But differences resulting from these concrete considerations are differences which we can model and examine on the basis of our data. Indeed, they are typical of the issues to which our modeling will be addressed.

B. THE DEFINITION OF EXTINCTION RATE

The question that we want to answer is brief but elusive: What proportion of the patrilines in the elite would ordinarily become extinct in a decade or a century? There are many ways in which this question can fail to have a meaningful answer. For instance, the pattern of extinctions may easily be irregular, responsive to historical events, leaping up and down according to special circumstances. Or, the relationship between numbers of extinctions and numbers of extant patrilines may not be expressible as a simple proportion, much less as the same simple proportion at different times. At the outset such troubles may appear more than likely, but that is no reason to abandon our analysis before at least examining the data that we have.

Our strategy is to generalize from the experience of one particular segment of the elite for which extinction dates can be obtained easily from published sources. In the next section we shall review this evidence, which has the great advantage over most historical data on social structure of being reasonably clean, as far as it goes. As we shall see, our sources appear to yield a quite complete and accurate set of numbers. But numbers are not measurements. In order to interpret our extinction data as measurements, we must tackle a whole sequence of questions, which amounts to choosing a model or models within the context of which our variables are well-defined. These questions are

1. Are the data sufficiently regular to uphold the claim that a few underlying factors are producing the same patterns over long stretches of time?
2. Are there signs of the intervention of political events, or other sudden effects, which would apply uniquely to the group of baronets rather than generally to the elite? Is it plausible to ascribe the main features of the pattern of baronetcy extinctions to ordinary rather than exceptional influences?
3. What adjustments are required if we want to generalize from the baronets to wider segments of the elite?
4. Can we suppose our process to produce extinctions on the average in some fixed ratio to a number of patrilines at risk? Or is the risk irrelevant to the number of extinctions, or related to it in some more complicated way? Is the relation sharp or vague? Is it fixed or changing over time?
5. Assuming some average relationship between extinctions and numbers at risk can be defined, how great a variance around such an average is it appropriate to expect?

C. CHARACTERIZING THE EVIDENCE

The evidence pertaining to patriline extinction which we shall analyze consists of information about dates of creation and extinction and numbers of successive holders of titles of baronet conferred by King James I. King James established the honor in 1611 and conferred it 204 times before his death in 1625. His successors continued to confer the title, and all such creations up to 1769 were listed and numbered by date by two authors named Kimber and Johnson in a work published in 1771. We shall confine ourselves to King James' creations, which are the ones at risk of extinction for the longest period and therefore the most informative to analyze. Kimber and Johnson mark 116 of these 204 baronetcies extinct by 1769. All but one of these 116 also appears in Burke's *Extinct and Dormant Baronetage* of 1838 with a list of the titleholders in each line. We shall ignore the one missing baronetcy, leaving a sample of 203 baronetcies of which 115 became extinct during our period of observation.

One baronetcy of the 115 which appears in Burke is registered as dormant, that is, unclaimed, as from the year 1675. We shall treat it as if extinct. Burke gives actual dates of extinction for 110 baronetcies. Nine of these dates are labeled as approximate, but they seem to derive from phrases like "shortly after the battle of Edghill" and to be reasonably reliable. We shall pool them with the 110 precise dates which Burke gives. Of the 5 baronetcies of James I which became extinct before 1769 and which Burke lists without dates, 4 are described as expiring with the death of the first holder and 1 at the death of the eighth holder, "much after 1702." We shall artificially assign these 5 baronetcies intervals between creation and extinction of 1, 14, 21, 30, and 148 years, based on the distribution of such intervals whose lengths are known, so as to avoid the small bias against early dates which would occur if we excluded the 5.

It seems fair to claim that Burke, in conjunction with Kimber and Johnson, furnishes us with a complete record of extinctions accurate to within a couple of baronetcies up to 1769. Later extinctions appear in Burke's volume, but a collection of extinctions from between 1769 and 1838 could not claim completeness without some source to make up for Kimber and Johnson's list of dates of creation. Of course with substantial effort further information could be recovered about many of the baronetcies mentioned by Burke, but our aim is not to carry out an exhaustive study of baronetcies. It is rather to exploit some readily accessible and relatively clean data for the sake of pinning down a single rate.

We are in the enviable position, rare in historical studies, of being able to discount one source of random variation, namely measurement error. But this situation will only serve to highlight the other sources of random variation with which we must cope in the modeling process itself.

D. ANALYSIS OF THE DATA

The questions that come first to the fore in our analysis are questions of the presence or absence of broad regularities in the data. It is thus sensible to begin by displaying the data in several forms to diagnose its general features.

Exhibit 7.1 shows the cumulative number of baronetcies in our sample created before each given number of years and extinguished before each

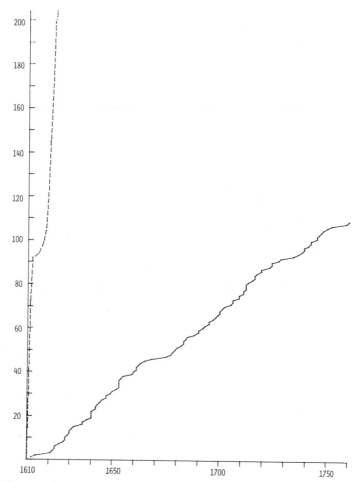

EXHIBIT 7.1. Baronetcies created by King James I. Dashed line indicates cumulative creations and solid line indicates extinctions by historical year.

given number of years from 1611 to 1769. The creations break into two bunches, one early and one late in King James' reign. The extinctions follow a remarkably regular pattern, rising along a nearly straight line whose slope is close to the net total of extinctions per year, 115/158. There are no obvious waves of extinctions during the Civil War or at other times and only one slight lull, which spans the later years of King Charles II's reign. The process of extinctions appears from this graph to be fairly immune to impact from historical events, so that we are encouraged to regard it as depending primarily on long-term social and demographic factors.

We may shift perspective slightly and count the number of baronetcies extinguished or surviving so and so many years after their creation. The numbers surviving invite comparison with the survivors columns of life tables, where the years of "lifetime" of baronetcies correspond to different historical years for the various cohorts of patrilines whose elevation occurred in different years. Graphs of extinctions or survivors resemble Exhibit 7.1 so closely that we omit them here. We include a graph of the logarithms of the numbers of survivors later in Exhibit 7.4. The following numbers of baronetcies are still surviving after each stretch of time: 187 after 20 years, 166 after 40, 154 after 60, 139 after 80, 120 after 100, 108 after 120, and 97 after 140 years. Extinctions are obviously heavy. They deplete the original pool of 203 baronetcies by nearly 60% in 150 years. We shall conclude, let it be said here, that such extinction represents intrinsic, normal processes and that the replacement mobility that it called forth represents intrinsic, normal replacement mobility.

Taking a third point of view, we display the numbers of baronetcies dying out after the death of the first holder, the second holder, and on up to the sixth holder. Each letter B stands for one baronetcy:

```
1: BBBBBBBBBBBBBBBBBBBBBBBBBBBBBBBBB
2: BBBBBBBBBBBBBBBB
3: BBBBBBBBBBBBBBBBBBB
4: BBBBBBBBBBBBBBBBBBBBB
5: BBBBBBBBBBB
6: BBBBBBBBBBBBB
```

Five of our 115 extinct baronetcies are not found here because they die out after the seventh, eighth, or ninth holder's death. The lengths of the bars are approximately numbers of extinctions per generation, although the title of baronet could pass from one holder without sons to a cousin in the same genealogical generation instead of a later generation. In this graph the wave of extinctions on the death of the first holder is unmistakeably large. But it is hard to say how to read the pattern of the later bars. Is there a systematic tapering of extinctions, modified by random surges here and there? Or do the numbers of extinctions remain relatively constant, up to randomness? To make choices about what to regard as systematic and what random, choices specific enough so that we can confront them cogently with the data, we turn to probability theory for help.

Our first impulse is to search for a probability model which incorporates as much as we can find out about the circumstances which were supposed to lead to the extinction of a patriline. The laws governing the extinction of baronetcies are very clear. A baronetcy would descend to any "heir male of the body" of the original holder, "haeridibus masculinis de corpore suo" to quote the authoritative Latin in Selden (1672) *Titles of Honor*, page 681. It would become extinct upon the death of the last male who could trace descent through an exclusively male line to the first holder. Brothers of the first holder could not succeed, but brothers of the second holder could. From our point of view, this rule introduces an undesirable complication. As generations passed from the conferment of the baronetcy, the pool of potential kin positions eligible to inherit the honor would increase. Thus we must foresee that the pattern of extinctions of baronetcies ought to change over time, due to the expanding pool of heirs.

In this respect, the sample of baronets will differ, or may differ, from the broader elite. The inheritance of a gentleman's manors and status was not governed by such strict rules. For the broader elite, the pool of inheritors embraced a circle of male kin still in touch with the patriline in the way that the Rev. George Austen was in touch with Thomas Knight II. The size of this pool must vary in a highly random manner but there is no reason to expect systematic change in it over time. Insofar as the inheritance of baronetcies in practice accorded with the laws of inheritance, we shall have to transform our extinction data in order to obtain extinction rates undistorted by the effect of the increasing cousin pool.

In theory we can trace out all possible trees of male descent from a single progenitor. Given assumptions about the probability of each male fathering various numbers of surviving male children, probabilities which depend on the demographic rates over the time concerned, we can also in theory go on to calculate the probabilities of finding various numbers of eligible heirs in each kin position at any point in time. The probability of extinction is the probability that all lines of descent will come to an end.

Discovering methods to carry through calculations like these efficiently is virtually the oldest subject of stochastic population theory. Francis Galton and H. W. Watson tackled the question out of interest in surname extinction in 1873. Their solutions were in error, but research by Heyde and Seneta (1975) has demonstrated that a correct solution had already been derived by I.-J. Bienaymé in 1845. The history of the theory makes diverting reading in D. G. Kendall's "Centenary Address to the London Mathematical Society" (1966) and "The Genealogy of Genealogy" (1975). The mathematical details are summarized in Harris (1963) and in Chapter 18 of Keyfitz (1968). Our interest in this theory is to have a set of predictions of extinction numbers that take detailed account of the increasing heir pool and thus give formal expression to our expectation that more baronets will have patrilines which die out early, before the pool of heirs increases, rather than late, after many potential cousin inheritors can have been born.

The theory of tracing lines of descent and calculating probabilities of extinction for them, branching theory, takes account of all the branches in the descent lines in a hypothetical genealogical tree. But in its most usuable form it pays for exactness in this respect by taking a stylized view of demographic variability. First of all, it reckons time in generations, so that the predictions are comparable not to data like that graphed in Exhibit 7.1, but solely to data like the bar graph shown previously. Second, the theory assumes statistical independence between the numbers of sons different fathers sire, whether or not these fathers are related to each other. Third, on a technical point, the distribution of numbers of surviving sons is customarily taken from the reduced geometric family of distributions. This family is a versatile one, but there is no direct evidence from our sample for or against its appropriateness here. Because our knowledge of family sizes in the segment of the elite with which we are concerned is inexact, we cannot narrow our choice down to a single set of predictions from branching theory. The predictions depend on our choice from the reduced geometric family of a set of probabilities of a father having various numbers of surviving sons. But the question of interest to us is a question of patterns. Even with several competing sets of predictions, we can ask, are there patterns in the predictions, not depending too severely on the exact choice of prediction, similar to empirical patterns in our baronetcies data?

To assess the agreement between predictions and data we resort to a logarithmic transformation. We predict numbers of patrilines surviving to each generation to compare against numbers of baronetcies surviving, and we then calculate the logarithms of these survivorship statistics. Logarithms constitute a natural transformation for at least two reasons. First, we are ultimately concerned with proportions, and logarithms convert expressions of interest to us, ratios, into simple expressions, namely arithmetic differences. Second, there is an asymptotic limit theorem (cf. Harris, 1963, page 16) making predictions from branching theory after logarithmic transformation for sufficiently late generations approach straight lines. Though this theorem tells us nothing about the first few generations, which are what we are observing, it endorses logarithmic scales in general for displaying branching processes.

The crosses in Exhibits 7.2 and 7.3 are the logarithms of the proportion of baronetcies surviving until after the death of each successive holder. The lines in Exhibit 7.2 pass through four sets of branching theory predictions. The predictions are representative of a dozen cases selected to span a range of generational replacement rates estimated to apply at various times during our era of interest to the children of British peers by Hollingsworth (1964) in his Table 23. (We specify each line by the mean

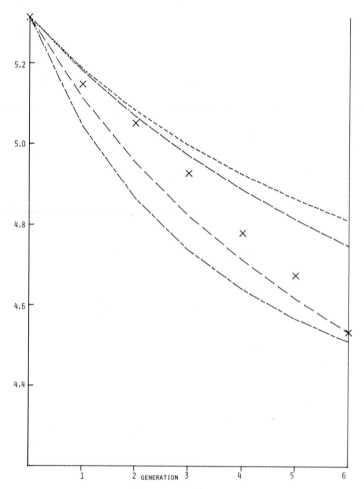

EXHIBIT 7.2. Logarithms of numbers surviving. Branching Theory predictions (dashed lines) and baronetcies data (crosses).

generational replacement rate and the proportion of fathers without surviving sons; from top to bottom these pairs of numbers are 1.10 and .120, 1.05 and .123, 1.05 and .182, 1.20 and .236.) This figure exposes a systematic difference between the predictions and the empirical data. The crosses for the baronetcies, strikingly enough, lie very close to a straight line all the way from generation one to generation six. The predictions, by contrast, all curve down and to the right. The data appear to have a simple kind of regularity, adherence to a straight line, which the predictions lack.

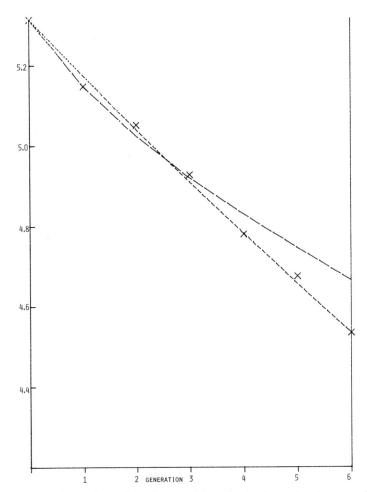

EXHIBIT 7.3. Logarithms of numbers surviving. Special branching theory predictions (dashed lines) and baronetcies data (crosses).

The sense of mismatch between data and predictions is partially, but only partially, relieved by Exhibit 7.3. These show two predictions from branching theory that fit the data much more closely. The line of long dashes is derived from a case of branching theory where the demographic rates change from generation to generation, unlike those behind Exhibit 7.2 which remain constant throughout the six generations. For this solid graph in Exhibit 7.3, the mean generational replacement rate drops (as do Hollingsworth's estimates) from around 1.15 for the first generation to stationary levels for later generations. Proportions of fathers without surviving sons rise from .081 to .150. We might obtain an even more closely fitting curve if we complicated our predictions further by allowing for a dip in replacement rates around the fifth generation, as Hollingsworth's estimates suggest. However, each change of rates commits us to a largely arbitrary choice of other parameters for the distribution of surviving sons. With as many parameters as we have at our disposal, it would be remarkable if we failed to fit a mere six points on a graph. Furthermore, our line of long dashes does not actually fit the data as well as the line of short dashes on Exhibit 7.3. That line corresponds to a branching process with rates unchanging over time, like those in Exhibit 7.2, with a mean generational replacement rate of .90 and 13.0% of fathers without surviving sons. In this process only 3% of all fathers have more than one surviving son, 84% having exactly one surviving son. Such demographic rates are highly implausible in our context, but they do achieve a notable fit to the data.

The process which generates the line of short dashes in Exhibit 7.3 is really a degenerate case of a branching process, for the only alternatives to which it assigns any sizable probability each generation are extinction or a single surviving son. A patriline either dies out or continues with a single representative, without any expanding pool of potential cousin heirs. Since we resorted to branching processes in the first place in order to model the effects of an expanding pool of inheritors, this outcome reads like a clue that our efforts were misdirected. The data seem to rebel against our attempts to take this possible effect into account.

Our exploration of the data so far casts doubt on the idea that the pool of potential inheritors of baronetcies did grow systematically as time passed. It may be that in practice families kept track only of close cousins, so that more distant relatives, even if they existed, were not members of the effective inheritance pool. Perhaps families like the Knights, even if they had baronetcies, did not usually know about cousins as distant as the Austens, let alone those further removed. That would mean that baronets kept only limited account of their eligible heirs and it would imply restrictions on what we have called the market. Social practice would be interfering with the more purely demographic factors we have been incorporating in our model.

It is still possible, of course, to take the opposite stance and assert the importance of the expanding heir pool in the light of the line of long dashes in Exhibit 7.3. We cannot deny that the data are compatible with a branching process with rates changing over time to a considerable degree. On the other hand, whatever the data, we could assuredly find a complicated branching model to fit them, since our inexact knowledge of the demographic circumstances within the elite leaves us so much free choice in specifying models with changing rates. A model of this kind would be explaining a very simple pattern—a straight line through the logarithms of the survival data—by an intricate succession of compensating changes. Is it better to trust our original expectations about the succession to baronet-cies and to adopt a complicated model of a simple pattern or is it better to demand that a simple pattern have a simple model, if we can find one? We are in a piquant inferential position. Our conclusions turn upon our attitude toward the time-honored principle called Occam's razor.

In our own discussion we shall pursue the search for simpler models, leaving behind us the complicated branching model with changing rates. We shall, in other words, wield Occam's razor. If this choice of ours is sound, then the baronets form a better sample for illuminating extinction rates among the whole elite than we might have feared. Any expanding pool of inheritors, which would have differentiated the baronets from mere gentlemen, fades from view in the rest of our analysis. Put other-wise, the simple straight line pattern in the data encourages us to forego special adjustments for differences in succession law and custom when we try to carry over conclusions about extinction rates from baronets to the elite as a whole.

Fortunately, it is easy to find a model from probability theory which incorporates the feature we have uncovered in Exhibit 7.2, the straight-ness of the log transform of survivors. The model we propose is a so-called pure death model with exponential lifetime, a special case of a birth-and-death process (cf. Keyfitz, 1968, Chapter 16) in which there are no random births. This model posits that out of all baronetcies which have survived until a given year or generation from their creation, the propor-tion which go on to survive until the following year or generation will be a fixed fraction on average, a fraction unchanging over time. We view the extinction of a given baronetcy as a wholly accidental occurrence, inde-pendent both of the time since its creation and of the fate of other baronetcies. We draw an analogy, that is to say, between the extinction of baronetcies and the burning out of lightbulbs or the mutating of genes by cosmic rays. This model is virtually the simplest model we could propose. It interprets the forces governing extinctions as very simple, stable, and straightforward and implies that no special influences have noticeable effects on the dying out of baronetcies. Demographically speaking it would be a reasonable model if, as we have just suggested, families only kept track of some more or less constant number of close heirs. We are emboldened to try out such a simple-minded scheme by the disappointing performance of the branching models which have incorporated more structure into them.

We are free to reckon time either in years or in generations in our pure death model. We choose to work with years, since the data on extinctions by years of patriline lifetime are more finely quantized data and since our conclusions about replacement mobility rates are better couched in years than in the looser scale of generations. For us, a pure death model is a highly desirable one. It relates the numbers of extinctions systematically only to the numbers at risk of extinction, so that it allows us to talk of a well-defined "extinction rate," and use a statistical estimator to estimate it from the data.

Exhibit 7.4 graphs the logarithmic transform of the number of baronet-

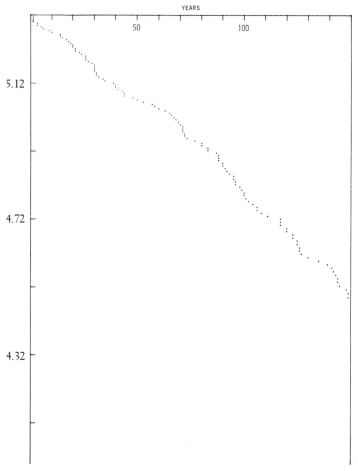

EXHIBIT 7.4. Logarithms of numbers of baronetcies surviving at least x years from their creation.

cies out of the original 203 which survive x years or more from their creation. Under a pure death model, the expected values of these logarithms would lie on a straight line. The locus of data points is relatively straight, but we are brought up against the question, How straight is straight? How do we evaluate the goodness-of-fit between model and data? We are in a position to make a formal statistical attack on this question with a classical hypothesis test. For our purposes, what we want to do is to see how great is the discrepancy between data and expectations based on our model, compared with the discrepancies that would be generated by chance alone through the random processes which the model takes into account.

The details of this program are very much complicated by the fact that our baronetcies remain in observation only up to 1769, so that our data is censored. Later extinctions are concealed from us. What is worse, because baronetcies were created at different moments, different subsets of the data are censored at different points. Furthermore, we are trying to test the empirical survival curves against a curve, the average predicted survival curve, which is characterized by an extinction rate that must first be estimated from our data. It is an amusing statistical exercise, whose details we here omit, to cope with all these complications and program a computer to find the conditions under which to reject the model, for an appropriate statistical test. We concoct a test based on the Kolmogorov–Smirnov statistic, the largest absolute difference between our observed curve of survivors and the predicted curve of survivors, calculating significance levels conditional on the value of the estimated extinction rate. It turns out that we should fail to reject our model even at significance levels as lax as 65%, much less at the customary 10% or 5% levels. In other words, the difference between predictions and extinctions measured by the statistic we have chosen is smaller than the differences we should expect from purely chance effects as often as 65% of the time. Thus we are doing no violence to the data if we do speak about an extinction rate and think of a constant proportion of patrilines dying out each decade in the normal course of events, more or less regardless of the other more complicated influences that might impinge.

Under our model our guess for the rate of patriline extinction per decade, the maximum likelihood estimator of that rate, is 5.2%. The proportion of patrilines dying out over any other time period t years in length may be predicted from the formula $1.0 - \exp(-.00532t)$ where "exp" stands for the exponential function. A 95% confidence interval for the decadal rate stretches from 4.2% to 6.1% and for rates over a time period t from around $1.0 - \exp(-.0043t)$ to $1.0 - \exp(-.0063t)$. Thus our calculations give us not merely a handle on the rate of extinction but tell us how big an allowance to make for random variability. The confidence intervals turn out to be easy to remember if we figure on a 65-year period. Over a lifespan of 65 years, between a quarter and a third of all patrilines should be expected to die away.

We should mention that had we calculated our extinction rate based only on the 72 baronetcies elevated by James I in the first year of the establishment of the honor, our answer would have been lower, in fact 3.5% per decade. Although the statistical reliability would have been less and the difference between 3.5% and 5.2% is not great, it is statistically significant. The pure death model with this lower rate still shows an excellent fit to the subset of data for the first cohort of baronetcies. It is odd that cohorts elevated in different years should have different extinction rates persisting over a century and a half and fitting all the while such a simple model as the pure death model. One might argue that the first wave of creations elevated patrilines of greater wealth and prominence than later creations, but we have no good reason to believe that family sizes varied sufficiently systematically with wealth and prominence to produce this effect on extinction rates. If they did so vary, of course, it would be logical to infer that the whole sample of baronets themselves had extinction rates lower than the elite as a whole and we should have to regard our extinction rates as underestimates for the wider elite.

Leaving these considerations aside, we have arrived at an estimate which we can use for the purposes proposed at the outset, namely, to consider as a benchmark or standard against which to judge the size of mobility effects. On the average a proportion between 12% and 17% of all extant patrilines are likely to have been dying out every 30 years, provided that no factors hidden from us and not represented in our data invalidate a generalization from our sample to the elite as a whole. Furthermore, this is a well-defined rate of extinction. Our models tells us how to apply it to different time intervals and estimates of the size of random fluctuations from it are within our grasp.

This brings us to the end of our statistical exploration of the data on baronets. At practically every stage our conclusions have been gratifying. Where we might have encountered erratic patterns of waves and lulls of extinctions stimulated by special historical events and rendering the baronets useless for any claims about normal extinction levels, we have found instead regular persistent patterns of extinctions. Where laws governing inheritance might have made extinctions of baronetcies a poor guide to extinctions of other patrilines, we have found the data encouraging us to discount those effects. Where extinction numbers might depend on time or patriline age or other factors besides numbers of lines at risk, making it meaningless to talk of an extinction rate on its own, we have found instead an excellent fit to our data by a model in which an extinction rate on its own makes perfect sense. Upon examination this data set does appear to offer us the opportunity to measure an ordinary or normal, sustained, presumably demographically-determined rate of extinctions. Our hope of pinning down one element of a picture in which we can distinguish between normal and exceptional levels of mobility appears to meet with success.

Let us in conclusion return to the implication of the rate of intrinsic replacement mobility which we have been able to calculate by the use of the baronetcy extinction figures. We can say that in England during the 1600s and 1700s upward social mobility had to go on at a high and steady rate if the elite was to stay at strength. The need to replace something like 40% of all patrilines constituting the elite each century must have meant a considerable amount of upward shifting that need not be accounted for in terms of the special economic necessities or social stresses of segments of the population during these centuries. The intrinsic upward mobility rate of a traditional society must have been of consequence in its effects on many patrilines and individuals, a feature of the social landscape of traditional societies, even perhaps of those with demographic regimes differing from the England of the Stuarts and Hanovers.

To go beyond the estimation of an extinction rate and to elaborate our broader picture of replacement mobility leads inevitably into speculation. Data are rarely as easy to garner as those on extinctions of baronetcies have been. It is hard to say how far the extinction of patrilines led on a regular basis to replacement mobility, how elastic or inelastic the total number of slots in the society can have been. It is equally hard to say how much replacement mobility took the form of patriline promotion and how much took the form of patriline repair by sideways motion such as we have described. It may be that the answers to these questions differ profoundly from generation to generation, from area to area, and from segment to segment. But it may also be that the impression of social regularity that our examination of extinction rates has stimulated may be sustained by detailed and quantitative study of these further questions by statisticians and historians.

8

The Income of Hilandar:
A Statistical Exploration[1]

A. INTRODUCTION

This methodological exercise examines property and taxation records of a handful of households in fourteenth century Macedonia, in an attempt to see what can be extracted from such records by statistical analysis. I pretend to no expertise in Byzantine history but present this work for what may be immediately gained in understanding the social structure of the time and place, and in the hope that others, more experienced in the substantive area, may find the same tools useful and wield them more expertly. Having said this, I will very briefly place the materials in historical perspective.

The Byzantine Empire, which had continued the traditions of the civilized Mediterranean world after the fall of Rome, came under increasingly heavy attack in the twelfth, thirteenth, and fourteenth centuries. Rivals to its power appeared in vigorous Serbian and Bulgarian states. In

[1] The research for this chapter was supported in part by grant RO 21959 75 197 from the National Endowment for the Humanities, research assistance from the Center for Slavic and East European Studies at the University of California, Berkeley, and grants for computer time from the University of California, Berkeley computer center to Eugene A. Hammel. Findings presented here do not necessarily represent their views of taxation in fourteenth century Macedonia.

the thirteenth century Constantinople was taken by Western crusaders, and the Byzantine territories were spotted with Frankish principalities. At the same time, the Ottoman advance from the east had begun, progressing through the Slavic collapse at Kosovo in 1389, the fall of Constantinople in 1453, and the victory at Mohacs in 1526. While the political, diplomatic, and military aspects of this turmoil are reasonably well documented, the life and conditions of the peasantry are obscure. There is little archaeological evidence of the kind that illuminates Greek and Roman antiquity. The most valuable documentary evidence is found in tax enumerations and transfers of property. The Church (as in the West) was a major proprietor. Donations by the lay nobility to monasteries were common, and the most stable element through these centuries of strife was monastery proprietorship. The monasteries seemed well organized, structurally equipped to persist as corporations despite turnover in personnel, as principalities and empires were not. Their records, often preserved in isolated havens such as those of Mt. Athos ("The Holy Mountain" in the Slavic tongues), surely provide the best, if a limited, insight into the condition of the peasantry.

The documents that clearly pertain to Slavic populations are of particular interest, because of the obscure roots of those peoples and the paucity of reliable data concerning their early social organization. The Balkan Slavs appear to have preserved some ancient features of Indo-European organization until recent times, and medieval data would be valuable in reconstructing it. Unfortunately, the documents that describe Slavic populations are later, and of lesser quality than the more strictly "Byzantine" ones. The systems of land tenure and taxation common in Byzantium appear to have continued in monastery practice, but details are obscure. The clarity lent the data by established systems of measurement of land and money, for example, is muddied in the Slavic texts, and comparison with parallel Greek texts sheds little light. Nevertheless, I believe that one can at least propose hypotheses for investigation by applying analytical methods uncommon in historical studies. If they show promise even with the relatively intractable evidence utilized here, they could be more effectively employed on richer data explicable by those with the necessary historical, paleographic and linguistic skills.

B. THE DATA

One of the most interesting of the medieval Balkan household listings is that of 127 households under the jurisdiction of the monastery of Hilandar (Mt. Athos). They were part of six villages in the "Struma" region of what is now Serbian Macedonia. The most recent and probably most accurate interpretation of the date of the original manuscript is 1315.[2] In an earlier analysis, I presented the kinship structure of the households and discussed the probable effects of demographic factors on their constitution.[3] The present paper explores the listed possessions of the households, comments on the implications for the economic system and social structure, and attempts to establish the basis for taxation. Although earlier commentators have described the economic holdings of the households and drawn their own inferences, they have not used modern statistical techniques, in part because some of those techniques had not been invented when they wrote.

The Hilandar listing is uniquely rich in economic detail (although unfortunately brief in its limitation to 127 households). It gives number of plowing yokes, bulls, beef cattle, cows, horses, sheep, swine, donkeys, trees, beehives, mills, and extent of patrimonial vineyard, dowry vineyard, garden, field land, and meadow for each household. It often notes occupation, social status, or (rarely) ethnicity, whether female heads of household were widowed, and the amount of money taxes paid. The data on individuals give their kinship relationship to the head of household and permit inference of sex, marital status, and approximate age. The document also gives important information on village lands not held by individual households, aggregate taxes, etc., but these are not analyzed here.

Interpretations of the data were of course necessary. Persons in the listing were assumed to be adult if they were married or widowed or had children. Others in the same household and genealogical generation as those deemed adult by the foregoing criteria were also taken to be adult even if the listing afforded no direct evidence of their marital status or parenthood. The overestimation of number of adults possible by this procedure is felt to be minimal, since the inferences are quite clear where

[2] The most recent and reliable transcription, with extensive commentary is Vladimir Mošin, "Akti iz svetogorskih arhiva," *Spomenik XCI*, Srpska Kraljevska Akademija, drugi razred, 70, pages 153–260, Belgrade, 1939. See also Th. I. Uspensky, *Materialy dlya istorii zemlevladeniya v XIV veka*, Odessa, 1883; Lj. Stojanović, *Stari srpski hrisovulji, akti, biografije, letopisi, tipici, pomenici, zapisi, i dr.*, *Spomenik III*, Srpska Kraljevska Akademija, Belgrade, 1890; Aleksandr V. Solovjev, *Odabrani spomenici srpskog prava (od XII do kraja XV veka)*, Belgrade, Geca Kon, 1926. I am indebted to Sima Ćirković for pointing out the Mošin source and to Gordon McDaniel for translating Mošin's transcription, against which I was able to check my own translation of Stojanović's. In all cases of disagreement, Mošin's transcription was accepted. Mošin dates the manuscript in 1315 in its Greek original, the Serbian copy some time later. He does not locate the villages precisely, although he mentions Gradac as being on the Struma. My own examination of modern maps suggests the Plačkovica area, although all such interpretations are doubtful, the names of some of the villages being quite common (e.g., Gradac, Kamenica).

[3] E. A. Hammel (1978). The deficiencies of the Stojanović transcription do not affect the conclusion of that paper, except in regard to the reported date.

kinship links are simple, and almost all links within households in the listing were simple. Occupation and social status, where given, usually attached to heads of households, but occasionally blocks of households were listed as serfs or freemen. If no occupation or status was given, the household was taken to be one of serfs. This interpretation is identical to Mošin's and is consistent with the internal evidence of the document, unlabeled households being more similar in organization and possessions to labeled serf households than to labeled free households. Other than serfs and freemen, there were eight households of artisans, two of priests, and one containing a hunter. Clear designation of ethnicity was too rare to be useful, and inference from personal names too risky. Measures of money and of land are difficult to define precisely in modern terms, but for internal analysis such definition is unnecessary. Money tax was measured in *perpers* or in *dinars*, with apparently 12 dinars to the perper. Most often, the tax is listed in whole perpers and/or fractions thereof, the fractions being ¼, ⅓, ½, ⅔. Since the highest tax was only five perpers, these crude divisions lend an unfortunate modularity to the data. Land was measured in *k6b16*, probably just under a hectare.[4] The land measure is referred to in this paper by its modern Serbian derivative, *kabao* ("bucket").

The six villages, according to Mošin, contained more households than the 127 listed in the document, and indeed portions of these villages were the subject of intermonastery property disputes. Since we cannot know with any confidence whether the households belonging to Hilandar were representative of the total population of the villages, the list of 127 cannot form a thoroughly reliable basis for inference to the village populations. Since we do not know the size of the village populations, we cannot even say anything about the proportion that these households constitute of the villages. The listed households are very differently distributed across the villages, with 71 in Gradac, 9 in Munzen, 9 in Gornji Lužac, 18 in Kamenica, 5 in Kondogrica, and 15 in Kumica. However, the information in this list is all that is available.

C. ANALYSIS

Exhibit 8.1 shows the mean values of variables. Classificatory attributes such as those pertaining to occupation, social status, and household

[4] The symbol 6 indicates an indeterminate vowel. See Djuro Daničic, *Rječnik iz književnih starina srpskih*, I–III, Graz, Akademische Druck-und Verlaganstalt, 1962 (1863–1864), s.v. *k6b16*; Vuk St. Karadžic, *Srpski rječnik istumačen njemačkijem i latinskijem riječima*, Belgrade, 1898, s.v. *kabao*. Mošin, "Akti," 1939, gives a value of $838.42m^2$ (page 53, note 6).

EXHIBIT 8.1.   Means and Standard Deviations

	Mean	S.D.
Men	1.01	.49
Adults	2.09	.74
Children	1.70	1.22
Persons	3.80	1.38
Yokes	.39	.49
Bulls	.32	.47
Beef cattle	.94	1.65
Cows	.03	.35
Horses	.04	.23
Sheep	3.31	8.40
Swine	2.11	4.28
Donkeys	.21	.61
Patrimonial vines	1.52	1.93
Dowry vines	.04	.20
Garden	.10	.39
Field land	21.18	33.63
Trees	.16	.74
Beehives	.69	3.44
Meadow	.10	1.15
Mills	.01	.09
Serf	.76	.42
Free	.15	.36
Artisan	.06	.24
Priest	.02	.12
Hunter	.01	.09
Nuclear household	.83	.38
Widowhood	.15	.36
Total tax	1.37	1.11
Residual tax	.94	.58

organization are dichotomous, and the means should be interpreted as proportions. These means can be phrased verbally and approximately as follows: There were about four persons per household, of whom two were children and two adult, one of the latter being male. A plowing yoke (interpreted as an ox team) was found in one out of three households, a bull in one out of three, and a beef on the average in each. There were only four cows (and all four were in one household), and five horses (in four households). Sheep averaged three per household and swine two; donkeys were rare. Vineyard land in patrimony averaged about 1.5 kabao per household; dowry vineyard was quite rare and in even smaller portions. (Nevertheless, its existence in any proportion is important, since land dowry is rare over much of the Balkans.) Garden land averaged but a tenth of a kabao per household; field land averaged 21 kabao. Meadow and mills were rare; only one household had any meadow and only one had a mill. Taxes averaged 1.4 perpers. About three-fourths of the households were of serfs, 15% of freemen, the rest consisting of artisans (including a scribe), priests, and a hunter. Eighty-three percent of the households were nuclear in organization (cf. Hammel and Laslett, 1974).

Exhibit 8.1 also shows the standard deviations for these same variables. It is clear from their magnitude, as well as from examination of the frequency distributions (not shown here for lack of space) that there was wide variability between households. For example, 85 of the households had no field land at all, and 61 had no vineyard in patrimony. There were 77 that had no plowing yoke, 34 with no draft animals, 68 with no small stock, and 20 with no animals at all. Taxes ranged from a low of ⅛ perper to a high of 5, in a bimodal distribution with one peak at ½ perper and another at 1 perper. (Possible reasons for this differentiation of households will be discussed in a following paragraph.)

Comparison of the households by village location yields few clues, partly because some village subsets of the list are so small as to make the statistics unreliable (see Exhibit 8.2). If we take average tax assessment as a measure of wealth, the poorest villages seem to be Kumica and Kamenica, with Kondogrica, Gornji Lužac, Munzen, and Gradac at

EXHIBIT 8.2.   Means by Village and Occupation[a]

	Gradac	Munzen	Lužac	Kamenica	Kondog	Kumica	Serf	Free	Non-agricultural
Persons	3.94	3.89	3.56	3.39	5.20	3.20	3.96	3.05	3.64
Yokes	.55	.44	.33	.17	.20	0	.46	.11	.27
Patrimonial vines	1.92	.44	.89	1.58	1.70	.47	1.81	0	1.55
Garden	.09	0	0	.17	.70	0	.10	0	.18
Field	30.42	33.33	25.56	0	0	0	26.39	4.21	4.55
Trees	.17	0	0	.44	0	0	.17	0	.36
Total tax	1.68	1.49	1.33	.69	1.30	.69	1.58	.55	.93
Nuclear organization	.79	.89	1.00	.89	.40	.93	.79	.95	.91
Serf	.83	.44	.44	.61	1.00	.93	1.00	0	0
Free	.10	.56	.56	.11	0	0	0	1.00	0
Nonagricultural	.07	0	0	.28	0	0	0	0	1.00

[a] Only some of the more interesting variables are presented here.

successively higher levels, but the meaning, as well as the reliability of the inference is in doubt. Somewhat more can be seen by comparison of serfs, freemen, and the remaining occupational groups, the latter being presumably "nonagricultural." Serfs are more prosperous than freemen, have larger families that are more frequently extended and have more adult males, and pay more taxes. However, the frequency distributions show that some freemen were more prosperous than some serfs, and Mošin notes that the distinction was fundamentally a legal one, perhaps based on length of residence. His suggestion is supported by the more frequent nuclearity of free families, since more recently arrived families would have had less time to form extensions. Where the listing permits inference of kinship links across household boundaries, free families show a lower incidence than do serf families. The nonagricultural households are intermediate between the serf and free families, were almost as nuclear as the free households, and had precisely one adult male each. There is thus some weak evidence for a relationship between occupational or legal status and economic and social organization, but a good deal is probably attributable to mere length of residence, not to social differentiation *on account of* legal or occupational status. The absence of dowry vineyard among freemen, suggesting no marriages with locally established households, supports this notion.

Differentiation of households on individual variables need not mean total differentiation of the households. Occupational or economic specialization could underlie diverse distribution of resources. However, there is little unambiguous evidence for such specialization. Although the average landholding for "nonagriculturalists" was small, three of the eleven had a plowing yoke, and one had 50 kabao of land. The simple correlation coefficients between legal/occupational status and holdings in land or animals are quite weak. Another possible explanation is that of functional substitution of economic activities in the agricultural sphere. For example, some families might have concentrated on field crops and others on garden and vineyard. If so, we would expect negative correlations between these kinds of "trade-off" possessions. The data do not show such negative correlations of any strength at all except that bulls may have been an alternative to draft oxen (Exhibit 8.3). On the other hand, there are frequent positive correlations, some of them strong. For example, the simple correlation between amount of field and of patrimonial vineyard is .59. All of this suggests that families with one type of property also tended to have other types of property, that some households were simply wealthier than others, in a way apparently unconnected with formal legal or occupational status, as detectable in the manuscript.

EXHIBIT 8.3.   Correlations[a]

	Yokes	Bulls	Cows	Sheep	Patrimonial vines	Garden	Field	Trees	Widowhood	Total tax	Residual tax
Yokes	1.00	−.56	.11	.23	.36	.00	.50	.13	−.11	.65	.66
Bulls		1.00	−.06	−.16	−.11	−.02	−.14	−.10	.04	−.21	−.24
Cows			1.00	−.04	.30	−.02	.21	.71	−.04	.29	.32
Sheep				1.00	.24	−.02	.38	.06	−.17	.44	.39
Patrimonial vines					1.00	.21	.59	.42	.00	.70	.67
Garden						1.00	.08	.14	.01	.16	.20
Field							1.00	.19	−.05	.90	.57
Trees								1.00	−.09	.24	.24
Widowhood									1.00	−.10	−.14
Total tax										1.00	.87
Residual tax											1.00

[a] Only those variables shown to be significantly correlated with total tax in the multiple regression, plus residual tax, are shown here to conserve space.

Even this kind of differentiation could be explained away if it were associated with the numbers of persons in households. That is, even in a purely subsistence farming economy, large households might have more possessions than small ones, but all households might be roughly equivalent on a per capita basis. The data do not strongly support this possibility either. The simple correlation coefficient between field land and number of adults is .30, with children .12, with number of adult males .31. If one takes the sum of all nonfield land (garden, vineyard, and dowry vineyard), these correlations are .32 with adults, .22 with children, and .27 with adult males. If taxes are taken as a measure of wealth, the correlation is .36 with adults, .27 with children, and .35 with adult males. The correlation between total number of persons and taxes is higher, .43, but none of these simple correlations is high enough to suggest a very strong relationship between producers and wealth, consumers and wealth, or the two of them together and wealth; only 5% to 15% of the variance in various measures of wealth can be "explained" purely by the demographic features available from the document.

Since neither occupational specialization, specialization within agriculture, nor simple sex-and-age estimates seem to explain the differences, we must conclude that, although the population was highly differentiated, such differentiation was apparently a matter of chance or of migration, or perhaps the result of the effects of the constant armed strife that seemed to characterize the area. The data do not permit direct exploration of any of these possibilities, although Mošin's suggestion of length of residence could be easily followed up if the census contained age data that would permit inference of position in the cycle of household development. Perhaps other censuses will be found that will allow this.

The analysis must therefore turn to the decomposition of wealth and examination of its components. The work underlying this paper employed a variety of measures of wealth—amount of various kinds of property, singly and in combination, taxes, and taxes paid on property after the probable effect of field land had been subtracted out. The most satisfactory explanatory model, presented here, utilizes total taxes as a measure of general wealth of households. Because the population of households is so small, the analysis rests on the total sample and does not further examine its subsets.

There are two ways to pursue the analysis of the relationship between wealth and other factors. One is through the use of contingency tables. These would be appropriate to the skewed, modularized nature of the data and the nominally scaled character of several of the variables. Variables had to be dichotomized in this approach, generally about their medians, to diminish the occurrence of cells with small expected frequencies. Simple 2 by 2 tables show strong relationships between taxes and the following: yokes, beef cattle, patrimonial vineyard land, and field land. The last of these relationships is very strong. When three-way tables were constructed, for example to examine the effect of yokes on taxes for particular values of land, they were difficult to interpret because the frequencies invariably fell heavily into only a few cells. For example, in the table just described, most of the observations fell into the cells for those households having land *and* yokes *and* paying higher than average taxes, and into those with *no* land, *no* yokes, and paying *less* than the average. The data again suggest that the rich were rich and the poor poor, but they make it difficult to get much of a feeling for the effects of individual variables when all others are held constant.

The second approach, multiple regression, is not ideally suited to the data in the statistical sense. However, since the document itself, in its regularity of listing of properties, leads one so easily to the idea of a checklist, it seems not unlikely that an ad valorem tax was applied or a tax on the productivity of land, stock, and labor. If tax collection was based on rates for individual kinds of possessions, for example, so much per kabao of land, so much per plowing yoke, then multiple regression only retraces the steps taken by the tax assessor and is perfectly reasonable regardless of the statistical nature of the data. I proceed on that basis. Some care must be taken, however. First, interpretations of significance levels in the regression must be cautious. Even if the tax collector was building a problem for multiple regression six and a half centuries later, the probability estimates in the regression *do* depend on the mathematical qualities of the distributions and must be taken with a grain of salt. Second, the basic distributions must be examined for nonlinearity. This was done; the bivariate relationships were either roughly linear or nonexistent. Third, the residual error after estimates are made from the regression model must be compared with the predicted values; if these are correlated or show some distinct pattern, the model is unreliable. This, too, was done, and no such patterning could be detected.[5]

The regressions were computed on three levels. At Level 1, all conceivable independent variables were employed, except those that were linearly dependent on one another. (For example, while numbers of adults, children, and adult men could be entered into the regression, numbers of adults, children and persons could not be.) The results at this level were screened to eliminate those independent variables that were not statistically significant; the level of significance was taken as 5%, keeping in mind the cautions given above. At Level 2, only the variables significant at Level 1 were entered, and these results were again screened in the same way, since one of the variables that was significant at Level 1 ceased to be at Level 2, when the effects of the nonsignificant variables at Level 1 were removed. Only the variables significant at Level 2 were entered at Level 3. No variables lost their significance at Level 3.

The results are given in Exhibit 8.4 and can be summarized here. Level 1, using 26 predictors (including some derived indices not shown in earlier tables) yielded a multiple regression coefficient of .974, "explaining" 94.9% of the variance in taxes, with a probability of chance occurrence vanishingly close to zero. On this basis we could say that we knew practically everything there was to know about taxation and, inferentially, about level of wealth. However, given the cautions on significance levels noted earlier, and the fact that 26 predictors is a lot of knowledge to begin with when only 127 households are involved, we should look further. Only nine of the 26 variable are "significant" at the 5% level at Level 1: yokes, bulls, cows, sheep, vines, garden, field land, trees, and widowhood. We enter these at Level 2, with a resulting multiple correlation coefficient of .968, explaining 93.6% of the variance in taxes, and with a

---

[5] I am much indebted to my colleague, Peter Bickel, for his comments on my statistical efforts and suggestions on cautionary procedures, and to Ruth Deuel for assistance in the more complex aspects of the programming. Neither of them is responsible for my remaining errors.

EXHIBIT 8.4.   Results of Multiple Regressions

Predictor	Regression coefficient	Standard error of coefficient	Standardized regression coefficient	p
	Level 1[a]			
Yokes	.625	.086	.276	0
Bulls	.177	.071	.075	.014
Cows	.546	.115	.175	.000
Sheep	.013	.004	.099	.002
Patrimonial vines	.111	.021	.194	0
Garden	.338	.099	.120	.001
Field land	.018	.001	.553	0
Trees	−.166	.060	−.111	.006
Widowhood	−.320	.124	−.103	.011
	Level 2[b]			
Yokes	.654	.075	.289	0
Bulls	.175	.069	.074	.010
Cows	.600	.107	.192	0
Sheep	.016	.003	.119	.000
Patrimonial vines	.136	.018	.238	0
Garden	.243	.069	.086	.001
Field land	.019	.001	.564	0
Trees	−.235	.054	−.157	.000
Widowhood	−.100	.074	−.033	.178
	Level 3[c]			
Yokes	.666	.075	.294	0
Bulls	.181	.069	.076	.010
Cows	.598	.108	.191	0
Sheep	.016	.003	.125	0
Patrimonial vines	.134	.018	.234	0
Garden	.244	.069	.086	.001
Field land	.019	.001	.563	0
Trees	−.228	.054	−.152	.000

[a] Dependent variable = total tax. Predictors = 26 basic and derived factors (see text). Only those predictors significant at the 5% level are listed in this summary. Multiple correlation coefficient = .974. Coefficient of multiple determination = .949. $p = 0$.

[b] Dependent variable = total tax. Predictors = 9 variables significant at the 5% level in Level 1. Multiple correlation coefficient =.968. Coefficient of multiple determination = .936. $p = 0$.

[c] Dependent variable = total tax. Predictors = 8 variables significant at the 5% level in Level 2. Multiple correlation coefficient = .967. Coefficient of multiple determination = .935. $p = 0$.

probability of chance occurrence again about zero. At this level only eight variables are significant—all of the above except widowhood. At Level 3 we enter all except widowhood, obtaining a multiple correlation coefficient of .967, explaining 93.5% of the variance in taxes, with probability of chance occurrence again about zero. Surely something was gained by moving from Level 1 to Level 2. A great many intercorrelated weak variables were eliminated, with a loss in explanatory power of only 1% or 2%. The selection of variables as "significant" seems reasonable because the differentiation of high and low probability levels is very sharp. The highest probability level accepted was .013; the next highest is .147. Whether the move from Level 2 to Level 3 is justifiable is less certain; widowhood loses its significance only because of the elimination of a lot of other weak variables, and it is sociologically interesting to contemplate that widowed heads of households might have enjoyed a tax break in the fourteenth century. Although it could be claimed that we would do almost as well by using field land *only* as a predictor, thus explaining 81% of the variance in tax, use of the simple relationship masks other interesting factors and loses more than 12% in explanatory power.

It is particularly interesting to note the regression coefficient for field land at all three levels—about .02. At the end of the manuscript, in the section dealing with aggregate taxes, there appear the following statements:

"The land controlled by the village Gradac is 8000 kabao outside the peasant homesteads and the tax for that area is 160 perpers."

"For the land of Munzen 1800 kabao outside of serfs' homesteads 36 perpers."

"The bounded property near the land of Metritopul . . . 600 kabao for 12 perpers."

"Kamena . . . 200 kabao . . . 4 perper"

"Prevlak . . . 300 kabao . . . 6 perper"

"For the place Luzac 2000 kabao 40 perpers."

". . . in Krusici 800 kabao of land 16 perpers."

The tax rate in all of these statements is .02 perpers per kabao of land. Our confidence in the multiple regression approach is strengthened by this independent evidence of the coefficient; it seems clear that the average rate for taxation of field land inside peasant homesteads was close to, although perhaps a bit lower than, the stated rate outside those boundaries. The regressions can be paralleled in a general way using as the dependent variable a residual tax that consists of the total tax minus .02

times the amount of field land held, thus subtracting out the effect of field land on tax directly, and eliminating field land as a predictor in the regression. The power of the explanatory model is somewhat reduced, but still strong. Exhibit 8.3 also shows that the correlation between total tax and residual tax is .87, suggesting that those wealthy enough to pay a large total tax still paid a large residual tax. This, too, strengthens the idea of an item by item tax, with high correlation between critical items such as land, vineyard, and stock, the rich being rich, and the poor poor.

One must, however, examine the possibility that the tax was one on productivity rather than on possessions. For some time the analysis led in this direction, but the idea cannot be strongly supported. Arguments for a tax on productivity would be strengthened by positive correlations between tax and number of persons, or of adults, or of children (but not necessarily of men, because the usual head tax on adult males, if applied, could confuse the issue). Such simple correlations appear, as noted, but they are weak. Furthermore, when the data are examined at a multivariate level, the correlations with these factors fade away. Thus, there appears to be no *marginal* effect of human labor on tax, as we would expect if productivity were the basis of taxation.

Although the basic component of taxation was field land, shown by its very high standardized regression coefficient, it cannot be the only component. If other factors, such as plowing yokes, vineyard land, and the like were nearly perfectly correlated with land, they would drop out of the regression. They do not. Were they taxed on an ad valorem basis or in anticipation of production? For example, it could be argued that the tax apparently assessed against a plow team was really one on the value added to production, since a household with land and a plow team could presumably work more efficiently than one with land but without a plow team. However, 21 of the households had a yoke with no field land at all; these constitute 42% of the households with yokes and 25% of those with no land; in these cases the tax must be on the yoke or plow team itself. The only reliable inference is a sociological one for cooperative plowing, and the probable use of individually owned plow teams on village-owned fields.

The most troublesome problem of interpretation is posed by the consistently negative correlation between trees and taxes. It holds up at all levels of the analysis and for both total and residual tax, with a very small probability of occurrence by chance. The regression model shows that for each combination of kinds of property, possession of trees resulted in a lower tax. There is no reason to suspect a negative tax on trees. Neither does there seem to be any reason to imagine a monastery program that encouraged arboriculture by giving tax breaks for land taken out of production for something else; such manipulations are a modern phenomenon. It is possible that trees provided an alternative to vines for the production of wine and brandy, so that a household could satisfy its consumption needs with less vineyard, thereby lowering its taxes *if* the *product* was not taxed *and if* trees were not taxed. In these circumstances one would expect a negative correlation between trees and vines, but it does not appear. In fact, the correlation is positive and reasonably strong (.42). It is conceivable that, if trees were located on field lands and lowered the productivity of those lands by taking part of a plot out of production, the negative correlation arises from a deliberate offset in taxes based on the number of trees, or taxation based on anticipated lowered productivity of the land as originally measured. No other ethnographically credible and statistically meaningful explanations suggest themselves. There were only seven households with trees and another with "a place with vines and fruit." The presence of trees may serve only as a proxy for the identity of these households (or of a few of them) which happened by chance to pay lower taxes than expected for their level of wealth. Exactly the same problem is raised by the effects of cows on taxes, when we know that all four cows in the sample were in one household. Some of these questions cannot be solved with the data at hand.[6]

It seems very unlikely that the economic resources of some, and perhaps of any households were completely recorded in the document. Those families that were without land, and particularly those that had no land but had a plow team, must have had access to the undivided village lands or to the lands of their wealthier neighbors. They might have had such access on a rental or sharecropping basis. Nesbitt presents data and arguments for rental arrangements in Byzantine documents of the same time period.[7] Whether the peasants had labor service obligations on monastery lands in addition is beside the point; the point is that the peasants had listed exploitable assets of their own and probably other exploitable assets as well. The possibility of additional resources may seem to vitiate the conclusions reached above about social differentiation, and

[6] Taking cows and trees out of the regressions does not lower total explanatory power much and is an easy way out of the dilemma. However, the persistence of these variables persuaded me to leave them in the presentation of data. Since they are so rare in the population, they have relatively little effect on the total problem, but they might be important in assessment of tax for individual households, particularly if the "checklist ad valorem" theory is correct.

[7] John W. Nesbitt. *Mechanisms of agricultural production on estates of the Byzantine praktika*. Doctoral dissertation (History), University of Wisconsin, 1972. University Microfilms, Ann Arbor. I am indebted to Rondo Cameron for bringing this reference to my attention.

the analytical implications of such additional resources should be examined.

If the intensity and distribution of rental arrangements was random with respect to possession of other resources, the general conclusions would not be affected. Different families might emerge as richer or poorer, but the extent of differentiation would be exactly the same.

If the intensity and distribution of rental arrangements was a response to subsistence need dictated by the number of consumers in families and the number of producers available to work rented lands, again the general conclusions would not change. It must be recalled that the correlations between demographic and economic variables in the data were very poor. For that reason, a distribution of rental activity highly correlated with demographic factors would be relatively random with respect to listed resources. Thus, this second possibility would not differ much in its implications from the first.

If the intensity and distribution of rental arrangements was a function of the intensity of other productive activities, so that wealthier and more productive households also rented land for further exploitation, social differentiation would be greater than shown in these data.

Finally, it is possible that owning and renting land and other resources were alternatives at every level of wealth. Under these conditions, households at the same level of wealth overall might differ in the degree to which their resources consisted of rented or owned land. In these data, the families that appeared wealthy would have rented very little land, while those who appeared poor would have rented more. Under these conditions one might find a population relatively homogeneous in wealth.

The last alternative does not seem likely because of the strong correlations observed between field land, vineyard, plow teams, and taxes. Surely it would have been the peasants with yokes and animals who would have been in the best position to till additional rented land. But it is just these peasants who were, on the average, wealthier in land of their own. Of the remaining three possibilities, the first—that rental arrangements were random with respect to owned wealth—seems unlikely, too. At least it is distinctly uninteresting. The second and third possibilities are not mutually exclusive, although the weight one puts on each depends on the view of society at that time. If there had been any emergent entrepreneurial activity, the second alternative—with rich peasants using rented land to expand their production—would be likely. There is some evidence for this in the households with plough teams but no land; why else would a family have a team except to accumulate the resources necessary to obtain land? But this alternative requires some degree of marketing for the accumulation of surplus and some activity in sale of land. These matters are unclear. The third possibility—response to subsistence—seems very likely, particularly if the economy was a subsistence one with little or no marketing or availability of land through sale. But in either of these cases there is social differentiation, as strong as or stronger than that indicated in the document.

We cannot of course assume that the economic basis of peasant life in these villages is well known as a result of this analytical exercise. It is entirely unclear how typical the households listed are of the villages from which they were drawn. Nevertheless, the results are intriguing and conformable with what we know from other sources. The population was fundamentally agricultural, engaged in mixed farming partly on the lands of individual households and, most likely, also on undivided village lands. Whether the exploitation of the village lands was through rental or labor service is not indicated in the document. The population was heterogeneous in wealth, and the kinds of wealth were correlated inter se. Wealth differences seem to have had little to do with formal legal status but may have reflected length of time in the area, social incorporation, and the opportunity to assemble resources over time. Taxation appears consistent, and although there are some hints of production as the basis for taxation, it seems more likely that stock and land were taxed on an ad valorem basis. The marketing of produce and sale of land and stock are certainly not precluded by the evidence in the document, but made more likely as a concomitant of one of the probable explanations of the relationship between rental and ownership.

9

Ancestors at the Norman Conquest[1]

There are few illustrations of the inevitability of math in history so apt as the popular puzzle about the number of ancestors anyone had during some great historical event like the Norman Conquest. Each of us has two parents. If we reason that two parents mean four grandparents, eight great grandparents, and twice as many ancestors more each generation back, then each of us should have had a thousand million ancestors alive when William the Conqueror stumbled up the sands toward Hastings. Carrying the fallacy a step further, the ancestors of an English person of today would have been so numerous at the time the Emperor Hadrian visited his northern province that there would have been one ancestor for every square inch of surface area of the globe—land and ocean.

The flaw in this reasoning, saving us from having such a myriad of ancestors, is not hard to pinpoint. People can marry their cousins, and so

[1] This chapter derives from a reply to a letter from Edward E. Green of Norwich, England, in January 1973. The author is indebted to comments of Mr. Green's. The original reply was widely circulated, and much interesting work on this problem has been done since then by David Kendall of Churchill College, Cambridge. The reader is likely to enjoy Kendall (1975), dealing with related questions. Work so far unpublished refining our model to allow for less than total mixing of populations in the distant past is also due to R. V. Simons, formerly of Clare College, Cambridge.

the distinct positions in a pedigree need not be filled by distinct men and women. But the question remains, how many distinct ancestors is a person likely to have had at any time? For how many generations back does the number of distinct ancestors grow larger? When does it start to shrink? Can a typical person expect to be descended, back beyond some date in the past, from the whole population of his country of origin, or at least from everyone in the population who had descendants? In this chapter we offer answers to these questions on the basis of a simple probability model. The exercise is an amusing one, and it exemplifies points of contact between model building and less formal varieties of speculation.

As a genealogist constructs a family tree, working backwards through time, he is effectively choosing for each individual in the tree two people out of some pool of possible candidates to record as the individual's parents. If the individual is generation $g = 0$, then at generation $g = 1$ there is one father and one mother. At generation $g = 2$ there are $2^2 = 4$ positions in the family tree, 2 for males, 2 for females. At generation $g = 3$ there are 2^3 positions in all in the tree, 2^2 of them for males and 2^2 of them for females. Thus g generations back there are 2^g positions in the tree, 2^{g-1} for males and 2^{g-1} for females. We shall suppose that the 2^{g-1} positions for males are filled by $m(g)$ distinct male ancestors and the 2^{g-1} positions for females are filled by $f(g)$ females. To fill the 2^{g+1} slots in the tree for generation $g + 1$, the genealogist must find $m(g) + f(g)$ fathers for all the distinct males and females of generation g. We suppose that he must find these fathers out of some collection of $x(g + 1)$ men. He must also find $m(g) + f(g)$ mothers out of some collection of $y(g + 1)$ women. Of these fathers, some $m(g + 1)$ will be distinct men, and of the mothers some $f(g + 1)$ will be distinct women. What we want is a model which allows us to calculate expected values for the numbers $m(1)$, $f(1)$, $m(2)$, $f(2)$, . . . going back in time.

Whenever two slots in a family tree are filled by the same person, it means that further down the tree a couple who married were in fact cousins. It seems sensible to distinguish between two sorts of cousin marriage, close and distant, and this distinction forms an essential step in our analysis. Marriages of close cousins, on the one hand, presumably involve a conscious choice of a cousin as marriage partner, and they may reflect social preference for cousin marriage, desires to keep property in families, special opportunities for acquaintanceship and affiliation through a kin network, and similar social factors. Such choice would be systematic rather than random. Marriages of distant cousins, on the other hand, must often arise from accident, without the couple knowing of the kin relationship. If a bride's and groom's ancestors come from the same country, there being only a limited number of people alive at any point in the past in that country, then chances are that the couple have ancestors in common. Duplicate people in the slots in the family tree are likely to occur at random, with more of these random duplications the larger the number of slots to be filled and the smaller the pool of people in the population from which these slots must be filled. A probability model ought to be able to predict chances of various numbers of duplications. On these grounds we propose to regard close cousin marriage as a systematic process and distant cousin marriage as a random process.

We should mention that there are arguments for opposite points of view, emphasizing the random character of close cousin marriage or the systematic character of distant cousin marriage. For close cousin marriage, Gilbert and Hammel (1966) have demonstrated by microsimulation that in one society where elaborate cousin-preference systems have been supposed, a simple random model based on geographical propinquity would explain a large fraction of the observed close cousin marriage. For distant cousin marriage, it is easy to hypothesize patterns of social or geographical stratification which would severely restrict the pool of plausible candidates from among whom not only each person's parents but his or her more distant forbears would be found. Such stratification would give less scope to randomness. Geneticists interested in coefficients of inbreeding more complicated than our simple measure, the number of distinct ancestors, have collected some data on consanguinity in western societies. This work is summarized in Chapters 7 and 8 of Bodmer and Cavalli-Sforza (1971), but strictness of stratification over long time periods is not readily estimable from it. For some groups, stratification may have been so rigid, pervasive and prolonged as to be an important determinant of distant cousin marriage, but it is hard to imagine this being true for a majority of any national population.

A genealogist filling in a family tree who talks of a choice of parents or a pool of candidates eligible to be ancestors is adopting an artificial but a useful point of view. In the world where clocks run forward, brides choose grooms and grooms choose brides or parents choose them for them, but the effect, as we should see it if we ran the clock backward, is that children acquire parents and their parents acquire parents, and more and more branches grow on the genealogical tree.

It may be right not only to think of the branches of the tree as spreading but to think of the ancestors on it spreading out through the country and through society. Even if the chance of mobility at any one generation is small, over many generations it can add up to a lot of movement. Furthermore, evidence is coming to light that geographical mobility may not have been infrequent, even in rural villages centuries ago. Chapter 2 of

Laslett (1977) contains interesting material along these lines. Immigration and emigration do complicate matters, and we shall restrict our treatment of ancestors to the case of an English person of wholly English ancestry. For such a person, we shall assume that over the span of time back to 1500 ancestors diffuse through most regions of the country and most social classes. This assumption may be wrong, but it is a good one for a first attack.

In our model we measure time in generations, each generation lasting 30 years. This is a handy figure. It would be elementary to change our calculations to allow for some change in the span of a generation as we go back in time, if we could agree on some account of how the span has changed. More effort would be involved in allowing for random spans of generation, letting the same person appear not only at different positions in the genealogical tree but at different levels. Such duplications between levels imply marriages between distant cousins "several times removed," as the phrase goes in some dialects. These certainly occur, although it is not obvious that the total number of distant cousin marriages is much altered by letting some of them occur between cousins several times removed.

For times when the number of ancestors is large enough for a random model of "parent choice" to be appropriate, we formulate our model in the following way: Consider $m(g)$ distinct males and $f(g)$ distinct females in the tree at the g-th generation back. At generation $g + 1$ we have $x(g + 1)$ males and $y(g + 1)$ females from whom the parents of these people must be drawn. Think of distributing $m(g) + f(g)$ "fatherhood markers" among the $x(g + 1)$ males, just as we might distribute $m + f$ balls among x bins. More than one ball may go into the same bin. The first ball may land in any of x bins, the second again in any of x bins, and so there are $x^m x^f$ possible combinations of balls in bins or fatherhood markers on eligible males. If we distribute balls among bins at random, giving each of the $x^m x^f$ combinations an equal chance, the probability of obtaining exactly u nonempty bins, or exactly u distinct fathers, is given by a formula on pages 60 and 102 of Feller (1968), namely

$$\frac{x!}{u!(x - u)!} \sum_{k=0}^{u} \frac{(-1)^k u!(u - k)^{m+f}}{k!(u - k)!x^{m+f}}$$

This is the probability that $m(g + 1)$ be equal to u given $m(g)$ and $f(g)$ in our model, in other words, the probability of having exactly u distinct male ancestors at the next generation back. The same formula applies to motherhood markers and female ancestors.

For this probability distribution the mean of u equals the expression

$$x - x(1 - 1/x)^{m + f}$$

Using exp $[z]$ to stand for the constant e raised to the z-th power, the quantity $x\{1 - \exp[(-m -f)/x]\}$ is an excellent approximation to this mean when x is large. Thus, given $m(g)$ and $f(g)$, the expectations of $m(g + 1)$ and $f(g + 1)$ are the following functions of the sizes $x(g + 1)$ and $y(g + 1)$ of the pools of eligible fathers and mothers:

$$Em(g + 1) = x(g + 1)\{1 - \exp[(-m(g) - f(g))/x\ (g + 1)]\},$$
$$Ef(g + 1) = y(g + 1)\{1 - \exp[(-m(g) - f(g))/y\ (g + 1)]\}.$$

Under the model just cited for $m + f$ balls in x bins, the number of empty bins $x - u$ has an approximately Poisson probability distribution when $m + f$ and x are large. Its variance is therefore close to its mean. Its standard deviation, being close to the square root of its mean, is very small relative to the mean, less than one thousandth of the mean for x in the millions, the range of values of x that we shall have. Thus for our purposes it is fair to identify the random variables $m(g)$ and $f(g)$ with their mean values. Then assuming a sex ratio close to 1.00 for the sizes of the pools $x(g)$ and $y(g)$, we have approximate equality at every generation between the number of distinct male ancestors $m(g)$ and the number of distinct female ancestors $f(g)$, and we may replace $m(g) + f(g)$ by $2m(g)$ and write our recurrence equation in the form

$$m(g + 1)/x(g + 1) = 1 - \exp[-2(m(g)/x(g)) \cdot (x(g)/x(g + 1))]$$

The quantity $m(g)/x(g)$ is the proportion that actual ancestors form out of the pool of those eligible to be ancestors at the g-th generation. The equation expresses this proportion as a function of its previous value and of the growth rate $x(g + 1)/x(g)$ of the pool.

We might be concerned that the probability distribution from Feller puts no constraints on the ratio of children $m(g) + f(g)$ to parents $m(g + 1) + f(g + 1)$. Our model might be unrealistic in producing arbitrarily large family sizes. It is a relief to notice, therefore, that the small standard deviation relative to the mean insures us that the probability of ratios out of line with the growth rate of the pool itself is negligible. Were we not using total population or some other pool that grew primarily by natural increase, the average family size in the model might stray from the plausible range.

We have now formulated our model for the effects of distant cousin marriage. We still need some assumptions about the effects of close cousin marriage. In the absence of better information on this subject, the author has consulted his own family tree researched by his mother. The first place where two slots are filled by the same person occurs six generations back, where a man named Ebenezer appears twice, being the grandfather of both Tabitha and Thomas Bishop, who are man and wife. Each of Ebenezer's parents of course then occurs twice, so there are only $2^6 - 1$ or 63 distinct males and $2^6 - 1$ or 63 distinct females, making $2^7 - 2$ = 126 distinct people at the seventh generation due to this close cousin marriage. Whether two duplications after a stretch of six generations back from the first are too many or too few is hard to say. Other duplications occur further back in this tree. Pending better evidence, we shall allow 63 instead of 64 male ancestors at the seventh generation, and again allow 63 instead of 64 distinct male ancestors for each of these 63 males back another six generations to the thirteenth. We do the same for females. These are our fixed allowances for close cousin marriage. Beyond the thirteenth generation back, the total number of ancestors is large enough that the number of duplications predicted by the random model for distant cousin marriage eclipses these adjustments. We shift to the random model at $g = 13$ with $m(g) = 63 \cdot 63 = 3969$ and $f(g) = 63 \cdot 63 = 3969$, proceeding on from there.

We begin our calculations with a child born in England of wholly English ancestry around 1947 who reaches the age of 30 in 1977. We trace the values of $m(g)$ back at intervals of 30 years. Assuming wide diffusion of ancestors throughout the society and the country by 1600, we take $x(g) + y(g)$ to be the total population of England for all earlier years. If desired, these values could be reduced by guesses at the numbers of infertile men and women, members of religious orders, and others not eligible to be the parents of each generation. Since there is wide uncertainty in the total population figures themselves, such guesses are not likely to improve our answers very much. We might consider taking the adult population at each 30-year interval instead of the total population. Taking total population, however, gives some leeway for the differing ages of marriage and childbirth among different members of the family tree.

In order to carry out our exercise, we need guesses at the population of England in medieval times. Unfortunately, all such guesses are speculative. We have taken values back to 1230 from the graph on page 386 and the remarks on page 387 of Hollingsworth (1969) and for dates before that we have interpolated between estimates of Josiah Russell (1948). The most accurate estimates pertain to 1377 and 1347. Although we should not trust any of the figures too far, they suffice for our purposes.

The results of our calculations appear in Exhibit 9.1. The last column shows the generation g. The first column shows an average date when the ancestors in this generation are reaching the age of 30, and the second

EXHIBIT 9.1.   Predictions of Numbers of Distinct Ancestors at Each Generation

Date	$x(g) + y(g)$	$m(g) + f(g)$	$m(g)/x(g)$	$x(g + 1)/x(g)$	2^g	g
1947	—	2	—	—	2	1
1587	3,500,000	7,938	.0022	.829	8,192	13
1557	2,900,000	15,833	.0054	.759	16,384	14
1527	2,200,000	31,438	.0142	.773	32,768	15
1497	1,700,000	61,728	.0363	.765	65,536	16
1467	1,300,000	117,776	.0905	.923	131,072	17
1437	1,200,000	213,874	.1782	1.167	262,144	18
1407	1,400,000	368,579	.2632	1.607	524,288	19
1377	2,250,000	628,576	.2793	1.622	1,048,576	20
1347	3,650,000	1,063,510	.2913	.877	2,097,152	21
1317	3,200,000	1,553,820	.4855	.906	4,194,304	22
1287	2,900,000	1,906,866	.6575	.931	8,388,608	23
1257	2,700,000	2,042,455	.7564	.926	16,777,216	24
1227	2,500,000	2,012,114	.8048	.800	33,554,432	25
1197	2,000,000	1,732,588	.8662	.850	67,108,864	26
1167	1,700,000	1,478,584	.8697	.824	134,217,728	27
1137	1,400,000	1,230,650	.8790	.929	268,435,456	28
1107	1,300,000	1,104,255	.8494	.846	536,870,912	29
1077	1,100,000	952,279	.8657	—	1,073,741,824	30

column shows our guess at the total English population $x(g) + y(g)$ at this year. The third column shows our estimate of the number of distinct ancestors $m(g) + f(g) = 2m(g)$. The proportion of ancestors in the pool, $m(g)/x(g)$, occupies the fourth column and the rate of growth of the pool, $x(g + 1)/x(g)$ the fifth column. Raising e to the power given by minus twice the fourth column divided by the fifth column and subtracting the result from unity gives the entry in the next row in the fourth column. In this way, given the population figures, we generate the next row of the table from the preceding row. The seventh column shows 2^g, the total number of distinct slots in the family tree.

The outcomes of our model are intriguing. Around the discovery of America, our individual has more than 60,000 distinct ancestors. Some 95% of the slots in the family tree at this level are still filled by different people. But back as far as the time of Wycliffe and the Peasants' Revolt, at the twentieth generation, the number of distinct ancestors has grown beyond 600,000, and nearly a third of the slots in the tree are filled by duplicate people. Just before the Black Death, nearly 30% of the 3,650,000 inhabitants of England turn up as ancestors. Moving back through the reign of King John, we find the number of ancestors starting to decline from its high point of around 2 million. Each person in the tree is occupying an average of 16 slots. The effect of distant cousin marriage on the numbers of distinct ancestors is becoming enormous. By then 80% of the population are ancestors of our single individual.

With 80% already ancestors under King John, we might expect that the whole population would be turning up as ancestors a few generations further back. Surprisingly, the proportion in the fourth column of our table never rises to 100%. In fact, it oscillates around 85% for all the generations of Plantagenet and Norman kings. Our individual is likely to be descended from only about 85% of the population at the Norman Conquest. The relatively constant proportion around 85% is a kind of equilibrium level, built into our formulas for $m(g)$. The numbers of distinct ancestors get smaller as the population gets smaller. But the proportion around 85%, once achieved, persists as we go back in time, in spite of the changes in population size and the perpetual rule of two parents for each child.

Thus our model leads us to imagine the population of Domesday England divided into two groups, the ancestors and the nonancestors of our individual. Five-sixths of the population are relations, one-sixth are of no particular kin. Of course the relations are not some identifiable group of the population like the Saxons or the husbandmen and servants. The assumptions of our model imply that the group is a random sample out of the whole population. Some other breakdown between five-sixths and one-sixth of the population is defined by the ancestry of any other English person. It seems likely that if people are not siblings or bilateral cross cousins, the groups they define are almost certain to be different, although we have not proved this result in our model. Far enough back in time, when the population is very small, it must start to be common for ancestor groups to coincide.

We have framed our discussion in terms of England and a person of English ancestry back to the Norman Conquest. The methods we have developed, of course, can be applied to the ancestors of other nations and races, so far as an identifiable pool of potential ancestors can be determined. It is strange to think of ourselves within our population today as divided into two groups insofar as we are or are not the ancestors of some specific unknown person in the distant future. It is also strange to think of the links which tie each of us by descent to most but not all of the population of our country of origin in the far past, to a group special in no way except in having one of us as their common descendant. Each link between parent and child is intimate and full of emotional associations, and only 30 such links back in time bring us to each ancestor at the Norman Conquest. Yet, these ancestors together, a random five-sixths of the population, seem almost beyond picturing. Each of us is connected to the historical past in many ways—through the language we speak, the changed face of the earth around us, the institutions we act within, our store of knowledge, images, emotions, and preconceptions. The "ties of blood," that is, of genes and lineal descent, in some sense the most real of all connections, are also the most mystical. Always hard to grasp imaginatively, they become still more elusive when a statistical element enters, when they connect us with millions of people, a part of a whole population that we can count but not identify. Our exercise in modelling numbers of ancestors opens the way to piquant speculations.

10

Living Forbears in Stable Populations[1]

Demography, by electing to employ certain concepts, gives them precedence over others. It pays attention to the evolution of populations and to their equilibria. Individuals are nothing but atoms inside gigantic molecules—"populations." The activities of individuals are stripped of all meaning except their meaning for "populations"—fertility, nuptiality, mortality.

But, to pursue the analogy, the atoms of these molecules are not chaotic. They do not wander at random, like the molecules of a pure gas. Not only do they belong to different types (ages, sexes, or socioeconomic groups), but there are quite precise links between these atoms, links between children and parents, ancestors and descendents, cousins, spouses—in one word, kinship. It is interesting to go behind the classical view of the molecule and the basic units that compose it, and add to it a structural view, a description of the links that bind together the atoms, a statistical mechanics of their positions vis-à-vis each other. How many cousins? How many orphans? How many grandparents and grandchil-

[1] This chapter was translated with revisions from the French article "Parents, Grandparents, Bisaieux" by Hervé LeBras in *Population*, January 1973, Volume 28, pages 9–37, by Kenneth W. Wachter in consultation with the author.

dren? To answer these questions is to describe the family in the broad sense, to touch on a region of demography that is perceived and lived through by each of us.

It is out of the question to try to describe in a single article all of the demography of these links and we shall be content here to study vertical links, links which unite children with their parents, grandparents, and great grandparents. First of all, using the demographic rates of present-day France, we shall ask, for each age group, how many will have lost either their father or their mother or both, and then carry our analysis on to grandparents and great grandparents. Our results have many ramifications—social ones in the study of orphans; economic ones, for orphans are holders of patrimony; psychological ones, pertaining to the roles of parents and grandparents and the impact of the experience of their deaths.

But the "family of forbears" depends on the demographic conditions of today. Different demographic regimes entail other types of families. To suggest the variety of possibilities, we consider two very different populations: that of contemporary Venezuela, with fairly weak mortality and high fertility, and that of France in the 1750s, where the fertility and mortality were high. In conclusion, we then set our findings on living forbears in the context of the age pyramids of the three societies studied, to better assess the relative importance of the different situations, not only at a single age but within the entire population.

A. THE DEATH OF PARENTS IN PRESENT-DAY FRANCE

In order to calculate who has a living father or mother and at what age he loses one or the other, we make a number of assumptions. In particular, we need to work within the assumptions of stable population theory. The results are not exact empirical results for France in 1972, but are results that would be observed in the long run on the average if the present-day fertility and mortality rates continued for several decades. Happily, the results are most sensitive to the mortality rates, which may be expected to remain fairly stable at present levels, and to the growth rate, which also is likely to remain near its present small level.

In any case, since we go on to study France in the 1750s, we have two extremes between which the real cases should fall, and the case we are about to describe can be mildly revised in the light of the next one we shall treat.

Method

Taking an infant at birth, we can calculate the probability that his mother is of any given age, depending on the general fertility $f(x)$ and the size $P(x)$ of the cohort of women aged x. In a stable population with growth rate r and probability $S(x)$ of surviving to age x

$$P(x) = P(0)S(x) \exp(-rx)$$

By a result of Lotka we may write the number of mothers giving birth at a given instant as

$$\int_{15}^{50} S(x)f(x)P(0) \exp(-rx) \, dx = P(0)$$

The probability density of the age x of mothers of newly-born infants is therefore

$$A(x) = P(x)f(x)/P(0) = S(x)f(x) \exp(-rx)$$

In order to derive the ages of fathers, we might proceed in the same way, using a table of masculine fertility, but that would be to assume independence between the ages of father and mother. It is therefore preferable to obtain the ages of fathers from the ages of mothers by using a two-way table of father's age given mother's age. To compile such a table is a reasonably complex task, which we summarize here.

We take a three-way table of feminine nuptiality by age at marriage and fertility. In a contracepting (Malthusian) population like modern France, we take account of the fertility by age at marriage. In the case of a population subject to high mortality, we take account of the differential mortality of men and women. Since errors may accumulate from the many operations performed, we fit each conditional distribution of fathers' ages by a curve of the form $T[(y - a)^b \exp[-(y - a)c]$, where $a, b,$ and c are least-squares estimates derived by simulation. We then check the sensitivity of the outcomes when we vary b and c, holding the parameter a constant. The sensitivity turns out to be very low, so that the imprecision of the table is not a dominant factor.

Having the table of fathers' ages, we are left to calculate ages at death for fathers and mothers. We adopt tables of recent male and female mortality, admitting that the concomitant assumption of independence between the death dates of the two parents is not entirely tenable here and is still less tenable for France in the past era of crises, catastrophes, and epidemics.

We may now put all the ingredients into the melting pot to obtain the age of children at the deaths of each of their parents. Call $S_M(y)$ and $S_F(x)$

the probabilities of survival for males and females and $q_M(y)$ and $q_F(x)$ the corresponding mortality rates. The probability of a child losing his mother at age u and his father at age v has a probability density $B(u, v)$ equal to

$$A(x)q_F(x + u)[S_F(x + u)/S_F(x)]q_M(y + v)$$
$$\times [S_M(y + v)/S_M(y)]T(x, y) \, dx \, dy,$$

where $T(x, y)$ is the conditional probability density of the age y of fathers given the age x of mothers, satisfying $\int T(x, y) \, dy = 1$ for all x. The preceding expression is already formidable and a similar expression for grandparents would contain a sextuple integral.

Since triple integrals and higher order integrals call for evaluation by simulation in any case, it is reasonable to introduce simulation at the level of the phenomena themselves rather than at the level of integral evaluation. Accordingly, we take 10,000 individuals one after the other and draw at random ages for their mothers and fathers and for their mothers' and fathers' deaths, following the probability laws A, T, S_F, and S_M.

The schedule of fertility rates from France in 1962 which we have used peaks at a level of .171 at age 26, rising steeply from .035 at age 18 through .105 at age 20 and declining more slowly through .085 at age 35, and .035 at age 40 to reach zero at age 50. The survival functions from France in 1968 are very nearly linear until the age of 50 for both males and females with slopes about $-.0080$ and $-.0076$ per year, respectively. Male survivorship then drops much more rapidly to about 13% at age 80 while female survivorship is around 20% at that age. The conditional distributions of ages of fathers given age of mothers are gamma distributions as we have said. For mothers aged 20 the conditional distribution peaks at age 22; for mothers aged 30, around age 35.

Age at Parents' Death

On Exhibit 10.1 the curve labeled 1 indicates the probability that a child age x has lost its mother. That probability is greater than 50% down to age 50. It is no surprise that the median age of offspring at their mother's death is around 50, since that age must be close to the difference between the average lifespan of mothers and their average age at childbirth.

Curve 2 on Exhibit 10.1 shows the probability of the father having died. It rises much earlier than that for the mother and reaches 50% at offspring's age of 40. Thirteen percent of children are still minors at their father's death; 20% are as old as 52 and 5% as old as 62.

The remarkable differences between ages at father's and at mother's

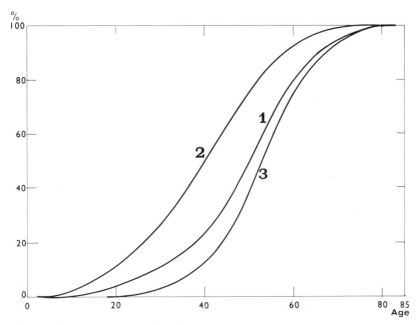

EXHIBIT 10.1.   Proportion of children of each age without parents. (Curve 1 = without mothers, curve 2 = without fathers, and curve 3 = without either parent.)

death are easily explained. The excess of male over female mortality is very high in France. Furthermore, fathers are older on average than mothers and reach ages of severe mortality more quickly, so that we find mothers still young matched with fathers already aged, but not the reverse.

Curve 3 on Exhibit 10.1 in a sense summarizes curves 1 and 2. It gives, according to age, the proportion of individuals with neither father nor mother living. Thus it gives the proportion of orphans in each age span. This curve is not the product of curves 1 and 2, since death dates of fathers are tied to death dates of mothers through the joint distribution of ages at marriage. The curve is quite remarkable. Less than 1% become orphans as minors. Orphanhood, so common in novels, turns out rare in reality. The 20% mark for orphanhood is not reached until the age of 43. The median is 55. After that point, proportions rise rapidly, coming to coincide with proportions having lost their mothers.

To complete our description, Exhibit 10.2 shows the distribution of all deaths, whether of father or mother, by age of offspring. The deaths peak between 30 and 60. The curve is asymmetrical, rising regularly from birth, falling abruptly after 60 years.

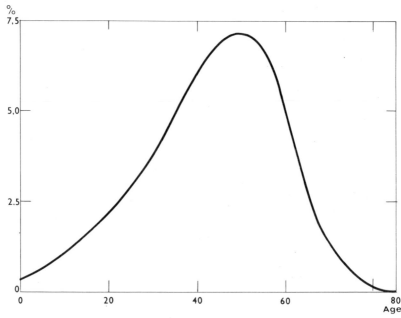

EXHIBIT 10.2.   Density of parental deaths by age of child.

If we wanted to portray a typical, better, a dominant, situation for offspring and their direct forbears, we would say

1. That an individual loses his or her father between 30 and 50; his or her mother between 40 and 60.
2. That at age 55 one out of two individuals has lost both father and mother, at an age, in other words, close to the end of active life. At that age undoubtedly the experience of loss has less impact on his life course, serving as a prelude not to maturity, but to old age itself.

By the same token, in the many callings in commerce and agriculture where a son succeeds his father, he only does so after age 40 in one case out of two. Rural exodus and stagnation of commerce and crafts might find an explanation here. Refusing long paternal tutelage, more dynamic individuals might have migrated to other callings, exacerbating by negative selection the aging of their fathers' professions.

Conversely, the problem of orphanage scarcely arises and the state can afford to treat orphans generously without emptying its coffers, for orphans form a tiny part of the population under 21 years old.

Instead, problems of patrimony, generational succession, and the accumulation of wealth rear their heads, in a form which further study of forbears including grandparents and great grandparents will make more precise.

B. GRANDPARENTS AND GREAT GRANDPARENTS

The study of grandparents poses no technical problems different from the study of parents. Grandparents are treated as the parents of parents, the same simulations being applied to them. The largest difference is a qualitative one, namely, that while two parents pose only four possibilities, presence or absence of each of them, adding grandparents lets us consider as many as 64 configurations; each of the four grandparents and two parents may be there or not. During an individual's life, one or the other of these 64 cases will be dominant. Let us begin by treating grandparents in the same terms as parents.

Death of Grandparents

One may read off of Exhibit 10.3 the frequency of absence of each grandparent as it varies with the age of the grandchild. The order of the

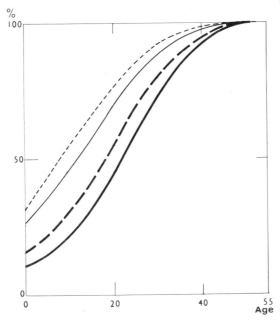

EXHIBIT 10.3.   Proportion of grandparents deceased by age of grandchild. Light dashed line indicates father's father, light solid line indicates mother's father, heavy dashed line indicates father's mother, and heavy solid line indicates mother's mother.

curves is easily anticipated. In order of decreasing survivorship, we have mother's mother MM, father's mother FM, mother's father MF, and father's father FF. Mean ages of a grandchild at the death of each grandparent separately are 9 (FF), 12 (MF), 18 (FM), and 21.3 (MM). These figures are less what we might expect than those for parents. It is especially noteworthy that half the individuals still have a living mother's mother at age 21, and 89% have one at birth. Going a step further, the decease of at least one grandparent is experienced by practically every child, and is undoubtedly for the overwhelming majority the first encounter with the death of someone close to them.

Exhibit 10.4 represents the frequency of death of a grandparent of any type by the age of the grandchild. These deaths peak between ages 15 and 20, and only at age 35 do they become fewer than parental deaths. More than 95% see one of their grandparents die after the age of 5 and before the death of either of their parents.

Thus grandparents are eminently present in childhood. Exhibit 10.5 makes the picture clearer. From bottom to top we see on four curves the proportions in each age group without living grandparents, with at most one, two, and three. The complement of the top curve shows the propor-

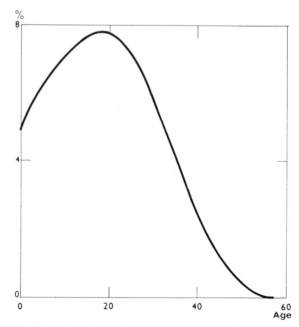

EXHIBIT 10.4.   Density of all grandparental deaths by age of grandchild.

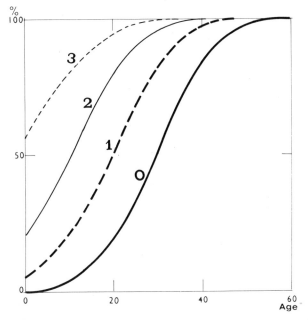

EXHIBIT 10.5.   Proportion of grandchildren with, at most, N grandparents (for N = 0, . . .
N = 3), by age.

tion with a full four living grandparents, amounting to 42% at birth. At
birth, only 1% have no grandparents. At age 20, half have at least two
grandparents left. One must wait 30 years before as many as half have no
grandparent. The presence of grandparents is thus the dominant condition of childhood. Until the age of 17 one out of two children has at least
one intact grandparental couple. He has a continuing frame of reference
for his own relation to his parents in the relation of one or the other of his
parents to their own parents. The relative permanence of grandparents
permits them to play the role of "parents à plaisanterie" in primitive
populations—a position charged with emotion free of authority,
foreshadowing the relationship of friendship. Finally, the role of grandparents helping and complementing parents in the education of children is
likely to increase in proportion to their permanence.

Thus in an epoch where the dissolution of the family is a byword,
demographic factors, on the contrary, reinforce the family nexus. They
promote the smooth overlapping of successive family nuclei. The conflict
between generations, between parents and their children, takes place
under the eyes of witnesses, the grandparents.

Dominant Situations

As we have already indicated, we can specify our description a bit further by considering, for each age, which of the 64 types of families prevails. Exhibit 10.6 represents the breakdown of individuals among the 64 types at four stages, birth, age 10, age 21, and age 30. Each cell corresponds to a family configuration; the numbers in the cells add to a full cohort of 10,000 persons for each age of child. The labels on the columns show which parents (F and/or M) are living and the labels on the rows show which grandparents are living.

Let us trace, age by age, the dominant types. At birth 41% have four grandparents and two parents, while 28% have lost one grandparent. The other cases are negligible. By age 10, 42% are still in one of the two preceding large categories, but 10% have lost both grandfathers, 7% have lost both their father's parents, 7% have no one left but their parents and their mother's mother, 2.7% have no intact couple left among their forbears.

At age 15 (not shown in any table), five situations each account for 10% of all cases: a complete set, a set missing only the father's father, missing both grandparents, containing only parents and mother's mother, and containing only parents. Three situations represent between 5% and 8% each: a set missing only father's mother, missing father's parents, or containing only parents and mother's mother.

No situation dominates the cases for the twenty-first birthday. The most important all include both living parents, along with no grandparents (17%), or only the mother's mother (12%) or only the father's mother (7%), or only the mother's parents (8%) or only grandmothers (8%). Other situations make up 50%, but the absence of all forbears comes to only 0.5%, while all parentless orphans are 1%.

By age 30, a single situation once again dominates. Thirty-one percent have no one but their parents left. Only two other situations are worth mention. Seventeen percent have only their mother; 10% have both parents and their mother's mother.

Thus from birth to the age of 30 one passes from one dominant situation of a complete set of parents and grandparents to another dominant situation, with only parents remaining. But 30 is the mean age of parents at the birth of their children. The generations truly overlap. Nothing could be more natural: While children have their grandparents, their parents have their parents. However, the quantitative importance of these two boundary cases and their near-perfect simultaneity is striking.

We also note that since at age 30 half of the population has at least one grandparent, their children will have at least one great-grandparent.

EXHIBIT 10.6. For Present-Day France, Frequency in 10,000 Cases of Each of 64 Configurations
(Margins List Relatives Living for Each Cell; MF = Mother's Father, etc.)

	At Birth				At Age 10				At Age 21				At Age 30			
	M,F	M	F	*	M,F	M	F	*	M,F	M	F	*	M,F	M	F	*
MM FM MF FF	4111	4	7	0	1794	52	21	0	310	28	9	1	27	6	3	0
MM FM MF —	1553	5	3	0	1341	35	19	0	535	41	19	3	109	15	6	2
MM FM — FF	1214	4	2	0	1119	30	11	0	479	37	15	0	100	10	7	1
MM — MF FF	504	1	3	0	427	13	4	0	150	15	6	1	36	3	2	0
— FM MF FF	385	1	0	0	339	14	1	0	161	19	3	1	31	5	1	0
MM FM — —	577	1	1	0	961	34	12	1	811	86	39	4	369	68	25	7
MM — MF —	418	2	3	0	678	28	12	0	668	81	22	1	260	72	9	4
MM — — FF	162	1	0	0	262	10	4	1	206	26	12	2	82	21	7	0
— FM MF —	194	0	0	0	259	12	3	0	222	27	14	1	101	21	9	3
— FM — FF	220	2	0	0	373	20	6	1	355	37	14	1	184	31	11	2
— — MF FF	52	0	0	0	88	5	1	0	71	10	4	2	31	9	3	1
MM — — —	222	2	1	0	647	47	18	0	1167	203	51	13	1001	316	85	32
— FM — —	146	4	0	0	447	19	9	0	793	109	56	11	684	162	66	20
— — MF —	62	1	0	0	195	15	5	1	337	58	15	5	265	84	25	16
— — — FF	39	0	0	0	17	3	5	1	243	46	14	2	203	55	19	9
— — — —	92	1	0	0	415	53	10	2	1724	441	117	46	3107	1451	408	298

Great Grandparents

On Exhibit 10.7 we have drawn four curves. The bottom one indicates the proportion of individuals, according to their age, having no living great grandparent; the next, those having at most one; the next, at most two; and the top, at most three. At birth 64% have at least one great grandparent; 12% have at least four. To have one or more living great grandparents is thus the normal condition for a new-born child, but that situation lasts only briefly. More than half of the 6-year-olds have no living great grandparents, and a paltry 8% of all 21-year-olds have one. Thus the deaths of great grandparents are concentrated in early childhood and prevent them from playing an important role in the family. On average, each child who lives out his three-score years and ten witnesses the deaths of 1.5 great grandparents, compared with 3.2 grandparental deaths.

These figures illustrate once more the point of the preceding section. The third generation completes its exit from the scene at the moment when its great grandchildren make their entrances. This overlapping of generations has an important effect upon inheritance and so upon possession of patrimony.

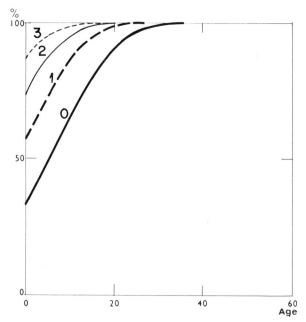

EXHIBIT 10.7. Proportion of great grandchildren, by age, with, at most, N living great-grandparents (for N = 0, . . . N = 3).

Age at Inheritance

Laws governing inheritance are extremely complex. The part of an estate inherited is difficult to distinguish from the part acquired, and no sure statistics exist on these subjects. But there are some points that help us frame an opinion about the ages that heirs are likely to be. We can be certain in the first place that anyone without living forbears of any degree whatsoever must have already inherited. Thus, we may cast one extreme case in the following terms: Due to bequests between spouses, the only inheritors are those who have lost at least the whole paternal or maternal line and have lost the parent in that line before the last of the grandparents.

The opposite extreme puts inheritance always in the descending line. There is a cascading effect. We assign to each grandparent an equal fortune, which he or she transmits to the parents upon death and which the parents transmit to the children. If a parent died before his or her parents, inheritance passes directly to the children.

These two extreme situations which we wish to describe can be reconstructed with the help of the distributions on the preceding pages. The problem of collateral inheritance, however, remains untouched. We are not able to treat it with our methods, but we claim that it does not alter our results at all. It only concerns people who have already inherited, who are therefore advanced in years, who die without descendants. Their collateral relatives are also advanced in years, and, if they are already deceased, the inheritance passes on to their descendants who have already inherited and so are to be found in our distributions.

The proportions of individuals in one or the other of the two situations to which we restrict ourselves may be found in Exhibit 10.8. For bequests between spouses, the median age of inheritance is 53. (These are net ages, like those for the other distributions, in the sense that we assume the children survive their forbears.) In the most favorable case of succession in a line of descent, the median age, the age at which half the patrimony has been inherited, falls around 46 years. At 21 years, 0.5% of individuals have inherited in the first manner and 7% in the second. At age 30, 4% and 17%, at age 60, 68% and 85%. Whatever the manner of inheritance—and the real case falls in between the two extremes which we describe—we conclude that heirs inherit at ages between 45 and 55. These are ages of full adulthood by which one's position in life is settled and sealed. They are ages at which one typically may have one's own family of teenagers and young adults. Thus, inheritors may find their inheritances often serving mainly to establish their children rather than to consolidate their own position. Use of inheritance jumps a generation.

These points deserve careful attention, for they have an impact both on

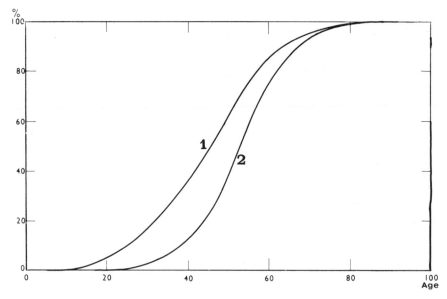

EXHIBIT 10.8.   Proportion at each age of inheritors by modes 1 and 2.

private lives and on public finances. Primarily, recall how far into adult-hood are inheritors and how old, therefore, the possessors of patrimony must be. Certainly there is also income and individuals accumulate pat-rimony themselves, but the amount accumulated is often proportional to their initial fortune.

Finally, leaving economics for psychology, we see that inheritors under the first mode of inheritance we have considered coincide almost exactly with terminal branches of the tree of living forbears. They are those without living ancestors themselves, those on the top line, so to speak, face to face with death. Their move to the top line occurs a dozen years before retirement at the start of grandparenthood.

In summary, we may describe an ideal average type who has at birth parents, grandparents, and a couple of great grandparents who die during his early childhood. His grandparents die during his adolescence and at the start of his working life. He still has his parents as he starts his own family. He loses them between 40 and 55. Inheriting, he establishes his children and between 50 and 65 is bereft of forbears. His grandchildren are born; he retires. His wife at least is likely to have the pleasure of surviving the births of great grandchildren before her death.

Of course this ideal type does not exist or at least not yet exist. It is based on the idea that fertility, mortality, and marriage rates which prevail today will continue to prevail for many years. What would happen if rates changed? What would happen in countries with other demographic rates or at other epochs? To these questions we now turn.

C. FORBEARS IN OTHER EPOCHS AND PLACES

We consider two examples, Venezuela in 1960 and France in the second half of the 1700s. For Venezuela age-specific fertility and mortality rates by sex and 5-year age groups are available. We convert them to yearly rates. However, a two-way table giving ages of fathers conditional on ages of mothers was impossible to obtain. Since varying that table appears to have little impact on the results, we keep the table discussed in the previous section. We check it by comparing the paternal fertility rates it entails against reported yearbook rates. Fortunately, the match is satisfactory.

For France in the 1750s we lift the fertility rates from Ganiage's (1963) monograph on three villages of the Isle de France. We use mortality rates from the model life tables of Ledermann (1969), Reseau 100, with expectation of life at birth of the combined sexes of 30. The table of father's by mother's ages is again impossible to calculate. We again keep the original table, but we have increased the variance of the conditional distributions of gamma type in order to take account of the greater variability in ages at marriage and especially at remarriage.

The combination of the fertility and mortality rates yield rates of natural increase (à la Lotka) of 3.6% for Venezuela and 0.7% for 1750s France. The growth rate for Venezuela is a bit high but not completely unrealistic. That for 1750s France is reasonable. Venezuela may be characterized as a country where women have early and high fertility, where mortality is already quite mild, and where, consequently, the population is exploding. The historical French case shows high but late fertility and severe mortality, especially at younger ages. For these two types of populations we have calculated all the sorts of tables as for present-day France, although our comments on them will be briefer.

1750s France

On Exhibit 10.9 we see the proportions of children of each age who have both parents living, one, or none. In spite of the high age of mothers at childbirth, the severe mortality, and the low growth rates, these figures are less catastrophic than one would have predicted. Half of the individuals still have their fathers at age 27. Half have their mothers at age 32. More than half have both parents up to age 18. Thus, not until age 21

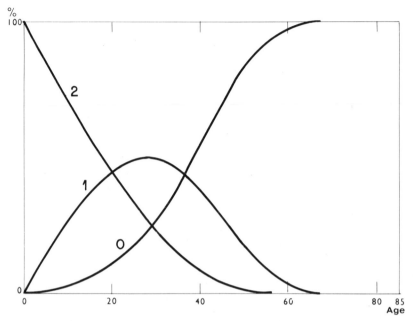

EXHIBIT 10.9.   Proportions at each age with 0,1, or 2 living parents, for 1750s France.

are there as many as 13% orphans. The popular notion that a son would immediately succeed his father is untenable. At age 21, 62% still have living fathers.

It might seem paradoxical that these figures accompany an expectation of life as low as 30, but the fault lies with expectation of life as an index of mortality, extremely sensitive as it is to mortality at the earliest ages. If mortality is high at these ages, it can be proportionately lower at adult ages than in a present-day life table. Since parents are dying largely with children between 25 and 35, one might still think that it is rare for children to have living grandparents. But Exhibit 10.10 showing from top to bottom proportions by age with none, one, two, and three or four living grandparents, again contradicts expectation. Only 16% have no grandparent at birth, and 5% have all four. At age 10, 38% have none; only by age 21 does this figure grow to 73%. Thus it must have been customary for a youth in his prime to have one or several grandparents. On average he would see the deaths of 1.65 grandparents. And these grandparents would often not have lost their spouses. At birth 42% of children would have had an intact grandparental couple. As children grew, these couples would be broken up but on the whole the grandparents would have been, potentially, more visible than the great grandparents today.

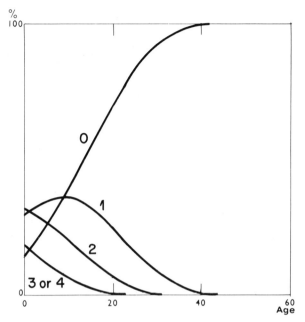

EXHIBIT 10.10. Proportions at each age with 0, 1, 2, or 3 or 4 living grandparents, for 1750s France.

Since children are born at the point where grandparental couples are beginning to disappear, there is no progression of dominant situations in Exhibit 10.11 comparable to those for present-day France in Exhibit 10.6. The most frequent situation at birth is to have parents only. From age 10 on, that condition dominates more clearly with 26%. Families comprising parents plus a single grandmother grow to 15%. At age 21, 30% have only their parents, 12% have only their mother, 9% only their father, and 12% both their parents and a single grandmother. The most widespread and stable situation is thus that of the first-degree family. One generation is succeeded by the following one, without the generational overlapping on which we have commented for modern France.

Another difference between earlier and modern France is the better apportioning of widowhood between the sexes. Whatever their ages, today there are never as many as 10% individuals with a widowed father. In 1750s France that proportion could reach 19%.

The presence of grandparents, however ephemeral, reinforces the family nexus. At age 5, two-thirds of all orphans (without fathers and mothers) have grandparents. At age 10 the figure is 60%, at age 15, 36%. Had we also studied sibling sets, we would surely have found the pro-

EXHIBIT 10.11. For 1750s France, Frequency in 10,000 Cases of Each of 64 Configurations

	At Birth				At Age 10				At Age 21				At Age 30			
	M,F	M	F	*	M,F	M	F	*	M,F	M	F	*	M,F	M	F	*
MM FM MF FF	482	5	6	0	72	10	12	1	4	4	2	0	0	0	0	0
MM FM MF —	560	5	8	0	143	20	28	7	6	6	8	3	0	1	0	1
MM FM — FF	443	5	8	0	135	20	23	0	10	0	6	0	1	1	0	0
MM — MF FF	391	4	4	0	92	20	16	7	6	4	2	0	0	1	0	0
— FM MF FF	310	3	3	0	70	15	7	0	9	2	1	0	1	1	1	0
MM FM — —	705	10	8	0	322	57	51	10	52	30	24	11	2	4	6	0
MM — MF —	776	12	6	0	382	62	49	18	60	34	22	14	6	7	2	4
MM — — FF	415	5	4	0	179	39	33	1	22	11	13	5	3	3	2	2
— FM MF —	443	8	11	1	202	44	39	5	32	15	12	7	3	4	3	1
— FM — FF	454	10	6	0	230	46	45	6	51	18	18	9	0	3	5	7
— — MF FF	288	1	3	0	115	21	19	7	22	13	9	1	3	2	1	1
MM — — —	1099	17	21	0	876	210	164	40	383	200	162	87	85	93	61	61
— FM — —	716	11	8	0	637	127	107	25	269	136	108	48	62	67	48	41
— — MF —	631	13	12	0	553	115	96	20	185	110	94	62	41	46	44	37
— — — FF	483	4	6	0	379	86	73	10	155	70	54	36	31	34	29	21
— — — —	1518	31	27	0	2618	607	467	110	2959	1954	1380	970	1994	2699	1806	2616

portions of completely family-less orphans reduced much further and practically vanishing for the very young.

Our somewhat dry description highlights the stability of the family. No need appears to appeal to collateral relatives to provide for the upbringing of children. Generations succeed each other without breaks. To the extent that demographic conditions in France in the 1750s are not widely different from those of other historical populations, it is tempting to conjecture that the family unit was always, on the average, equal to the upbringing of its children, having recourse to the wider community only for marriage partners and for subsistence. On the other hand, we must bear in mind that the demographic crises characteristic of periods before 1700 might be responsible for a very different story.

Venezuela

Unlike France in the 1750s, modern Venezuela packs no surprise for us. Young mothers and rapid population growth partly counterbalance heavier mortality than in modern France and lead to results close to those of the first section. Exhibit 10.12 shows proportions at each age with both

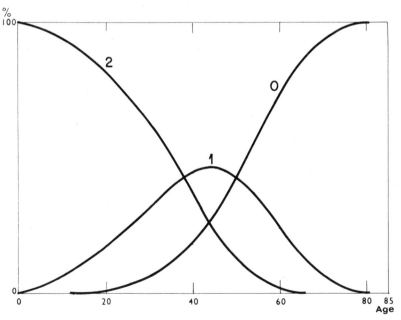

EXHIBIT 10.12. Proportions at each age with 0,1, or 2 living parents, for Venezuela.

parents, one parent, and none. Median ages at the deaths of father and mother are 41 and 47, respectively, compared to 40 and 50 for contemporary France. A much smaller excess male mortality explains the smaller difference between median ages at father's and at mother's death. As regards grandparents, the similarities between Venezuela and France are still more striking. Forty percent of new-born children have all four grandparents, just as in France. The same succession of dominant situations can be observed; the same overlapping of generations.

Contrary to what ill-founded intuition might suggest, fertility plays a small role in the position of a child vis-à-vis his living forbears. One might think that heavy fertility would mean large families and large numbers of late children with aged parents, but the early children born to very young parents redress the balance.

D. MATCHING CASES IN THE AGE PYRAMIDS

Up until now we have studied the life course of an individual, in probabilistic terms, but we have not grouped individuals together into age groups or considered the overall population.

When we take the differing sizes of age groups in the population into account, the ages and frequencies we have been discussing come to depend further on mortality and the rate of natural increase. Taking the three demographic cases with which we have been working, we mark off the proportions with different configurations of living forbears on the age pyramid for the appropriate stable population. While the position of the different groups tallies nicely with our intuition, the parameters which dictate them are much less evident.

Parents, Inheritance, and Fortune

Exhibits 10.13, 10.14, and 10.15 represent for France in 1968, Venezuela in 1960, and France in the 1750s the proportions in a stable age pyramid with both parents living, only mother living, only father living, and both parents deceased. The calculations for the modern French case yield 25% of men without parents, 22% with one parent, and 53% with both parents. The median age of persons without parents is 62, compared with a median age at which an individual loses his second parent equal to 55. Neglecting the grandparents who outlive their children, these people without parents are those who would have inherited their patrimony under the first, most gradual, mode of inheritance considered in the first section. Under the second, more rapid, mode of inheritance, that in the

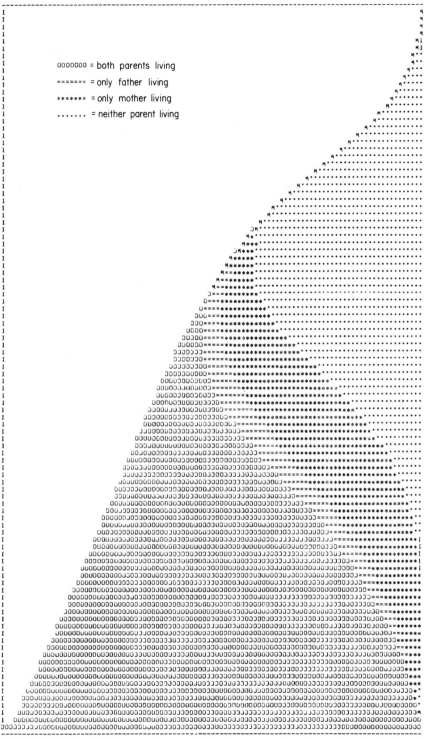

oooooooo = both parents living

======= = only father living

******* = only mother living

······· = neither parent living

EXHIBIT 10.13. Distribution by age of the four parental configurations in the female stable age pyramid for 1970s France.

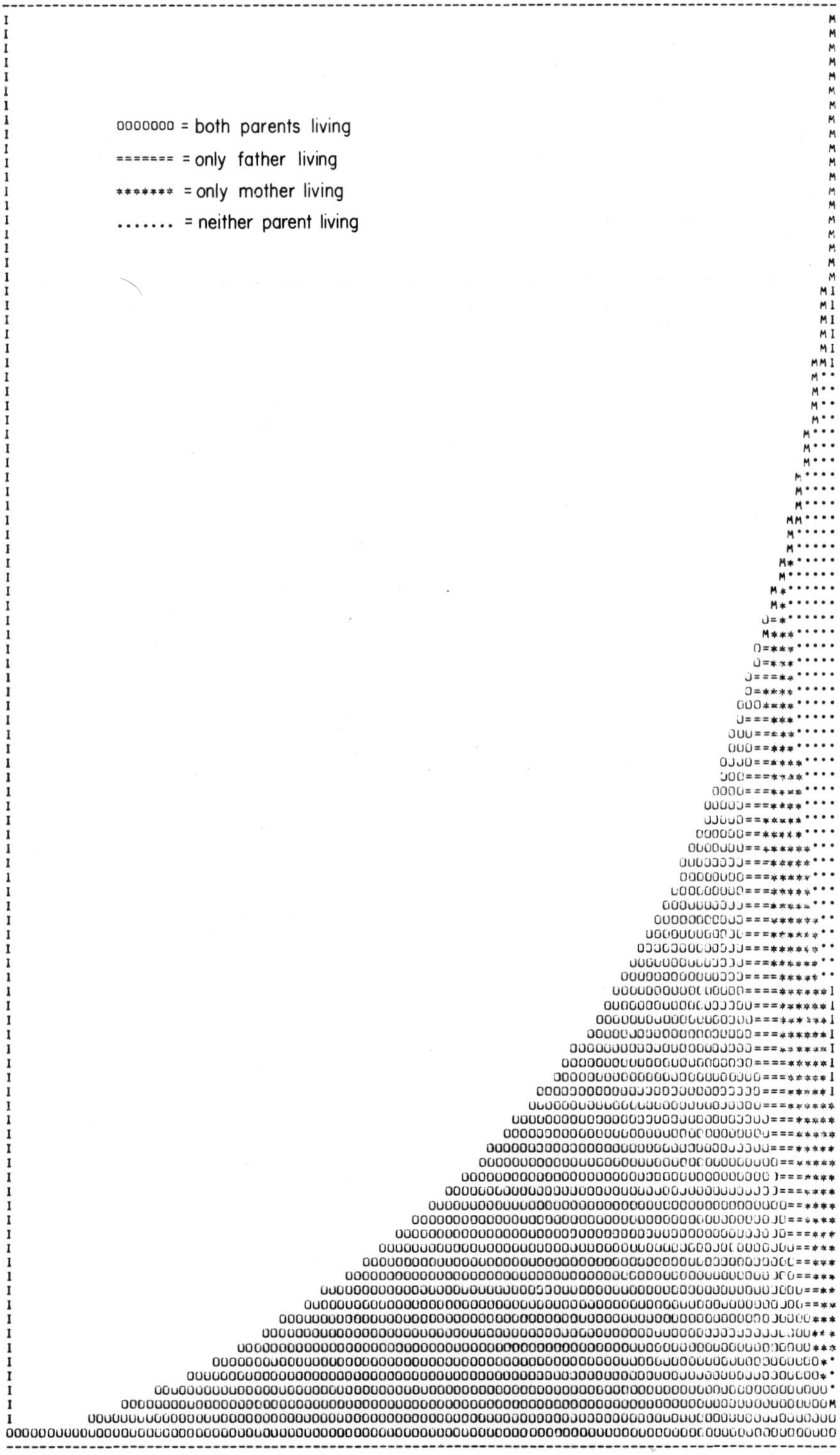

ooooooo = both parents living

======= = only father living

******* = only mother living

.... = neither parent living

EXHIBIT 10.14. Distribution by age of the four parental configurations in the female stable age pyramid for Venezuela.

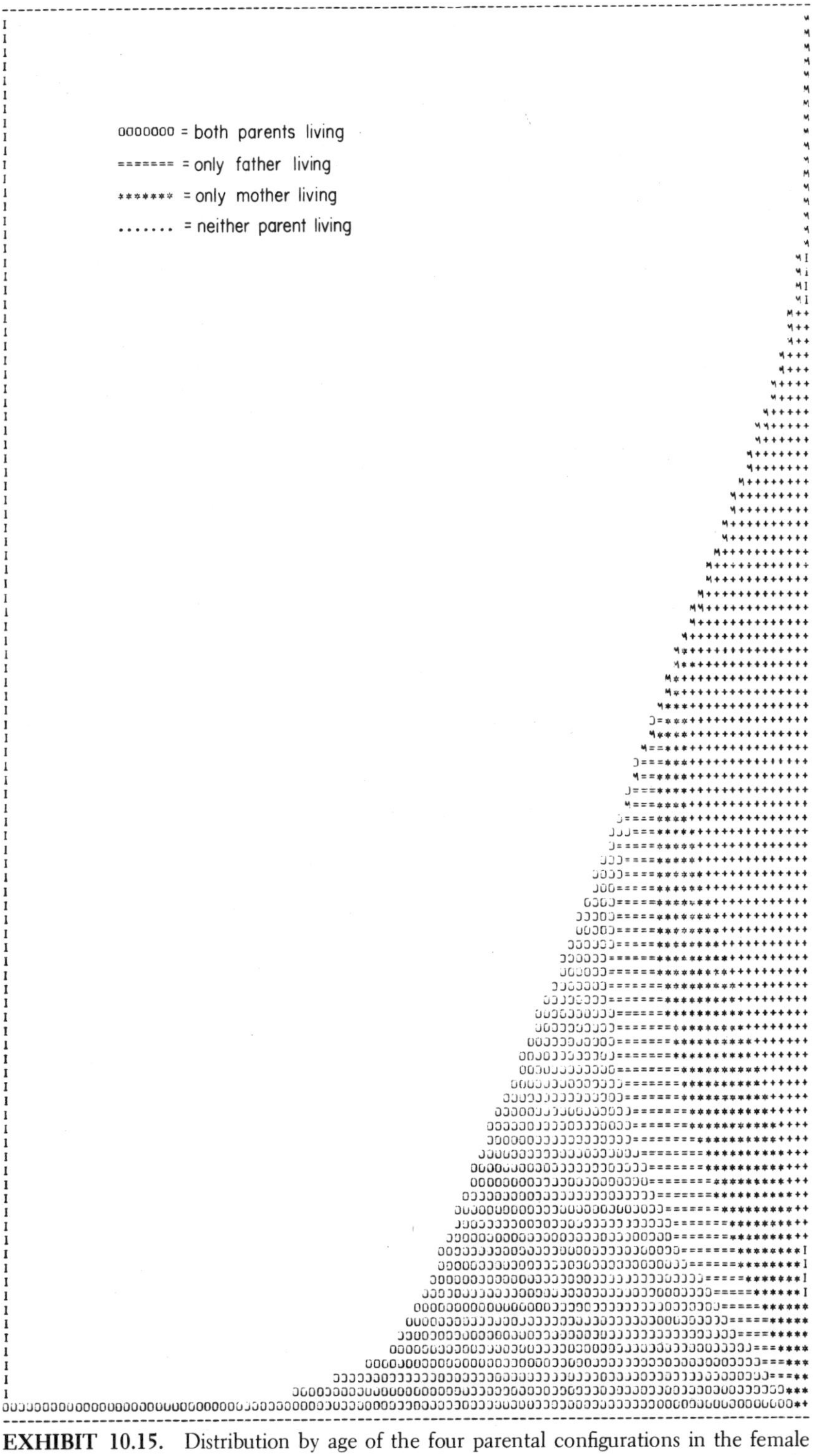

oooooo = both parents living

====== = only father living

****** = only mother living

.... = neither parent living

EXHIBIT 10.15. Distribution by age of the four parental configurations in the female stable age pyramid for 1750s France.

direct line, we must add to the people without parents about half of the people with only a living father or with only a living mother. Median age at inheritance would be around 56 years. The real world falling between our two extreme cases, we may take the age of 60 as a good round figure for inheritors. Thus, the age of those who possess patrimony is close to the age of retirement. If one were to identify capital with patrimony, one would come up with a stereotype of an elderly man of perhaps dubious flexibility regarding risk and innovation in the position of Schumpeter's beloved entrepreneur, the man supposed to risk capital on innovations and provide the cornerstone to economic progress.

The advanced age of the holders of capital would help explain the phenomenon of technocracy and our "era of managers." Managers would be younger individuals who have not or at least not yet inherited. We must mention, however, that France had higher mortality in the recent past and that the war of 1914 to 1918 has left its mark, so that the actual age of holders of patrimony must be lower than the age we have calculated for the stable age pyramid. On the other hand, the age is likely to rise in the near future.

Information on the distribution of ages of owners and inhabitants by size of dwellings would also be interesting.

Are these situations reproduced in a population like Venezuela in the grip of population explosion? Exhibit 10.14 suggests that they are not. Of the people 9% have neither mother nor father, 16.8% have one of their parents, and 74% have both their parents. Thus only one-quarter could be holders of patrimony. The median age of those without parents is 53. Adding half of those who have lost one of their parents, figuring on the second of our two modes of inheritance, the median age drops to 37. While for individuals the pattern of forbears is practically identical for France and Venezuela, in the age pyramid there is a wholly different story. Inherited holdings—even if they were to be found among all classes of the population—would be concentrated, in our model, in the hands of a quarter of the population, whose mean age would be in the neighborhood of 45 years, 15 years lower than in France.

The difference in ages is the most impressive of the contrasts. The difference for the proportions of heirs diminishes if we focus our interest on adults, putting aside the children. Only 22.1% have lost both parents and 53.7% at least one, compared with 38.2% and 67.6% in modern France.

France Around 1750

Finally, let us examine the case of France around 1750 in Exhibit 10.15. Around 31% of the population have no living parents, 28% have one, and

41% have both. The figures limited to adults older than 20 are interesting: Fifty-five percent have neither father nor mother, while 86% have lost at least one parent. The median age of orphans is 48. The median age of holders of patrimony under our second mode of succession, in direct line, is 40. These figures allow us to resolve the paradox encountered in our study of individuals. Children almost always have a family. Orphans are rare. But their families disappear as they reach adulthood. The rate of natural increase being small (.007) the proportion of adults is large and those who have one or both of their parents are submerged in the mass of those without parents, whose median age is 48. The median age of 40 for holders of patrimony is close to that for Venezuela. In spite of severe mortality and expectation of life no greater than 30 men and women in full adulthood are the controllers of patrimony.

Combined Effects of Mortality and Fertility

We may summarize the effects of mortality and fertility on proportions with living forbears in a stable age pyramid. High fertility entails younger orphans, younger holders of patrimony, and younger occupants of the terminal branches of a tree of living ancestors. High mortality entails larger proportions of adults without living forbears counteracted only slightly by the effects of high fertility.

Two populations with different mortality and fertility can have the same stable age pyramids. To distinguish two such populations one might study the density of relationships of various kinds between different age groups. Although we have studied only a single type of relationship here, that of lineal descent, our results confirm this idea. The stable age pyramid for France in the 1750s is intermediate between those for modern France and modern Venezuela, but the same is not true of the numbers of lineal links, which are very high in Venezuela, somewhat less in modern France, and rare in France 200 years ago.

One passes from a pattern of superposition of generations to a pattern of succession. But the family unit still proves its resilience. Even in the most severe situation, 90% of the individuals still have a living parent or forbear at the age of 21.

These results give us a concrete image of the family, whose structure influences individual behavior. Yet we also obtain global results, especially about inheritances, which constitute a substantial segment of capital, whose study should not be futile in a capitalist society. This is a somewhat unexpected angle, and our results should be compared against the little empirical evidence that exists, for many questions still remain.

We emphasize that our models are based on stable population theory, and they would have to be adapted to apply to real populations in which demographic rates are in continual change. By considering changing rates one might date the period at which three-generational populations replaced two-generational populations. It is also important to compare our results with empirical evidence, for the questions we are answering in theory are easy to ask of people: "Do you still have your father? Your mother? What is your age?"

Forbears are only one kind of relative. Descendants, siblings, and cousins are also of interest, although simulation models for them will be more complex.

Our results might be applied in countries with highly imperfect statistics. One might seek to express fertility and mortality as functions of the percentages of children having parents or grandparents at birth and the percentages of individuals having this or that configuration of forbears in the whole population, constructing a kind of combined model table of mortality and fertility with entries given by these percentages. However, if such procedures were to be applied to community populations, it is necessary to reckon with the random fluctuations which appear in any population of finite size. All of our results, derived from stable population theory, deal with mean values or with populations so large that randomness can be neglected. In this respect our results form a prelude to a much broader subject.

11

Age Pyramid Variances

A. AGE PYRAMID VARIABILITY AND
POPULATION THEORY

An age pyramid is a picture representing the numbers of males and females in each different age group in a population. Customarily the age groups are five-year age groups whose sizes are the lengths of horizontal bars emanating from a central axis, men on the left, women on the right, the elderly at the top, and infants on the bottom. For populations with more children than aged, the diagram tapers from a broad base to a narrow top like a pyramid, hence its name, and this name carries over to the numbers which are being graphed. To study the age pyramid of a population means to study its composition by age and sex.

Historians lucky enough to possess listings of settlements which include ages face the problem of interpreting the age pyramid. For large modern populations age pyramids reveal much about the history of births, deaths, migrations, and the historical forces affecting them which lie behind the snapshot of a population at a given moment of time. They reveal so much that it is an easy and amusing textbook exercise to guess countries' and cities' names from their unlabeled age pyramids as in Drake (1974, page 26). For Europe before 1800, however, listings with ages are rare and consequently precious. Only eight listings by household with ages are known for England before 1800, five of which figure in the tables of Chapter 5 of this volume as numbers 24, 32, 35, 50, and 61. The other

189

three are Buckfastleigh in 1680, Lichfield in 1696, and Grasmere in 1774. With data this rare, any help that theory can provide in matters of interpretation is sorely needed.

Population theory as it applies to age pyramids has two parts. One part deals with mean values, the other part with random variability. The theory of mean values of age pyramids is very thoroughly worked out and readily found in Keyfitz (1968, 1977) and Coale (1972). Its core is stable population theory, which assumes age-specific rates of death and childbirth for women unchanging over time along with no migration and predicts mean age pyramids given only a growth rate and age-specific death rates. Marriage, migration, and changing rates cause troubles, but all can be incorporated to some extent. The theory can be used in two directions. In one direction, age pyramids can be read as evidence about growth, death and migration; extensive tables based on mean value calculations which will aid such inferences will soon be available in Dupâquier and LeBras (1978). Reasoning in the other direction, guesses about fertility and mortality can be translated into conclusions about age pyramids to compensate for faulty or scant direct evidence about age-dependent features of social structure. Chapter 10, a translation of an essay by LeBras, treats questions of orphanage and inheritance by this method. All in all, for populations large enough that randomness can be neglected and mean values trusted, social scientists have at their disposal sophisticated tools.

Unfortunately, most of the populations for which data survives from preindustrial times are not large, and randomness, far from being negligible, is the dominant feature. The smooth tapering age pyramids from the theory for mean values bear little visual resemblance to the jagged, unbalanced age pyramids of actual settlements like Grasmere or Ealing. Exhibit 11.1 shows the age pyramid for the 427 inhabitants of Ealing in 1599. Exhibit 11.2 shows the theoretical mean age pyramid for the North Two model of Coale and Demeny (1966) with zero growth. Each capital M stands for a male and each F for a female. Some systematic errors like bunching of ages are apparent in the Ealing pyramid, perhaps some gaps represent interesting migration, but the jaggedness of the sides must also be due to the random ups and downs in births and deaths in the community. For populations of this sort, before we reason in either direction, from age pyramids back to vital rates, migration rates, and historical events, or from demographic guesses forward to age-dependent features of social structure, we need to know about randomness. We need to know what sizes of bulges and gaps in the pyramid are likely to reflect structure and what are safely written off to chance.

The mathematical theory for describing random variability in populations is, like the theory for mean values, very extensive. Unlike the theory

```
                                     M 70 F F
                                   MMM 65
                          MMMMMMMMMMMM 60 F F F F F F F
                                 MMMMM 55 F
                   MMMMMMMMMMMMMMMMMMM 50 F F F F F F F F F F F F F F F F F F F F
                                    MM 45 F F F F F F F F
                        MMMMMMMMMMMMMM 40 F F F F F F F F
                              MMMMMMMM 35 F F F F F F F F F F F F F F
                 MMMMMMMMMMMMMMMMMMMMM 30 F F F F F F F F F F F
                     MMMMMMMMMMMMMMMMM 25 F F F F F F F F F F F F F F
                        MMMMMMMMMMMMMM 20 F F F F F F F F F F F F F F F F F F F F F F F F F F F F F F F F F
      MMMMMMMMMMMMMMMMMMMMMMMMMMMMMMMM 15 F F F F F F F F F F F F F F F
    MMMMMMMMMMMMMMMMMMMMMMMMMMMMMMMMMM 10 F F F F F F F F F F F F F F F F F F F F F F F F F F F
                 MMMMMMMMMMMMMMMMMMMMM 05 F F F F F F F F F F F F F F F F F F
            MMMMMMMMMMMMMMMMMMMMMMMMMM 00 F F F F F F F F F F F F F F F F F F F F
```

EXHIBIT 11.1. Observed Age Pyramid in Ealing, 1599.

```
                                       80 F
                                     M 75 F
                                    MM 70 F F F
                                  MMMM 65 F F F F F
                                MMMMMM 60 F F F F F F F
                              MMMMMMMM 55 F F F F F F F F F
                            MMMMMMMMMM 50 F F F F F F F F F F F
                          MMMMMMMMMMMM 45 F F F F F F F F F F F F
                        MMMMMMMMMMMMMM 40 F F F F F F F F F F F F F F
                      MMMMMMMMMMMMMMMM 35 F F F F F F F F F F F F F F F F
                    MMMMMMMMMMMMMMMMMM 30 F F F F F F F F F F F F F F F F F F
                  MMMMMMMMMMMMMMMMMMMM 25 F F F F F F F F F F F F F F F F F F F
                MMMMMMMMMMMMMMMMMMMMMM 20 F F F F F F F F F F F F F F F F F F F F F
               MMMMMMMMMMMMMMMMMMMMMMM 15 F F F F F F F F F F F F F F F F F F F F F F F
             MMMMMMMMMMMMMMMMMMMMMMMMM 10 F F F F F F F F F F F F F F F F F F F F F F F F
           MMMMMMMMMMMMMMMMMMMMMMMMMMM 05 F F F F F F F F F F F F F F F F F F F F F F F F F
  MMMMMMMMMMMMMMMMMMMMMMMMMMMMMMMMMMMM 00 F F F F F F F F F F F F F F F F F F F F F F F F F F F F F F F F F F F
```

EXHIBIT 11.2. Theoretical Mean Age Pyramid for North Two Model, rounded for display.

for mean values, however, there is a serious gap between the problems which this theory has been able to tackle and the answers which would be most usable by historians. A relevant probability model can be found in David Kendall (1949) and is called an age-dependent birth and death process. Specializing this model to five-year age groups, as we usually do, yields a multi-type branching process. Unfortunately the equations for variances and other indices of random variability of age pyramids for that process have resisted solution. Much is known only about what would happen over infinite timespans or in case birth and death rates did not depend on age. Recurrence relations based on Kendall's model applying to all timespans have been pursued by Pollard (1966; 1973, Chapters 6 and 9). In principle they could yield the kind of information needed for historical data analysis, but as yet no work on practical characterizations of the random spread in human age pyramids for small populations in finite time periods seems to have been done.

This chapter takes up the challenge of bridging the gap between what probability theory provides and what historical data analysis needs, in the area of results about randomness in age pyramids. Our bridges bear comparison with rope footbridges swinging across a wide deep chasm; our results in this chapter are cruder than those in other chapters of this book. They are based in part on mathematical theory and in part on the technique of microsimulation that has also played a leading role in Chapters 1 through 5.

The organization of this chapter is motivated by the desire not to hide our proposed tools among the technical intricacies of the arguments that lead us to them. We have chosen first to present the tools and then the arguments. The first sections, B through E, are frankly applications-oriented. They describe things our formulas let us do, most of them paralleling standard statistical procedures, one of them introducing a new procedure. They leave the basis for these formulas and the limitations on their validity to Sections F through I. Those later sections are un-avoidably technical, and previous acquaintance with mathematical popu-lation theory is likely to be helpful with them. According to interest, the reader will want to pick and choose.

A precursor of this chapter based on earlier simulations was presented at the Historical Demography Symposium sponsored by the Social Sci-ence Research Council of London at Clare College, Cambridge, in July 1973.[1] The original study, more narrowly conceived, dealt with variances only at a single point of time. During the research on household composi-

---

[1] At this meeting and afterwards this investigation has profited from suggestions by John Hajnal and David Kendall and later by Joel E. Cohen and John Tukey.

tion reported in the first five chapters of this volume, age pyramid variability and its change over time has come to seem more and more central to the relevance of population models to historical settlements. Consequently, this chapter has grown; near its conclusion, in Section I, these issues of the relevance of models become our theme.

B. RULE OF THUMB FOR VARIANCES

There are many situations in statistics where an estimate of the mean of a random variable can be plugged into a simple formula to generate an estimate of the variance of the variable. Starting with any estimate p of the mean proportion of successes in n trials under a binomial probability model, we have pq/n where $q = 1 - p$ as an estimate of the variance. Under a Poisson probability model, any estimate of the mean is itself an estimate of the variance, since the mean of a Poisson random variable equals its variance. In an opposite kind of situation, like normal probability models, the value of the mean tells us nothing about the variance at all, since no functional relationship holds between them.

The usual basic probability model for describing random growth and change in human populations, the age-dependent birth and death process model of Bartlett and Kendall in Kendall (1949) is analogous to the binomial and Poisson models rather than to the normal in entailing connections between means and variances. The exact connections are poorly understood and very complicated. Approximate connections, however, may be useful, if we are willing to trade off exactness in return for simplicity and restrict attention to cases of interest to historians and social scientists. In this particular work, we restrict attention to moderately small and moderately stationary populations evolving over time-spans of a few generations. By moderately small populations we have in mind settlements like those discussed in Chapter 5 appearing in Exhibits 5.1 and 5.2. Two-hundred and fifty each of women and men is a convenient average figure. We also restrict attention to formulas that underrate rather than overrate the magnitudes of variances within our models, since our models themselves probably underrate the extent of random variability in historical populations. Broad and approximate connections between means and variances interest us more than finely-tuned connections, not only because they may be easier to uncover but also because they may continue to hold valid when we relinquish some of the simplifying assumptions in the basic probability model. Through microsimulation we can do without many of these assumptions. The real world does without many more.

In this chapter we propose the following approximate Rule of Thumb relating the variance $V(a)$ to the mean $M(a)$ of the number of women a years old or older and less than $a + 5$ years old in a population governed by the probability model defined on pages 254–255 of Kendall (1949):

$$V(a) = M^2(a)/c \qquad \text{for } a < 40 \text{ years}$$
$$V(a) = M(a) \qquad\quad \text{for } a \geq 40 \text{ years}$$

where

$$c = [M(35) + M(40) + M(45)]/3.$$

The evidence and arguments for this formula are set out in Sections F through I of this chapter. The age groups are often called cells of the age pyramid; the means and variances of the cell sizes are the quantities in the formula. The probability distributions, as we shall see in Section I, are well enough behaved that the means and variances are good indicators of location and spread, and we need not apologize for focusing on them rather than on more robust estimators. For applications, we are actually more interested in standard deviations, the square roots of variances, than in variances themselves. In words, our Rule of Thumb asserts that for younger ages the standard deviations of the cell sizes are roughly proportional to the means, whereas for older ages the variances are. For the younger cells we guess the constant of proportionality from an average of means of middle-aged cells. For the older cells, the constant of proportionality equals one.

Our formulas apply to the numbers in age groups, not to the proportions in age groups. Even if we could neglect all randomness in the proportions in age groups, our variances would not be zero, due to variance in total population size. The random variability with which we are concerned is the variability that would appear if we could look at many independent settlements all subject to the same long-term demographic rates and initiated in the same way at the same epoch. Small populations identical in all their underlying demographic characteristics still would differ from each other due to the haphazard timing of births and deaths. The counts of people by age and sex for the separate settlements would spread out from each other. The variances are summary statistics describing this spread. In this framework the mean values are indicators of systematic structure and the variances measure the size of chance effects.

This variability is the usual kind at stake in probabilistic or "stochastic" models of social processes and it is the kind we have discussed in our study of household structure in Chapters 1 through 5. It must not be confused with two other sorts of randomness with which we are not dealing, random fluctuation over time and sampling error. Our variances describe how different independent populations with the same structure would differ from each other, not how the same population observed at different points of time (and of course not independent of itself) would differ from itself. Furthermore, we are not interested in a collection of people who are a sample chosen at random out of some much larger population. Our variances are not sampling errors measuring how much the age pyramid of such a sample could differ from that of the whole population. Formulas for such sampling error are well-known and given, for instance, in Chiang (1968). Each of our populations is a whole population. Men and women are brothers and sisters and children and parents and cousins and spouses of each other, enmeshed in a network of statistical dependencies that reflects itself in the feature we are studying, the degree to which chance factors can express themselves in the age pyramid's shape and size.

Our Rule of Thumb for variances derives from computer microsimulation results for a relatively simple case combined with analytic arguments, described in Sections F through I. How widely our rule remains accurate enough to prove useful we do not know. We have not permitted underlying demographic rates to vary at all randomly in response, for instance, to putative economic and social factors, and therefore our variances, like the variances in our household studies in Chapters 1 through 5, are underestimates of the randomness for which allowance should be made.

Our study has been confined to the female half of the age pyramid, since the ordinary age-dependent birth and death process is a model of a one-sex case. Conceivably the variances for the male cells differ in pattern from the female cells, due for instance to the wider range in ages of fatherhood than motherhood. It is not likely that the differences are large, and until refinements of our formula become available through further research, it seems forgivable to use it for either sex. In Section H other possible limitations on the generality of our formula will be reviewed; none are so severe as to discourage use of the formula pending improvements.

C. USING THE RULE OF THUMB FOR CLASSICAL STATISTICAL PROCEDURES

The formula for variances puts us in a position to carry out classical statistical procedures like significance tests for any cell of the age pyramid. In the next section we suggest that there are better ways to work with age pyramids than to rely on significance tests, but here we illustrate how a test would be performed. Suppose we wanted to test whether the number of girls under 5 years old that would be produced on average by the (unknown) demographic rates in Ealing in 1599 could be as large as 30 (around 15% of all women), even though the observed number is as low as 20. To begin, we need estimates of the means. We might just take the counts themselves, but inspection of the full Ealing list published in Allison (1962) shows heavy clumping of ages at round numbers like 50. To correct for this clumping, we reassign half of the women of each boundary age from the cell above to the cell below the boundary. The female half of the age pyramid corrected for clumping is shown on the left in Exhibit 11.3. Each letter C stands for one woman. The changes in cells between 35 and 50 increase the constant c in our formula. Assuming that much of the jaggedness in the age pyramid is due to randomness we also smooth the pyramid. If $X(a)$ is the count in the revised pyramid, we let the count in the smoothed age pyramid equal

$$[X(a - 5) + 2 \cdot X(a) + X(a + 5)]/4$$

The smoothed female age pyramid, which serves for our estimates of the means $M(a)$, is shown on the right of Exhibit 11.3, each letter S standing for one woman. Our constant c in our Rule of Thumb is now $(11.25 + 10.25 + 12.00)/3 = 11.17$. If we hypothesized a mean of 30 for the number of girls under 5 years old, our variance would be $30^2/11.17 = 80.6$. Pursuing the usual procedure based on a normal approximation, we divide the difference in means 20–30 by 8.98, the square root of the variance. (Our sample is a sample of size 1.) Consulting a table of unit normal percentage points, we find the difference insignificant in a one-sided test at significance levels as lax as 13%.

It is interesting to go on and test the plausibility of our smoothing technique by seeing whether we would reject the hypothesis that each of the observed counts (in the pyramid of Cs) could arise by chance from means equal to the smoothed counts (in the pyramid of Ss). To test this

```
70 CC                                          70 S
65                                             65 SS
60 CCCCC                                       60 SSS
55 CCC                                         55 SSSSS
50 CCCCCCCCCCCCC                               50 SSSSSSSSSS
45 CCCCCCCCCCCCC                               45 SSSSSSSSSS
40 CCCCCC                                      40 SSSSSSSSS
35 CCCCCCCCCCCCCC                              35 SSSSSSSSSS
30 CCCCCCCCC                                   30 SSSSSSSSSS
25 CCCCCCCCCCCCCC                              25 SSSSSSSSSSSSSSSS
20 CCCCCCCCCCCCCCCCCCCCCCCCCCCCCCCCC           20 SSSSSSSSSSSSSSSSSSSSSSSS
15 CCCCCCCCCCCCCCCCCC                           15 SSSSSSSSSSSSSSSSSSSSSSS
10 CCCCCCCCCCCCCCCCCCCCCCCCC                    10 SSSSSSSSSSSSSSSSSSSSSS
05 CCCCCCCCCCCCCCCCCCCC                         05 SSSSSSSSSSSSSSSSSSSS
00 CCCCCCCCCCCCCCCCCCC                          00 SSSSSSSSSSSSSSSSSSS
```

EXHIBIT 11.3.   Ealing female age pyramid corrected for clumping (c) and smoothed (s), rounded for display.

simultaneous hypothesis about 14 counts at the 10% level, we test each separate hypothesis at the $10\%/14 = 0.7\%$ level. We fail to reject the null hypothesis by a wide margin. The farthest from zero of the differences in means divided by the square roots of our guesses at variance is -1.33, occurring for the age cell starting at 40, computed as $(6.00 - 10.25)/(10.25)^{1/2}$. A full 18% of the probability mass of the standard normal distribution lies farther from the origin than -1.33. This outcome reassures us that the effect of smoothing is small relative to the size of the effects that could be ascribed to chance.

D. NO-CONFIDENCE INTERVALS

The significance tests of the last section are informative, but there is an artificial ring to them. The null hypotheses sound more refined and specific than the questions we might naturally ask of the data were we not tutored by statistical tradition. We really want guidance more primitive than significance tests supply. In this section we propose a new way of phrasing the guidance that guesses at variance provide us. This new scheme is not limited to age pyramids but might have a role more widely in statistical data analysis.

Denouncing sham preciseness is a gut-level job of statistics. Points on graphs are really clouds; lines are strips of fuzz. These are basic tenets of a statistical viewpoint. If we deck our data out with the right amount of fuzz, many patterns disappear that would have caught our eye and preyed on our attention.

Classical confidence intervals, if we forget about their mathematical definition, have the look about them of pinning fuzz on data in this way. This look, rather than their formal properties, may be a source of their popularity. In our case, as often happens, we are not in a position to compute confidence intervals, because our guesses at variances, as we have said, are frank underestimates. They incorporate some but not all of the sources of randomness in real historical populations. If we tried to build confidence intervals from our variances, all we could say would be that we cannot have the confidence in the intervals that we are supposed to have.

This problem deprives us of confidence intervals, but it does not thwart us in doing what we want to do, namely pinning fuzz on observations and discounting patterns likely to derive from chance alone. If we apportion too little fuzz because our guesses at variance are too low, that merely means that we weed out fewer spurious patterns than we might. We still weed out some such patterns. In this spirit we propose constructing intervals like confidence intervals but bearing an opposite interpretation, to be called "no-confidence intervals." A random interval which is a function of the data is a no-confidence interval for a parameter at a level of $C\%$ if the maximum probability that the interval contains the true value of the parameter does not exceed $100 - C\%$, where the maximum is taken over all the probability models and values of the unknown parameter that we are willing to entertain.

This chapter is not the place to discuss the properties of no-confidence intervals in detail. Three remarks should suffice to show how they may be applied to the analysis of age pyramids. First, notice that in a normal probability model with a variance known to be greater than a fixed value, ordinary $100 - C\%$ confidence intervals calculated for that value for the variance turn out to be $C\%$ no-confidence intervals. Thus to construct no-confidence intervals we perform the usual calculations for confidence intervals. We simply interpret the outcomes differently. Second, notice that our definition does lead to the interpretation that we want. Patterns that rely on having the true value of a parameter falling within our no-confidence interval rather than outside it do not deserve our confidence. That is, they are suspiciously capable of having arisen by pure chance. Third, notice that, unlike confidence intervals and like critical regions of significance tests, the larger our no-confidence interval, the more stringent are the requirements that a pattern has to fulfill to avoid being discounted. Thus, every subinterval of a no-confidence interval is another no-confidence interval for the same level, but a less informative one.

Let us compute a 33% no-confidence interval for the number of women between 20 and 25 years old in Ealing. Our estimate of the mean from the smoothed age pyramid is 24. Our constant c in our Rule of Thumb is 11.17, and so our (probably somewhat low) guess at the variance is $24 \cdot 24 / 11.17 = 51.6 = 7.2^2$. If this were the true variance, then a 67% confidence interval computed via the usual approximation from normal probability tables would stretch from $24 - .98 \cdot 7.2$ to $24 + .98 \cdot 7.2$. This interval from 17 to 31 is our 33% no-confidence interval. This spread is revealing, for it suggests that the considerable observed bulge in the age pyramid among women of typical servant ages may not be as worthy of attention as it might seem at first glance.

E. SIMULTANEOUS INFERENCE

Most of the time we are interested not in a single cell of an age pyramid but in patterns stretching over several cells. Single cell calculations imply some results for simultaneous inference about several cells, as we have seen at the end of Section C, but when we are looking at more than a couple of cells, such results have little power. To do better, we require more guesses than our Rule of Thumb supplies, because the cells of an age pyramid are not independent. They tend to be large or small together, having positive covariance. If we ignore the covariance, we badly under-estimate the potency of chance.

Guessing covariances is a big problem. There is one covariance for each pair of cells, and the number of pairs of cells is much greater than the number of cells alone. For pyramids like ours for Ealing with 15 cells, there are $15 \cdot 14/2 = 105$ covariances to guess. Kinship relationships link people of some ages more often than others and give rise to genuine differences among covariances. In Section G, however, we do argue that the expression $b \cdot M(a) \cdot M(a')$ indicates a rough minimal level for covariances between age cells starting at ages a and a' when a and a' are less than around 40 or 50, above which ages covariances can more safely be neglected. Here b is a constant calculated from the constant c in our Rule of Thumb along with the estimated mean size of the smallest age group $M(0)$ by the formula $b = [1/c] - [1/M(0)]$. Our expression for covariances is a very rough guide, much rougher than our Rule of Thumb, but probably better than nothing.

We do not have space to embark on a full exposition of the statistical procedures which guesses of covariance make feasible. We confine our-selves to a sketchy description of two procedures; filling in the details is a matter of lengthy but standard statistical arguments. Abbreviated as it is, this section should convey how rich a repertory of tools becomes available to us for the analysis of age pyramids.

Our rough formula for covariances has the advantage that the inverse of the covariance matrix for a collection of age groups can be written in closed form. It follows that we can write down algebraic formulas for test statistics for performing classical significance tests for any k cells of an age pyramid at once. By way of illustration consider k age groups of women younger than around 40. For testing whether the differences between k observed cell sizes $X(a_1) \ldots X(a_k)$ and k hypothetical mean cell sizes $M(a_1) \ldots M(a_k)$ would be statistically significant under a normal model, compute $D(a_i) = [X(a_i) - M(a_i)]/M(a_i)$ and its sum $D1$ and sum of squares $D2$ over the k age groups. Then evaluate

$$D2 \cdot M(0) - D1^2 \cdot [M(0) - c]M(0)/[kM(0) - kc + c]$$

Compare the outcome against a critical value from a chi square table for k degrees of freedom.

Along those lines, suppose we wonder whether the apparent outward bulge in the smoothed Ealing female age pyramid is statistically significant. We might test the differences between observed cell sizes after our correction for age clumping and a set of hypothetical cell sizes unchanging up to age 25, say with values all equal to 23. The values $D(0)$, $D(5)$, . . . , $D(20)$ are then $-.13$, $-.13$, $.09$, $-.17$, $.35$. D1 vanishes, D2 is $.193$, b is $.046$, and our test statistic equals 4.44, which would not be significant even at the 45% level according to chi square tables on five degrees of freedom.

Turning to less classical procedures, we may extend the no-confidence idea to several parameters. A data-dependent region defined by conditions on several parameters at once is a $C\%$ no-confidence region so long as the probability that the conditions are ones that the true values of the parameters satisfy does not exceed $100 - C\%$. Correct, though rather uninformative, simultaneous no-confidence regions are easy to concoct. For instance, a rectangle one of whose sides is a no-confidence interval for one of two parameters is itself a no-confidence rectangle for the pair of parameters. More informative no-confidence regions can be constructed using our rough formula for covariances. For younger age groups, as we shall see in Section G, it turns out that one simultaneous $C\%$ no-confidence region for k cells consists of all sets of values $X(a_1)$ . . . $X(a_k)$ satisfying for all i from 1 to k the condition

$$[1 - q/M^{1/2}(0)]M(a_i) \leqslant X(a_i) \leqslant M(a_i)[1 + q/M^{1/2}(0)]$$

as long as a portion $(C/100)^{1/k}$ of the mass of the standard normal distribution lies closer to the origin than q. For a 50% no-confidence region for the eight cells under age 40 in the smoothed Ealing age pyramid, we have $(.50)^{1/8} = .917$, so that $q = 1.73$ and $q/M^{1/2}(0) = .39$. Thus we should put into the 50% no-confidence region all values within 39% of the values in the smoothed pyramid, a hefty allowance for randomness.

There are many other ways in which to bring our guesses to bear on the analysis of age pyramids, but the ones we have mentioned form a good selection. It is now necessary to turn to the arguments on which these applications rest and describe the basis for our Rule of Thumb and our other formulas.

F. ANALYTIC ARGUMENTS

The arguments leading to our Rule of Thumb are of two kinds. First there are results from probability theory for processes simpler than our process of interest in various respects. While the correct extensions of these results to a fully age-dependent birth and death process for small populations in finite time are unknown, the simpler cases suggest plausible forms for a relationship between means and variances in the more complicated case. Second, there are observations from computer microsimulation. Using the SOCSIM computer microsimulation routines, we have generated artificial random samples of such populations from which to estimate means and variances of age pyramids directly. We proceed in a data-analytic fashion to hunt for relationships between them.

In this section we speculate how far simple probability models capture features of a more complicated probability model. Our more complicated probability model is still much simpler than the processes we are able to mimic using computer simulation, and those processes are themselves simpler than the world of living human beings. We are starting up a ladder whose rungs are levels of increasing complexity. The first rung is our collection in this section of simple solvable probability models. The second rung is a full age-dependent birth and death process, to which most space will be devoted, and which we call "our complicated analytic model" or simply "our process." The third rung is a process with all the demographic complications that are in force in the SOCSIM household simulations described in Chapter 2 of this volume. In this section we are trying to mount from the first to the second rung. Section H will consider the climb to the third rung. The fourth rung, complete realism, is beyond our reach.

In both our analytic and our simulation studies we assume vital rates unchanging over time. We take no account of migration. There is no feedback between population size or structure and vital rates.

Our complicated analytic model, at the second rung of our ladder of increasing complexity, is still a one-sex model, treating only females and neglecting marriage. We restrict ourselves to the situation where the population is neither increasing nor decreasing on average, the case of a "stationary" stable population or a "critical" branching process, with a net reproductive rate or mean generational replacement rate equal to one. The initial age pyramid at time zero is taken to be a stable age pyramid for the birth and death rates we assume. That is, the initial ages of the women are such that (neglecting rounding errors) the expected mean values of the age pyramid cells never change over time. Our complicated analytic model is the age-dependent birth and death process defined by Kendall (1949, page 253) satisfying these extra conditions. For the simulations of Section G we maintain these assumptions for the sake of comparison with the analytic model; in other sets of simulations in Section H we relax them.

In this section we examine six probability models, tracing what consequences follow from them for the random variability in age pyramids, what complexities of our full age-dependent birth and death process they neglect, and what approximate predictions might be salvaged from them. We treat them in some detail, because it is important to understand why our problem does not have easy answers and why our proposed Rule of Thumb is tentative. Furthermore, the value of simulations is enhanced when we can interpret them in the light of analytic models.

The first and simplest of our six models is the multinomial probability model. We neglect all the relationships between individuals in our population and imagine them as a sample consisting of a fixed number of independent observations from an infinitely large population sorted into bins according to age. If n is the fixed sample size and $p(a)$ is the parameter in the model denoting the expected proportion in age group a, the cell means are $n \cdot p(a)$ and the variances are $n \cdot p(a) \cdot [1 - p(a)]$. Since we are interested in populations where no 5-year age group will have a monopoly on women, the values of $1 - p(a)$ should hug unity and vary little on a percentage basis. Thus the means should stay roughly proportional to the variances with a constant of proportionality slightly less than one and falling a bit for large age groups. A plot of variances against means should show a line at an angle below 45° bending down at the far right. The covariance between cells a and a' equals $-n \cdot p(a) \cdot p(a')$, negative covariance due entirely to the restriction that the sample size be fixed.

Of course for our process the assumption of fixed sample size is entirely unrealistic, since we expect considerable randomness in total population size. The simulations of Section G, as we shall see, show strong positive rather than weak negative covariances. The assumption of independence between individuals is equally unrealistic. Individuals in the same or adjacent age groups are often children of the same mother. The sizes of adjacent age groups should vary together and vary in response to the size of the age groups in which the mothers are found. Thus, as a function of the separation between age groups, the covariance between cells should start high, drop, and then rise again at about the span of a generation. We call the correlations operating here siblinghood and parenthood correlations. Weaker correlations should be associated with other kinship dependencies. No such patterns are contemplated by a multinomial model.

A second simple far-fetched model is a birth and death process where the same birth rates and same death rates apply for all ages. The lack of realism, especially about births, in this model needs no advertising. But the model has the advantage that we can derive closed-form formulas for the means and variances of age cells from equations of Kendall (1949, equations 117 on page 259). In our case, the variance for cell a turns out to be a linear combination of the squared mean and the mean. In terms of an instantaneous death rate parameter d, an initial population size n, and the time t, we have

$$V(a) = (2td - 1)(1/n)M^2(a) + [1 + 2H(d, a)]M(a),$$

where

$$H(d, a) = (ad + 5d) \exp(-ad - 5d) - (ad) \exp(-ad).$$

For death rates up to .045 per year, the coefficient of the second term is close to unity. For small, old age groups the second term dominates the sum, at least for times around 100 years, and variances are roughly equal to means. For large, young age groups and times around 100 years, the two terms are comparable in size. For young age groups and large times, the first term begins to dominate and variances become proportional to squares of means. Even before the first term starts to dominate, the quotient $V(a)/M^2(a)$ stays more nearly constant as a function of a than $V(a)/M(a)$.

The lack of age-dependent rates smooths away any siblinghood or parenthood correlations in this model and the covariances are also simple functions of the means. We find:

$$Cov(a, a') = (2td - 1)(1/n)M(a)M(a') \\ + H(d, a')M(a) + H(d, a)M(a').$$

The last two terms are a good deal smaller than the first one, so covariances are roughly proportional to products of means.

Before dismissing the formulas from our second model, we should notice that they strikingly resemble formulas from a third, rather different, simple model. Suppose we build a model in which total population size is a random variable N with some unspecified probability distribution and in which, conditional on the population size having a fixed value, the age pyramid cells are multinomial random variables like those in our first model. This third model is a compound multinomial model. In our earlier notation the variances and covariances are

$$Var(a) = bM^2(a) + M(a) \\ Cov(a, a') = bM(a)M(a')$$

where

$$b = [var(N) - mean(N)]/[mean(N)]^2.$$

Under our second model the variance of total population size is $2tdn$ and the mean is n, so we would have the same formulas as from the compound multinomial if $H(d, a)$ were not just close to zero but equal to zero.

Like the multinomial model, the compound multinomial model still assumes independence between ages of individuals. It is still far-fetched. It treats variability in total population size as the source rather than the outcome of variability in the 5-year age groups, whereas the opposite point of view would be more natural. Nonetheless, we might motivate this third model, somewhat loosely, along the following lines: Siblinghood and parenthood correlations, absent from this model, are mainly positive. In our more complicated process, the variations in the different age groups may only rarely cancel each other out when we add them up to a total population figure. Thus taking the variance of total population size and redistributing it among the cells in relation to their size, as the compound multinomial does, may give better answers than we might think.

For our fourth model we abandon 5-year age groups and deal with infinitely many infinitesimally small age groups. In this limit, the age pyramid cells in the age-dependent birth and death process reduce to Poisson-distributed random variables whose (infinitesimal) means equal their variances. It is tempting to jump to the conclusion that this relationship between variances and means might be preserved when we sum up all the infinitesimal cells into 5-year cells. But that is wrong. The different Poissons are not independent but are connected by a covariance function. The variance of a 5-year cell is the sum not only of all the variances of its pieces, but also of the covariances between all pairs of pieces. The number of pairs of pieces is the square of the number of pieces. Hence the "self-interference" between different pieces of a 5-year age group most likely dominates over the sum of the variances of the pieces, which is what equals the sum of the means. Because the covariances are positive, the 5-year age group variances should be greater than the means.

Now comes a crucial point in the arguments. If the correlations between infinitesimal pieces are relatively constant, then the covariances will be proportional to products of means and their sum over all pairs of pieces will be nearly proportional to the square of the means. However, the older the age groups the more total effect the occurrence of random deaths will have had. The variability in deaths will slowly overshadow the variability in the births by which a cohort begins its career, and the siblinghood correlations should diminish in importance. For elderly age groups we might even treat the infinitesimal cells as independent and recover equality between means and variances for 5-year cells. Thus, going from bottom to top in the age pyramid, we might expect variances to begin proportional to squares of means and end up proportional to the means themselves. This pattern is consistent with the formulas from both our second and third models, and so it gains in plausibility. It is the pattern that our Rule of Thumb expresses, and which we consider carefully in Section G.

We study variances from a different coign of vantage with our fifth model, which describes age pyramids in the "asymptotic" limit where an infinite span of time has passed since initialization. More research has been devoted to this limit than to any other aspect of multi-type branching processes. Chapter V of Athreya and Ney (1972) contains a wealth of information. Although the mathematics is deep, our process in terms of 5-year age groups does become simpler as time goes to infinity. The results are most easily described if we imagine a large number of independent replicas of our process, like the independent runs of our simulations. For our special case, which is a stationary or "critical" process with some initial size n, the theory makes four main assertions: First, the number of replicas in which the whole population has not died out before time t becomes proportional to $1/t$ for large t. Second, since the average size of the populations is not changing, the average size of those that have not died out before time t must increase linearly with t for large t, to balance those that do die out. Third, the proportions in different age groups for the replicas not yet extinct lose their randomness and converge to fixed constants. The only randomness remaining for large t is randomness in total population size. This loss of randomness is not surprising, inasmuch as the surviving populations are growing infinitely large. Random effects stand out less in large populations. A consequence is that all the correlations between age pyramid cells tend to unity. Fourth, the total population size of the populations not yet extinct at time t, divided by t, is a random variable which converges in distribution to a gamma-distributed random variable, the sum of n exponentially distributed random variables each of whose variances equals the square of its mean. It follows that the variances of the age cells for the populations not yet extinct grow nearly proportional to the squares of the means.

Unfortunately these four properties, to which we return following Section H in Section I, make asymptotic theory irrelevant to small human settlements. A model which says that with high probability a settlement has zero members and otherwise is infinitely large is less than helpful. Nor do the perfect correlations between age groups in the asymptotic limit recommend this model to us. The age pyramids of historical communities obviously have random shapes as well as random sizes and that is why the whole question of age pyramid variability is of interest to us. The four properties we have listed are logically related to each other in the proofs of the theorems, although nothing rules out the possibility that some of their corollaries might appear in the age pyramid for some other reason before all four take effect together. In the light of our second, third, and fourth models, the proportionality in this fifth model between variances and squared means is intriguing. From this fifth model we also learn that over long timespans variances depend very much on time, an issue we investigate in Section I.

A sixth model deserves mention. It is not a simplified model but a formulation of the full age-dependent birth and death process in terms of matrices due to Pollard (1966; 1973, Chapter 9). In this formulation the eigenvalues and eigenvectors of a certain matrix fully describe the evolution of means and variances of age pyramid cells. Annoyingly, in our case of a critical process this matrix has a multiple leading eigenvalue that complicates analysis. In the case of increasing populations, as Pollard remarks, the leading eigenvector contributes to each covariance between age cells a term proportional to the product of the means. This result recalls the formulas from our second and third models. Analysis of the contributions of other eigenvectors does not appear easy, but it is a possible path toward explaining the regularities which can be observed in simulation outputs, to which we are about to turn.

G. RESULTS OF THE STYLIZED SIMULATIONS

The key evidence from our simulations comes in the form of plots like Exhibit 11.4. This figure is typical of several we have for various time points in various batches of simulations. Let us see what it has to tell us before we set out in detail in the next section the specifications for the batches.

The 14 points sprouting bars in Exhibit 11.4 correspond to the 14 female 5-year age groups between ages 0 and 70, younger larger age groups toward the upper right. On the x-axis are logarithms of the mean sizes of the age groups. On the y-axis are logarithms of the variances. Because we have only 228 and not infinitely many simulations in this batch, our estimates of the variances are subject to sampling error. The stars are maximum likelihood estimates of the logarithms of the variances. The bars give 95% confidence intervals for the logarithms calculated from normal approximations. The means are not subject to sampling error in this plot because we predict them from the input rates instead of estimating them from the simulation outputs. The logarithmic scales for the axes obligingly make all the error bars the same length. Any upward-sloping curve defines a relationship between variances and means for which the variance is automatically zero when the mean is zero, a constraint which the variances and means of age pyramids naturally

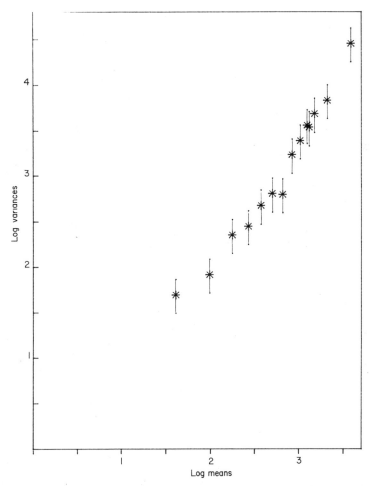

EXHIBIT 11.4. Log variances versus log means for age pyramid cells (228 Labor Day simulations after 100 years).

ought to satisfy. The curves slope up, not down, because means tend to decrease, not increase, with increasing age.

As always happens with curve fitting, many possible curves would fit our points. We could draw a single straight line which would pierce all but one of the confidence bars. We could draw a quadratic sweeping gently upwards which would graze almost all the points. We could draw two straight lines each catching with high accuracy half the points. All of these options achieve fits good enough that formal statistical inference is not going to decide between them, nor would larger sample sizes relieve our uncertainty, since our models themselves only approximate the historical processes which interest us.

If we view our plot in the light of the mathematical models of the last section, however, we find a clearer picture. As regards our first model, the simple multinomial distribution, our plot speaks unambiguously against it. The locus of points on our logarithmic scale bends upward. On a non-logarithmic scale it would bend even more sharply upward, rather than starting straight and bending down as the model predicts. The plot confirms our verdict that the simple multinomial model is misguided. Our second and third models lead us to try linear combinations of means and squared means. On our logarithmic scales such combinations are straight lines with a small quadratic bend at both ends determined by the slope of the line, as can be derived from a Taylor expansion. Though the log scales complicate the form of the function they simplify its use, since they let us weight errors for all points equally. The least-squares fit by functions of this form translates into $V(a) = (.036)M^2(a) + (.700)M(a)$, with a squared multiple correlation coefficient from the log plot of .976. The fit is excellent but the discrepancy between the second coefficient .700 and the predicted value close to one is disturbing. In fact, a whole variety of choices of coefficients give excellent fits. The curve is not very well determined within this family of curves because the bends are small.

We may think of the shape of the curve $\log V(a) = \log[bM^2(a) + M(a)]$ as a tug-of-war between a curve $\log(b) + (2) \log M(a)$ of slope 2 and a curve $\log M(a)$ of slope 1 on the log scales. The bigger the means the more slope 2 dominates. The smaller the means, the more slope 1 dominates. Thus it is hard to distinguish all these curves from the proposal from our fourth model of proportionality between variances and squared means for young age groups and between variances and means for old age groups, that is, of lines of slope 2 on the right and slope 1 on the left on the log plots. This proposal accords neatly with the visual impact of the plot. A line of slope 2 is an excellent predictor up to ages around menopause. Then, the points could be said to turn a corner onto a line of slope near unity heading toward the origin, which corresponds to the equation $V(a) = M(a)$. A linear regression based on the rightmost eight points yields the line $\log V(a) = -2.54 + (1.952) \log M(a)$ with a squared correlation of .97. A linear regression with the leftmost seven points yields a line $\log V(a) = 0.02 + (1.011) \log M(a)$ also with a squared correlation of .97.

In general a pattern like this broken line would possess little practical value, because we should need to know the unknown constant of proportionality for the right-hand piece before we could use it for prediction. But in our case we can solve for the constant of proportionality by setting the height of the lower line equal to the height of the upper line at their point of intersection. Allowing for some uncertainty in the position of the intersection, we may average over the heights of several adjacent age groups, taking, among other possibilities, $c = [M(35) + M(40) + M(45)]/3$. This trick supplies the crucial missing link and gives the broken-line reading of Exhibit 11.4 a practical significance that other readings would not share. The broken line along with the solution for the constant of proportionality constitutes our Rule of Thumb.

Applications of our Rule of Thumb to the analysis of age pyramids have been our theme in Sections B and C. It is a rough and ready formula. It makes sense with respect to what we know from simplified mathematical models and it is compatible with the evidence from simulation. It is not the only formula which would fit the evidence, but it is the only formula without unknown constants among those we have reviewed. It therefore seems a good point of departure, both for use and for refinement.

Simultaneous inference for age pyramids in Section E requires not only our Rule of Thumb but guesses at covariances between age cells. The evidence about covariances both from models and from simulation is much more equivocal than that for variances. None of our models represents the parenthood and siblinghood correlations that we foresee and that are easy to document in the simulations. Exhibit 11.5 shows the correlation matrix for the same output data as in Exhibit 11.4. The youngest age group is split into a 1-year and a 4-year group. The largest correlation in each column is circled twice, and all correlations within 80% of this column maximum in each column are circled once. Ridges of high correlation loom up between age groups where sibling links and parent–child links are likely. We also notice that all correlations diminish where elderly age groups are concerned. We cannot draw too many conclusions from these figures, however, for sampling error is substantial. It takes a correlation at least .13 to be significantly different from zero at the 5% level for our sample size.

The compound multinomial model, we recall, predicts the covariance between cells a and a' to be $bM(a)M(a')$, where b is a function of mean and variance of total population size. Such an expression is also the leading term in formulas for covariances from age-independent birth and death processes, our second model, and from Pollard's matrix formulation, our sixth model. Although it ignores parenthood and siblinghood correlations, this formula may at least capture the overall level of covariances between cells. The differences between simulated covariances and predictions from the compound multinomial model plugging in for the constant b are full of patterns, but they are not excessively large. For age groups over about 40 or 50 the covariances are in any case small enough to ignore, but for younger age groups the formula for covariances

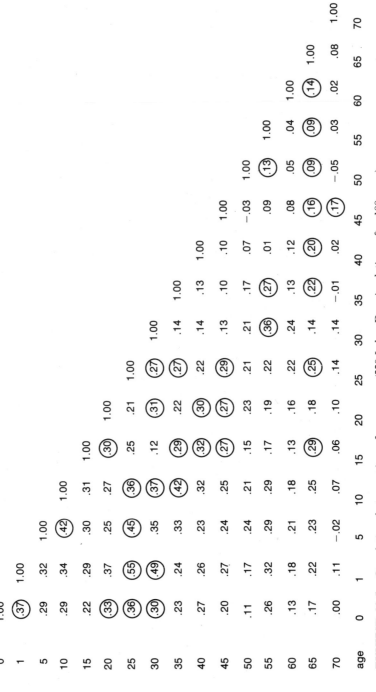

age	0	1	5	10	15	20	25	30	35	40	45	50	55	60	65	70
0	1.00															
1	.37	1.00														
5	.29	.32	1.00													
10	.29	.34	.42	1.00												
15	.22	.29	.30	.31	1.00											
20	.33	.37	.25	.27	.30	1.00										
25	.36	.55	.45	.36	.25	.21	1.00									
30	.30	.49	.35	.37	.12	.31	.27	1.00								
35	.23	.24	.33	.42	.29	.22	.27	.14	1.00							
40	.27	.26	.23	.32	.32	.30	.22	.14	.13	1.00						
45	.20	.27	.24	.25	.27	.29	.29	.13	.10	.10	1.00					
50	.11	.17	.24	.21	.15	.23	.21	.21	.17	.07	-.03	1.00				
55	.26	.32	.29	.29	.17	.19	.22	.36	.27	.01	.09	.13	1.00			
60	.13	.18	.21	.18	.13	.16	.22	.24	.13	.12	.08	.05	.04	1.00		
65	.17	.22	.23	.25	.29	.18	.25	.14	.22	.20	.16	.09	.09	.14	1.00	
70	.00	.11	-.02	.07	.06	.10	.14	.14	-.01	.02	.17	-.05	.03	.03	.02	1.00

EXHIBIT 11.5. Correlations between sizes of age groups (228 Labor Day simulations after 100 years).

from the compound multinomial may be good enough to improve our inferences.

Capitalizing on the formula $bM(a)M(a')$ requires a method for guessing b, since we cannot observe variance in total population size directly from historical data. One possible approach equates the compound multinomial prediction of variance to the prediction from our Rule of Thumb for some age group. The different age groups imply different guesses at b. The old age groups yield $b = 0$, which is no help. The young age groups yield bigger guesses. Anticipating the best match between models when the squared mean term most dominates, we should choose the largest, usually the youngest, age group, and guess $b = 1/c - 1/M(0)$.

Putting together our guesses for variances and covariances, the covariance matrix for any k younger age groups takes the form UFU, where U is a diagonal matrix whose nonzero elements are the means of the age groups and $F = [1/M(0)]I + ebe^*$, where I is the identity matrix and e is a column vector of ones whose transpose is e^*. We can check directly that the inverse of the matrix F is the matrix $M(0)I - [bM^2(0)]/[1 + bkM(0)]ee^*$. A standard statistical method based on the multivariate normal distribution takes the inverse of the covariance matrix $(UFU)^{-1} = U^{-1}F^{-1}U^{-1}$, combines it with the differences $X(a) - M(a)$ between observed and expected cell sizes in a quadratic form, and compares the value against a chi square table. That is the derivation of the chi square statistic of Section D. Because the term involving ee^* in the inverse of F is negative, in the sense that every element in it is negative, we may neglect this term without increasing the probability assigned to any convex region around the origin by the multivariate normal model. Once we neglect this part, the variables $[X(a) - M(a)]/M(a)$ for different age groups a become independent with the same variance $1/M(0)$. That is the basis for our simple formula for simultaneous no-confidence rectangles at the end of Section D.

The whole argument about covariances is shaky, but in the absence of better ideas it is one path to pursue. Fortunately, the applications of Sections B and C rest only on our Rule of Thumb, so that they have a firmer foundation.

H. CONDITIONS OF THE SIMULATIONS

Our results in the last section rest on a simulation experiment that is limited in a number of respects, and we need to list its special features. We also need to say how our Rule of Thumb fares under less stylized conditions.

A discussion of the nature of microsimulation and the SOCSIM program can be found in Chapter 2 of this volume, with full technical details in the *SOCSIM Manual* (Hammel *et al.*, 1976). The experiment on which Exhibits 11.4 and 11.5 are based is a highly stylized one-sex simulation with zero average growth rate. We call the simulations the Labor Day runs because they were run on Labor Day 1973. The experiment attempts to adhere to all the assumptions of the age-dependent birth and death process, except that dates are rounded to the nearest month and two events of childbirth or childbirth and death cannot occur to the same woman in the same month. No further constraint restricts intervals between births. All women have the same age-specific fertility rates. Each simulation run begins with the same population of 244 women whose age distribution up to rounding is a stable state for the given death rates under zero growth. That means that, except for effects of rounding, the true average numbers in age groups never change. Rounding does produce a small growth at the start, about 0.7 per thousand per year in the first 40 years. We have adjusted the mean values for this slight growth. The mortality rates, from the North Two model life table of Coale and Demeny (1966, page 221), are severe. The expected age pyramid is drawn in Exhibit 11.2. Of these conditions, the size of the initial population is the most important. We are specifically investigating variances for populations of a size relevant to historical settlements like those in the early chapters of this book. For populations of much larger or much smaller size, the whole story would be different.

Our batch of simulations consists of 228 independent runs, each lasting for 140 years. Exhibits 11.4 and 11.5 pertain to the age pyramids after 100 years. In the next section we consider the relation of the 100-year age pyramids to those of other years.

How far our analytic arguments and our particular simulation experiment have led us to general features of stochastic population structure and how far they only reveal features present in special circumstances is a large question that must await another study. We can, however, review briefly the performance of our Rule of Thumb in four batches of two-sex simulations aiming at greater realism. These simulations were run as part of another experiment studying demographic constraints on the composition of the immediate kin group, paralleling the studies of demographic constraints on the composition of households in Chapters 1 through 4. The demographic model is the same as that documented in Chapter 2 and the input rates and initial populations are the same as those for batches R1, R2, R3, and R4. We call the new batches K1, K2, K3, and K4. Marriage, population growth or decline, and an initial population differing somewhat from a stable state are taken into account among other complicating features. Exhibit 11.6 gives the sample size, values of the constant c, and, for each age cell, the observed standard deviation and the standard deviation predicted by our Rule of Thumb. Batches $K1$ to $K4$ are shown alongside the Labor Day runs. The age group from 0 to 5 is divided between 0–1 and 1–5 for $K1$ to $K4$. All columns pertain to the hundredth year after initialization. The rows labelled "Error Bounds" show the factors by which each entry must be multiplied to form 95% confidence regions. Thus they indicate the uncertainty due to finite sample size.

On the whole the figures in Exhibit 11.6 are gratifying. The predictions generally lie below the observed standard deviations, as we desire, and the differences between them are small enough that the predictions are a usable guide. There is some evidence, however, from simulations not recorded in this table with large growth rates approaching 26 per thousand per year that the shortfall of the predictions can become quite large under rapid growth. Wide scope for further research remains.

EXHIBIT 11.6.   Standard Deviations Observed in Simulations and Predicted by Rule of Thumb

Batch	K1		K2		K3		K4		Labor day	
Year	100		100		100		100		100	
c	17.700		15.123		14.533		8.900		14.876	
Sample	100		200		100		100		228	
Error	.85		.90		.85		.85		.90	
bounds	1.13		1.09		1.13		1.13		1.09	
Age	Ob.	Pr.	Ob.	Pr.	Ob.	Pr.	Ob.	Pr.	Ob.	Pr.
80	1.7	1.7	1.7	1.6	1.5	1.6	1.1	1.0	—	—
75	2.0	2.0	1.8	1.9	1.8	1.8	1.4	1.3	—	—
70	2.4	2.5	2.5	2.4	2.6	2.3	1.9	1.8	1.5	1.6
65	3.7	3.1	3.2	2.9	3.2	2.9	2.2	2.1	2.3	2.2
60	3.7	3.4	3.5	3.2	3.4	3.2	2.7	2.5	2.6	2.7
55	4.3	3.7	3.9	3.6	4.2	3.4	2.7	2.6	3.2	3.0
50	4.2	3.9	4.1	3.6	4.0	3.7	3.0	2.8	3.4	3.3
45	4.7	4.0	4.2	3.8	3.6	3.7	3.0	2.8	3.8	3.6
40	5.3	4.2	4.8	3.9	4.2	3.7	3.4	2.9	4.0	3.8
35	5.2	4.3	4.9	4.0	4.8	4.0	3.3	3.2	4.0	4.3
30	4.7	4.6	5.5	4.5	5.0	4.3	3.8	3.3	5.0	4.8
25	5.6	5.2	5.5	4.7	5.0	4.4	3.9	3.5	5.4	5.2
20	6.2	5.7	5.4	5.1	6.3	5.0	4.5	4.0	5.9	5.7
15	5.7	5.7	6.2	5.2	5.4	5.1	4.1	4.2	5.8	5.8
10	7.0	6.0	6.4	5.2	5.4	5.3	4.4	4.1	6.3	6.2
5	6.3	6.2	6.1	5.4	5.6	5.1	4.7	4.1	6.7	7.1
1	6.4	5.7	5.6	4.7	5.7	4.5	4.3	4.0	9.2	9.3
0	2.6	1.6	2.4	1.3	2.5	1.2	2.1	1.2		

I. THE STOCHASTIC PLATEAU

We have been postponing until this final section a deep question, the dependence of variances on the time from initialization of the process. Asymptotic theory reveals variances for age pyramid cells going to infinity as time goes to infinity. They go to infinity in our stationary process, as we have said in Section F, and they also go to infinity for an increasing population process. For a declining process they go to zero. Thus for large enough times our models lose their applicability to historical populations. For small enough times they also lose their applicability; initialization in our models is a time of zero variance, when the process starts from a fixed state. These models have a bad start and a bad finish. Is there a good middle sprint, during which we can honor their suggestions?

Exhibits 11.4 to 11.6 belong to the hundredth year after initialization. Dates in our model do not match dates in history in any special way, and there is nothing sacred about the hundredth year. If most different years show different variances, we are in a quandary. We do not know what dates to choose. Constantly changing variances are the rule for the late time periods on which most mathematical research in branching processes has been concentrated, and the literature is silent on the possibility of an earlier period of steadier variances or on its importance. The whole defense we have constructed at the end of Chapter 2 for these processes as models of random variability in small historical populations is open to challenge if no such period exists.

Our passing remark in Section G that Exhibit 11.4 is typical of the figures that we have for different times is therefore of some import. A fuller picture is given in Exhibit 11.7, which represents the probability distributions of the sizes of selected typical age groups as functions of time at 20-year intervals for our Labor Day runs. The top and bottom lines on each plot show the maximum and minimum size of cell observed in the 228 separate runs. The middle line shows the median, which in our cases differs only trivially from the mean. The other two lines are the "hinges" or "quartiles," the values above and below which one-quarter of the 228 cases fall. The lines indicate the changing spread of the whole set of runs. Following a line does not mean following any single run through time. Which run is the largest or the smallest or the median changes from year to year and age to age. An age group for any single run bounces up and down much faster than these lines. These are summary statistics for the batch. Information about variances is not lost on these plots, for the distance between the hinges times .74 is a good robust estimator of the standard deviation and its square is an estimator of the variance, close to

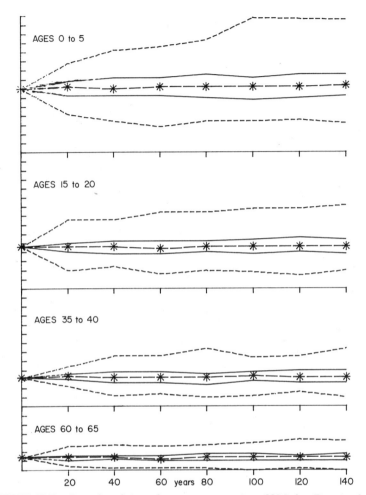

EXHIBIT 11.7.   Quartiles of sizes of age groups over time (228 Labor Day simulations).

though not identical with the maximum likelihood estimator used for Exhibit 11.4.

The graphs are enormously encouraging. All of the lines spread apart rapidly in the first 20 to 40 years. From that time on the hinges are very steady. The bulk of the distribution which is concentrated between and around the hinges spreads so slowly that every time slice from 60 to 140 years resembles every other. The maximum does keep growing, so that the distributions become long-tailed on the upper tail, but the maximum in its wanderings carries few of the 228 cases with it. What is worth more notice, the minimum stays very steady and does not drop to zero over this whole time period, except for a few older age groups.

Evidently, the constraints of initialization wear off long before asymptotic theory comes into force. After 140 years, no populations have died out and no upward linear trend marks the medians or hinges. The opposite effects, extinctions proportional to time and linear average growth for nonextinct populations, are the first two of the four asymptotic properties we have listed in Section F. The third property, perfect correlations between age groups, fares no better in our simulation data during the first 140 years. The largest correlation in all 140 years is .66, between 0 to 5-year-olds and 25 to 30-year-olds at 140 years. A typical series of correlations over time is the one between groups 5 to 10 and 20 to 25, which runs −.06, .00, .13, .24, .26, .43, .42. The fourth asymptotic property requires gamma distributions for the cell sizes. It is possible to see in the later distributions in Exhibit 11.7, with their long upper tails, embryonic gamma distributions. The implied proportionality between variances and squared means does set in early among younger age groups and persists. But the four asymptotic properties together are certainly not apparent, and so our data indicates a substantial preasymptotic period before the unrealistic aspects of the asymptotic limit gain the upper hand.

We name this period we are observing in our simulations the "preasymptotic plateau." It is a stretch of fairly level or gently rising amounts of random variability bounded on one side by a drop down to the zero level at initialization and on the other side presumably by a steepening rise toward asymptotic heights. During this period of temporary stability in the probabilistic structure of age pyramids, our models hold out hope of being relevant to small historical populations. Our simulations have not run long enough to reveal how far the preasymptotic plateau extends nor whether it ends gradually or abruptly. Nor of course do we know whether a preasymptotic plateau is a general feature of age-dependent birth and death processes with rates suitable for human populations, or whether it only occurs in cases like the one we have tried. Having found it in one case can only encourage us to look for it in others.

J. CONCLUSION

In this chapter we have proposed procedures for gauging the extent of random variability in the age pyramids of small, relatively stationary human populations. Looking back over our examples, we can see that the recommended allowances for randomness are large, large enough to affect inferences from data on age distributions of historical settlements in a major way. Our results reemphasize how misleading a theory of mean values for population processes can be for small populations, and therefore how important it is to bridge the gap between existing theory for random population models and the needs of data analysis.

In trying to swing one bridge across this gap, as far as age pyramids are concerned, we have relied on a combination of analytic arguments and simulation experiments, putting together tentatively some pieces in a large puzzle. The problem is sufficiently difficult that conclusive results appear distant. But we have managed to go far enough to propose concrete methods for assessing data. Furthermore, while previous theoretical results on asymptotic behavior might seem to bring into question the relevance to historical settlements of the standard random models for populations, our simulation outputs indicate a "preasymptotic plateau" for which the models are more plausible. Preasymptotic processes deserve the same attention as has been devoted in the past to the asymptotic limit. Not only are results in this domain capable of being useful, but the mathematical problems are intriguing. Mathematics and statistics have usually grown through the challenge of new areas of application. A more complete theory of randomness in population and social structure could be a happy outgrowth of the burgeoning in the last two decades of historical demography.

References

Allison, K. J.
1962   *An Elizabethan "Census" of Ealing.* Ealing Local History Society, Members' Papers No. 2.
Andorka, R.
1975   "Peasant family structure in the eighteenth and nineteenth centuries." *Ethnographia* 86: 340–367.
Athreya, Krishna B., and Peter E. Ney
1972   *Branching Processes.* Berlin: Springer.
Berkner, Lutz
1972   "The stem-family and the developmental cycle of the peasant household: An eighteenth century Austrian example." *American Historical Review* 77:398–418.
1975   "The use and misuse of census data for the historical analysis of household structure." *Journal of Interdisciplinary History* 5:721–738.
1976   "Inheritance, land tenure and peasant family structure: A German regional comparison." Pages 71–95 in Jack Goody, J. Thirsk, and E. P. Thompson (eds.), *Family and Inheritance in Rural Western Europe 1200–1700.* Cambridge: Cambridge University Press.
1977   "Peasant household organization and demographic change in lower Saxony (1689–1766)." Pages 53–69 in Ronald D. Lee (ed.), *Population Patterns in the Past.* New York: Academic Press.
Berkner, Lutz, and J. W. Shaffer
1978   "The joint family in the Nivernais." *Journal of Family History* 3: 150–162.

Berry, William
  1833   *County Genealogies. Pedigrees of the Families in the County of Hampshire.* London: Sherwood.
Bodmer, Walter, and L. Cavalli-Sforza
  1971   *The Genetics of Human Populations.* New York: W. H. Freeman.
Bradley, Brian, and Franklin F. Mendels
  1977   "Can the hypothesis of a nuclear family organization be tested statistically?" To appear in *Population Studies.*
Burchard, Max, and Herbert Mundhenke
  1940–
  1972   *Die Kopfsteuerbeschreibung der Fuerstentuemer Calenberg-Goettingen und Grubenhagen von 1689.* Thirteen volumes. Hanover and Hildesheim: August Lax.
Burke, John, and John Bernard Burke
  1838   *A Genealogical and Heraldic History of the Extinct and Dormant Baronetcies of England.* London: J. R. Smith.
Coale, Ansley, J.
  1965   "Estimates of average size of household." Pages 64–69 in M. J. Levy, Jr. (ed.), *Aspects of the Analysis of Family Structure.* Princeton, N.J.: Princeton University Press.
  1972   *The Growth and Structure of Human Populations.* Princeton, N.J.: Princeton University Press.
Coale, Ansley J., and P. Demeny
  1966   *Regional Model Life Tables and Stable Populations.* Princeton, N.J.: Princeton University Press.
Chiang, C. L.
  1968   *Introduction to Stochastic Processes in Biostatistics.* New York: Wiley.
Drake, Michael
  1974   *Historical Demography, Problems and Projects.* Milton Keynes, England: Open University Press.
Dupâquier, Jacques, and Hervé LeBras
  1978   *Repertoire des Population Stables.* Forthcoming. (Cf. pages 297–309 in R. D. Lee (ed.), *Population Patterns in the Past.* New York: Academic Press.)
Dyke, Bennett, and J. W. MacCluer (eds.)
  1974   *Computer Simulation in Human Population Studies.* New York: Academic Press.
Feller, William
  1968   *An Introduction to Probability Theory and its Applications.* Volume 1, Third Edition. New York: Wiley.
Fischer, Jack.
  1958   "The classification of residence in censuses." *American Anthropologist* 60:508–517.
Fortes, M.
  1949   "Time and social structure." In *Social Structure: Studies Presented to A. R. Radcliffe-Brown.* Oxford: Oxford University Press.
Ganiage, J.
  1963   *Trois Villages de l'Ile de France.* Institut National d'Études Démographiques, Cahier 40. Paris: Presses Universitaires de France.
Geoghegan, William H.
  1975   "Decision making in a complex environment: Selecting a drift route in Samal lantern fishing." Unpublished manuscript.

Gilbert, John, and Eugene A. Hammel
  1966 "Computer analysis of problems in kinship and social structure." *American Anthropologist* 68:71–93.
Goodenough, Ward
  1956 "Residence rules." *Southwestern Journal of Anthropology* 12:22–37.
Goody, Jack, J. Thirsk, and E. P. Thompson (eds.)
  1977 *Family and Inheritance in Rural Western Europe, 1200–1700.* Cambridge: Cambridge University Press.
Hammel, Eugene A.
  1961 "The family cycle in a coastal Peruvian slum and village." *American Anthropologist* 63:989–1005.
  1978 "Household structure in fourteenth century Macedonia." In J. K. Campbell (ed.), *Seven Studies of the Traditional Family in Southern Europe.* Oxford: Clarendon Press.
Hammel, Eugene A., and Ruth Z. Deuel
  1977 *Five Classy Programs.* Research Series No. 33. Berkeley: Institute for International Studies, University of California, Berkeley.
Hammel, Eugene, A., D. W. Hutchinson, K. W. Wachter, R. T. Lundy, and Ruth Z. Deuel
  1976 *The SOCSIM Demographic-Sociological Microsimulation Program Operating Manual.* Research Series No. 27. Berkeley: Institute for International Studies, University of California, Berkeley.
Hammel, Eugene A., and Peter Laslett
  1974 "Comparing household structure over time and between cultures." *Comparative Studies in Society and History* 16:73–109.
Hammel, Eugene A., and K. W. Wachter
  1977 "Primonuptiality and ultimonuptiality: Their effects on stem-family-household frequencies." Pages 113–134 in R. D. Lee (ed.), *Population Patterns in the Past.* New York: Academic Press.
Hareven, Tamara K. (ed.)
  1978 *Transitions: The Family and the Life Course in Historical Perspective.* New York: Academic Press.
Harris, Theodore E.
  1963 *The Theory of Branching Processes.* Berlin: Springer.
Heyde, C. C., and E. Seneta
  1975 "I.-J. Bienaymé: Statistical Theory Anticipated." Forthcoming. (Cf. Kendall, 1975).
Hollingsworth, Thomas H.
  1964 "Demography of the British peerage." Supplement to *Population Studies* 18.
  1969 *Historical Demography.* London: Hodder & Stoughton.
Kendall, David G.
  1949 "Stochastic processes and population growth." *Journal of the Royal Statistical Society.* Series B. 11:230–264.
  1966 "Branching processes since 1873." *Journal of the London Mathematical Society* 41:385—406.
  1975 "Branching processes before (and after) 1873: The genealogy of genealogy." *Bulletin of the London Mathematical Society* 7:225–253.
Keyfitz, Nathan
  1968 *Introduction to the Mathematics of Population.* Reading, Mass.: Addison-Wesley.
  1977 *Applied Mathematical Demography.* New York: Wiley.

Kimber, E., and R. Johnson
 1771 *The Baronetage of England*. Volume 3. London.
Laslett, Peter
 1966 "The study of social structure from listings of inhabitants." Pages 160–208 in E. A. Wrigley (ed.), *An Introduction to English Historical Demography*. London: Weidenfeld and Nicolson.
 1971 *The World We Have Lost*. Second Edition. London: Methuen.
 1972 "La famille et le menage: Approches historiques." *Annales Économies, Sociétés, Civilisations* 27: 847–872.
 1977 *Family Life and Illicit Love in Earlier Generations*. Cambridge: Cambridge University Press.
Laslett, Peter, and R. Wall (eds.)
 1972 *Household and Family in Past Time*. Cambridge: Cambridge University Press.
Ledermann, Sully.
 1969 *Nouvelles Tables-Types de Mortalité*, Cahier 53. Institut National d'Études Démographiques. Paris: Presses Universitaires de France.
Lee, Ronald D. (ed.)
 1977 *Population Patterns in the Past*. New York: Academic Press.
Le Play, P. G. Fredéric
 1864 *La Réforme Sociale en France*. Volume I, Book III. Paris: E. Dentu.
 1871 *L'organisation de la famille selon le vrai modèle signalé par l'histoire de toutes les races et de tous les temps*. Tours: A. Mame et fils.
Levy, Marion J., Jr.
 1965 "Aspects of the analysis of family structure." Pages 1–63 in M. J. Levy, Jr. (ed.), *Aspects of the Analysis of Family Structure*. Princeton, N.J.: Princeton University Press.
Levy, Marion J., Jr., and L. A. Fallers
 1971 "Some aspects of sex, generation, and modernization." *Journal of the National Sociology Honor Society* 41:73–84.
Mols, Roger
 1956 *Introduction à la Démographie Historique des Villes d'Europe du XIVᵉ au XVIIIᵉ Siècle*. Three Volumes. Louvain: J. Duculot.
Pollard, John H.
 1966 "On the use of the direct matrix product in analysing certain stochastic population models." *Biometrika* 53:397–415.
 1973 *Mathematical Models for the Growth of Human Populations*. Cambridge: Cambridge University Press.
Russell, Josiah C.
 1948 *British Medieval Population*. Albuquerque: University of New Mexico Press.
Selden, J.
 1672 *Titles of Honor*. Third Edition. London: Tyler and Hult.
Tukey, John W.
 1977 *Exploratory Data Analysis*. Reading, Mass.: Addison-Wesley.
Wall, Richard
 1977 "Changes in English household structure in British regional populations." Paper presented to the Liverpool Conference, September 1977, Department of Geography, University of Liverpool.
Waters, John J.
 1976 "Patrimony, succession, and social stability: Guildford, Connecticut in the eighteenth century." *Perspectives in American History* 10:131–162.

Wrigley, E. A.
  1966   "Family limitation in pre-industrial England." *Economic History Review* 19: 82–109.
  1969   *Population and History*. London: Weidenfeld and Nicolson.
Zimmermann, C. C., and M. F. Frampton
  1936   *Family and Society*. New York: Van Nostrand.
Zubrow, Ezra
  1977   *Demographic Anthropology*. Albuquerque: University of New Mexico Press.

Index

A
B
C 8
D 9
E 0
F 1
G 2
H 3
I 4
J 5